INTERGOVERNMENTAL RELATIONS IN THE UNITED STATES

AMERICAN FEDERALISM
The Urban Dimension

This is a volume in the Arno Press collection

Advisory Editors
Robert M. Fogelson
Lawrence E. Susskind

Editorial Board
Bernard Frieden
Richard P. Nathan

*See last pages of this volume
for a complete list of titles.*

INTERGOVERNMENTAL RELATIONS IN THE UNITED STATES

Edited by

W. BROOKE GRAVES

ARNO PRESS

A New York Times Company

New York / 1978

Editorial Supervision: JOSEPH CELLINI

Reprint Edition 1978 by Arno Press Inc.

Reprinted from a copy in the University of Illinois Library

AMERICAN FEDERALISM: THE URBAN DIMENSION
ISBN for complete set: 0-405-10474-X
See last pages of this volume for titles.

Publisher's Note: This book has been reprinted from The Annals of The American Academy of Political and Social Science, Volume 207, January, 1940.
The pagination is correct.

Manufactured in the United States of America.

Library of Congress Cataloging in Publication Data

American Academy of Political and Social Science, Philadelphia.
    Intergovernmental relations in the United States.

    (American federalism)
    Reprint of the 1940 ed. published by the American Academy of Polictical and Social Science, Philadelphia, which was issued as v. 207 of its Annals.
    Bibliography: p.
    CONTENTS: Federal relations with other units.--Interstate relations.--Regionalism.--Interrelations of local units.--Some considerations for the future.

    1. United States--Politics and government--1933-1945. 2. State governments. 3. Local government--United States. I. Graves, William Brooke, 1899- II. Title. III. Series. IV. Series: American Academy of Political and Social Science, Philadelphia. Annals ; v. 207.
JK325.A64   1977   353   77-23000

FOREWORD

IN VIEW of recent developments in the field of American government, it would be difficult to overemphasize the importance of the subject of this volume of THE ANNALS. These developments, conspicuous prior to 1933, have been accentuated since that date, due jointly to the influence of the depression and to the legislative policies of the dominant party in the Nation and in a large majority of the states. Many students have attacked particular aspects of the problem, in restricted areas; it now seems appropriate to attempt for the first time a broad survey of the entire field, which includes most governmental functions and all levels.

The Special Editor of this volume is deeply indebted to a great many persons. When the project was first undertaken, a letter was addressed to each of the members of a consulting group of fifty individuals who were known to be interested and to have worked in some portion of the field. Nearly all of these consultants replied, many of them presenting valuable suggestions as to subject matter or possible authors or both. In choosing the authors, the effort has been made to get a representative group—to give an opportunity to some of the younger men to contribute; to avoid the odor of the lamp by bringing in some men with no academic connection; but withal, to present a well-balanced view of the various aspects of the subject.

I should indeed be remiss if I should fail to express my very real appreciation of the splendid co-operation that has been accorded me by all of the contributors. To them belongs the credit for whatever merit the volume may possess.

W. BROOKE GRAVES

Politics and Administration in Intergovernmental Relations

By G. Homer Durham

THE rise of a new American federalism has been seen in recent Federal-state co-operation.[1] This is but a single, though commanding, aspect of intergovernmental relations in the United States where today one worker in every nine holds a public position within the 175,000-odd units embraced in our system. The relationships possible among such personnel, distributed through so many areas and groups, are practically unending in their number, complexity, and variety.

Outside of the work of a few pioneering scholars, little is known of this development and the interlocking of these many units. The legal devices of Federal and state aid have been generally recognized as important factors in forging such relations; as has the compact, the administrative or legislative agreement, and the contract. Such inventions have served to bridge the gap between various agencies, but form only another phase of the problem. Professor William Anderson points out:

If we think only in terms of constitutionalism and strict legality, we shall miss some of the most important functions . . . in understanding the working relations among governmental units. The problem is essentially a human and not a legal one.[2]

Structure and Function and the Problem of "Consent"

As intergovernmental functions have increased to meet the demands of an expanding nation, the administrator has come to have dominating influence in the American political scene. Presidents, governors, and lesser executives have long received attention, even in that aspect of public affairs which brings them into intergovernmental activity. But universities and colleges, and to a greater extent the public schools, have been slow in presenting the place of such activities in the political process.[3] In general, the American public, including many of those in active political life, prefer to view the scene in terms of traditional thinking about American government; namely, the states perform certain functions reserved to them, the Federal Government performs certain others; both, and the localities, take too much for taxes; and the Supreme Court will straighten out everything for the good of mankind. Career politics has been looked upon as a necessary evil. The administration of policy, fathered by such "evil," has been thought of as an automatic result of acts of Congress and local legislation.

The growing maze of relationships, legal and extra-legal, within the federal system has radically altered any ancient bases-in-fact for such views, and today affords particular challenges to the interests of regions and localities, to the nature of our federalism, and to the intelligent citizen's effort to understand the nature and control of his government.

Writing in The Annals in 1933,

---

[1] Jane P. Clark, *The Rise of a New Federalism; Federal-State Co-operation in the United States,* New York: Columbia University Press, 1938.

[2] *American Government* (New York: Henry Holt and Co., 1938), p. 275.

[3] In five important college textbooks on American Government produced since 1938, only one makes systematic effort to analyze this problem and two make no significant mention of it whatever.

Luther H. Gulick [4] forecast the need of a new theory of what he there called "division of powers"; not to be made up of checks and balances, nor yet as between policy and administration; but to be concerned "with the division between policy veto on one side and policy planning and execution on the other." [5] A moment's thought will show that the usual agencies of government classified as courts, legislatures, elected executives, the administration, and such devices as the initiative, may one and all affect both the veto of public policy and its planning and execution. So, for many reasons, a discussion of "politics" and "administration" in intergovernmental affairs may well recognize the basic oneness of the two in the political process, but likewise fall back on the advantages of differentiating them for the time being as posited by Professor Goodnow,[6] recognizing with Dr. Gulick that inasmuch as continued effort by legal prohibitions has failed to take "administration" out of "politics," henceforth more attention should be directed towards removing certain features of "politics" from "administration." [7]

Perplexity of the citizen

In the realm of intergovernmental relations, a separation into "politics" and "administration" defies realistic analysis. The structure and function of American political institutions is such that the two tend to become a single entity when agencies co-operate or otherwise come into association. Each brings to the association its own legislative background, rule-making power, and political and administrative controls. Such relations tend to obscure from the citizen the essential knowledge requisite to an intelligent "consent," and they also absorb the traditional outlets for expressing policy, with the result that the personal relationships between administrators become paramount. Thus, whereas we formerly had administration by campaigning office-seekers and their allies, today we have policy-making by administrators and the molding of a new American politics.

Such a situation imposes a serious problem on the befuddled citizen who, in paying lip service to his ideal of a mechanical, liberal state as an instrument for the common weal, is confronted by an administrative mechanism with whose complex workings he is unfamiliar; which seemingly directs and controls his activities while eliminating the traditional recourses for relief, manipulation, or direction to which he has been accustomed. The analysis of relationships which follow neither the vertical lines of financial aid nor the horizontal lines of co-operative agreement is possible only to those "in the know." To a less extent the same thing is true of relations between overhead service agencies, such as personnel or finance, to operating agencies in the same jurisdiction. It is in these areas that the politics of management, entering with varying content to affect the political process, must seek and win "consent," while yet remaining responsible. How may responsible administration be secured?

Somewhere behind the maze of structure lie the statutes, the campaigns, the elections, the groups, and the interests basic to broad legal decisions. In company with them stand the civil service examinations and other forms of recruit-

---

[4] "Politics, Administration, and the New Deal," Vol. 169, Sept. 1933, pp. 55–66.

[5] *Ibid.*, p. 66.

[6] Frank J. Goodnow, *Politics and Administration*, Macmillan, 1900. Leonard D. White claims a renewal of this distinction in a recent work by his colleague, Professor M. E. Dimock (*Modern Politics and Administration*, American Book Company, 1937). See White, *Introduction to the Study of Public Administration* (revised edition, Macmillan, 1939), p. 12.

[7] Gulick, *op. cit.*, p. 59. Cf. p. 55 for the reference to "prohibitions."

ing and appointing administrators. The campaign and the election are of little significance beyond admitting to legislative and other offices the personnel for approving or rejecting basic decisions as to structure and function. Behind the process of approval or rejection stand the administrators and their legislative aids, determining the loci of such decisions after they are made and influencing their making. And in certain recent large-scale additions to the intergovernmental field, the importance of administrative personnel has increased.

Example of unemployment compensation

The administration of unemployment compensation, for example, requires direct relations between operating personnel in the Federal capital, in a Federal regional office, in a state central office, and in a local public employment office. To this relationship, Congress, legislatures, court decisions, and the rules and regulations of nearly a dozen Federal and state agencies [8] (two of the former bearing different types of Federal aid to the state agency),[8a] plus a vociferous development in administrative adjudication, have contributed "policy" along well-beaten though complex paths. But where do these outlets for formulated policy converge in order that popular consent may be invoked? If policy is the determination, says the citizen, of what an agency does, then when, where, and with what personnel in this vast new enterprise has policy converged? Probably at the conference table in state offices (or in telegraphic communication with regional and national offices) where state officers have defended their quarterly budgets, and wheedled with Federal representatives of the Bureau of Unemployment Compensation over various specific items presented therein as the exact item-expenditure basis for the 100 per cent grants [9] administered by the Social Security Board to the states.

In 1935 Congress gave its legal consent, upheld by the Supreme Court, to a basic policy: "Let there be unemployment compensation." The specified pattern, connecting joints, and related controls have served to cloud the more detailed aspects of the policy process to all except those competent to know on the inside. The same factors have interfered with the process of administrative management in perfecting the service, in informing unemployed persons as to their legal rights, and in winning an intelligent "consent." The public has given a (produced?) apathetic consent to the *workings* of the entire system, including the significant activity of the Interstate Conference of Unemployment Compensation Administrators in piecing together the details of a plan for paying interstate benefits, now in effect.[10] Although recognizing the ultimate and present benefits of unemployment compensation, such public consent nevertheless is difficult to distinguish from that which a primitive aborigine would give to his incomprehensible gods aided by the tribal priest instead of the necessary

[8] The Bureau of Internal Revenue (Treasury), United States Employment Service (Labor), Post Office, Social Security Board and its operating Bureau of Unemployment Compensation and the new over-all Federal Security Agency; state treasuries, departments of finance, controllers, tax commissions, attorney-generals, and the complex state organizations themselves which combine the administration of compensation and systems of public employment offices.

[8a] This situation has been changed by a reorganization order effective July 1, 1939. The United States Employment Service was transferred to the new Federal Security Agency and its function merged with those of the Bureau of Unemployment Compensation in a "Bureau of Employment Assurance."

[9] Including additional sums for state employment services.

[10] The conclusion of this agreement bears added witness to the potency of the tax offset combined with a 100 per cent Federal grant in securing state co-operation.

public relations bureau. An organically controlled politics under such conditions is the inevitable result of administration, which factor requires analysis.

POLITICS AS A BY-PRODUCT OF ADMINISTRATIVE MANAGEMENT

In his clarifying analysis of forty years ago, Goodnow, while recognizing the essential unity of the governmental process, posited that execution (or administration) must be subservient to the law-making authority if popular government is to be insured. In order to keep the administrative arm in such control, Goodnow idealized the necessity of responsible party formulators, with centralized administration as an instrument for their popularly approved policies. "Politics" as the interrelations between human political beings would not be, and is not, thereby abolished. But the presence of politics within the instrument was to have been concentrated in content around the controls, with a minimum elsewhere as expressive only of a free regime.

The concentration of responsible political authority at all points of effective administrative control is impossible in intergovernmental relations thus far. Divergence in party dominance from district to district and from county to county has seen Democrats and Republicans of all shades and hues standing side by side, especially in the dramatic Federal-state and Federal-local relations which have been occasioned since the passage of the Emergency Relief and Construction Act of 1932. There has been therefore a remarkable jockeying of party politics in administration to produce through that instrument many aberrations of what normally appears as the political by-product of modern administrative management.

Administration is a problem in the association of human personalities. Their interrelation in the performance of services requires organization. Organization requires or entails hierarchy. Hierarchy entails descent of authority, decisions, and administrative orders, with resulting obedience or degree of compliance. Decisions require certain rationalizations in terms of human good will (else threats or violence) in order to obtain this compliance. Hence an inevitable political effect is produced in the usage by management of its staff aids, with stress on personnel training, in order to secure smooth operations and *esprit de corps*. Training, said to be inherent in supervision, requires direction as part of the supervisory process, transfer of ideas and instructions. Operations marked by staff co-ordination and personnel training can therefore in one sense be identified as a specialized miniature of that which appears to be the essence of the larger political process as developed in the party and other groups.

Viewing the nation as a whole with its divergent elements, the "essential" aids to management, even when operating in their assigned spheres, become instruments for producing "administrative politics." Under pressure the content of operations and training may assume the form of propaganda where professional standards are weak or do not exist. Without strict co-ordination and training, ambitious individuals utilize available areas of administrative discretion in order to "capture" additional areas of control. A dog-eat-dog type of administrative imperialism, of which the public is not conscious while services operate at the minimum required for tolerance, is the undesirable fruit in such instances.

The structure of intergovernmental relations, by and large, affords a wider play for administrative politics of this nature than is possible in a direct service. This may be traced to: (1) diverse administrative as well as diverse party and policy controls; (2) lack of responsible personnel trained in the details of maintaining the delicate balance between varying contents of public interest and popular consent; (3) the rapid expansion of intergovernmental services to localities, preceded or accompanied by the decline of local responsibility, thus opening the way for the atrophy of state and local service agencies as an outlet for the reserved powers of the states under the Constitution; (4) the influence of a growing Federal parallelism accompanying the latter atrophy with direct Federal provision of services, funds, or personnel, complementary to local or even existing intergovernmental services of Federal-local character; [11] (5) the very presence of connecting jurisdictional "joints" involving "no man's land" for administrative discretion between two or more agencies. Administrative politics may therefore be conceived in this sphere not only as (1) essential aids to management, (2) propaganda for self-perpetuation and other ends, and (3) administrative imperialism, but also as (4) the basis and core of a rising federal politic in which the generic concept of "administrative politics" threatens to replace the traditional "politics *and* administration," and embrace the entire process.

A Rising Federal Politic

It is along the lines of heavy expenditure for highways, public works, relief of all sorts, and the provision of new social services that the field referred to above has been prepared. The seeds have been sown for new and significant political alignments in which the parts will adhere to the national whole, rather than the whole being composed of and controlled through its many parts. Repeated emergencies and the pressure of international events aid and abet the development, of which the channels of intergovernmental relations are symbolic. Said relations have cut through state and local lines in an era of centralization and integration with subsequent widening of the area in which orders descend from a central, federal organism. Some of the largest and politically most powerful state agencies, such as highway administration with an almost total absence of merit personnel, are no longer dependent on their operating jurisdictions for funds, and especially is this true in the west where recent developments have been extensive. And in the heavily populated metropolitan centers, mayors and other officials look to the party in power in Washington for entering financial wedges. Governors, mayors, councilmen, and county officers no longer stay at home to enlist local aid during the period between their election and their assumption of office. Instead they are seen in the national capital, closeted with Federal officials and the officers of such groups as the United States Conference of Mayors.

With this rising federal politic a reality, even a Congress in revolt, however strong the local administrative ties engendered through "senatorial courtesy," may come to have little influence over the administration of policy except where its basic decisions alter the outline and structure of the governmental organization. No state legislature is likely to strip itself of the advantages of participating in Federal funds and relationships merely for the glorious thrill of exercising dominance over state administration, even if that were still possible. And to the office of President of the United States, such a nationalization of the political line only increases and enhances that executive office with further marks of political leadership and importance as source of policy. For, contrary to the Goodnow philosophy as

---

[11] Provision of the National Re-employment Service paralleling Federal-state employment services developing under the Wagner-Peyser Act from 1933 to 1937 affords a good example.

crystallized in the council-manager idea, the Presidency unites in one office and one personality the functions of "politics" and "administration." Reorganization as response to public need, interest, or national crisis, as a further interpretation of that philosophy in recent months, does not promise any separation but integration of the same.

The party and administrative politics

So what of politics and administration in intergovernmental relations? Their interlocking indicates the unreality of checks, balances, and division into politics *and* administration. As a guide to a "new theory of the division of powers,"[12] the idea of *administrative politics*, or the interrelations of public administrators in what appear to be increasingly more permanent offices with tenure, forms a more realistic concept. Too, with the importance of the Presidency emphasized, the political party emerges as an instrument of policy and consent in a new light. Questions of structure and function in the federal system preclude, under present boundaries and constitutional restrictions, the emergence of a more significant factor than the party in clearly defining the policy-phase of a new "administrative politics."

The realization of the importance of the party, which will increasingly tend to revolve around associations of administrators in spite of the Hatch Act of 1939, must bear effect in a decentralizing of the national party power. To attain this, wide participation in local political affairs, plus an eschewment of that traditional "clean-hands-stay-out-of-politics" policy which too many have followed in the pursuit of happiness through business opportunity, must be accomplished. The party cannot be a responsible instrument in any other way. Otherwise the essential unity of the governing process which the party directs, and the growing importance of administrative politics as the shaper of the party instrument, are such that instead of "towering above Presidents and State governors, over Congress and State legislatures, over conventions and the vast machinery of party,"[13] as Lord Bryce once had occasion to write, "public opinion ... in the United States, as the great source of power, the master of servants who tremble before it,"[14] will only become a technique whereby a dominant group may find occasion to perpetuate itself without active consent. It is all too evident in recent world history that the "people" may be made to "tremble" before services sugar-coated with propaganda.

In this aspect of government the decision to take the undesirable features of "politics" out of "administration" must be a human and not a legal one. Such a decision is within the range of competent administrative management, aided by basic legislative decisions directed towards securing this end. The party as the best available instrument for dealing with the administrator must accordingly undergo a metamorphosis, becoming more mechanical as government becomes more organic. In this change the party must be held accountable, through local participation, for the enforcement of such human decisions as may be required to administer intergovernmental and all other activities within the purview of popular, though an intelligent, consent.

[12] Called for by Luther Gulick, *op. cit.*, p. 66.
[13] *The American Commonwealth* (rev. ed., Macmillan, 1906 printing), p. 258.
[14] *Idem.*

G. Homer Durham, Ph.D., *is instructor in political science at the Utah State Agricultural College, Logan.*

State Legislation Facilitative of Federal Action

By V. O. KEY, JR.

THE traditional theory of federalism postulates a division of legislative powers between central and constituent governments and presumes that the legislative body of each unit will perform its lawmaking functions relatively independently. In several articles Professor W. Brooke Graves has shown that agencies of the Federal Government have come in recent years to exercise influence over the state legislatures.[1] Professor Graves has been primarily concerned with the fact of Federal influence—a matter of great significance in the evolution of federalism—rather than with the differentiation of situations in which that influence occurs. It is proposed here to carry the study a step farther by analyzing one type of Federal relationship to state lawmaking.

This discussion is concerned with the enactment of state legislation, under varying degrees of Federal persuasion, to facilitate direct Federal administrative action affecting individuals, corporations, or political subdivisions of the state. A complete systematization of the field of Federal leadership in state legislation need not be attempted, but the scope of the inquiry may be roughly marked out by differentiation from certain other phases of Federal influence on state legislative action. Through grants-in-aid to the states, legislatures are brought to enact laws meeting Federal requirements, but such statutes lay the legal groundwork for a continuing financial and administrative relationship between the Federal Government and the state itself. The Bureau of Narcotics seeks to bring about passage of the Uniform Narcotics Act, but this relationship is in its essence the same as that of a nonofficial pressure agency promoting legislation. In other instances Federal agencies are interested in state action to the end that the state will exercise powers parallel to the jurisdictional area occupied by the Federal agency. The National Labor Relations Board, for example, has looked with favor on the adoption of state labor relations acts on the order of the national act.

In the type of situation under examination, state legislation, generally in the fields of private and municipal corporation law, is sought to facilitate direct Federal action affecting individual or corporate subjects of state law. State legislation may be essential for the conduct of the Federal activity, or it may merely simplify Federal action. It may be related to Federal administrative action directly, or only indirectly. It may be enacted by the state legislature to meet a condition precedent to the enjoyment of Federal services by the citizens of the state, or it may be induced through advice or by confronting the legislature with the findings of research.

[1] "Stroke Oar," 7 (1934) *State Government* 259–62; "Federal Leadership in State Legislation," 10 (1935–36) *Temple Law Quarterly* 385–405; "The Future of the American States," 30 (1936) *American Political Science Review* 24–50; "Influence of Congressional Legislation on Legislation in the States," 23 (1938) *Iowa Law Review* 519–38. Jane Perry Clark has called attention to the interdependent character of certain types of Federal and state legislation. See *The Rise of a New Federalism* (1938), Chap. V. Similar relationships were earlier noted by W. Beard, "Government by Special Consent," 25 (1931) *American Political Science Review* 61–68. Since the present analysis was outlined there has appeared an excellent study of the interest of government corporations in the passage of state facilitative legislation. See Ruth Weintraub, *Government Corporations and State Law* (New York: Columbia University Press, 1939), Chap. V, "The State Legislates in Favor of the Government Corporation."

Federal Housing Administration

Illustrative of the type of state legislation under consideration is that enacted to facilitate the mortgage insurance operations of the Federal Housing Administration. The program, inaugurated in 1934, contemplated a system of mutual insurance of mortgages covering home loans made by banks, insurance companies, and other lending institutions. The policy was adopted of insuring mortgages covering a high percentage of the value of property offered as security, in order that the impositions on borrowers in connection with second and third mortgages might be avoided. It was also made a policy to insure mortgages evidencing long-term loans to be amortized by frequent payments, on the presumption that this sort of mortgage was more suited to the needs of the average borrower than short-term, lump-sum mortgages.

The Federal program immediately encountered the obstacle of state legislation that prevented state-chartered lending agencies from taking advantage of mortgage insurance. State-chartered commercial banks, for example, were commonly permitted to lend only 50 to 60 per cent of the appraised value of the property, and under mortgages payable in from three to five years. "With a loose system of appraisals and with mortgages traditionally a nonliquid form of investment, there were plausible reasons for the restrictions, at least as applied to certain classes of lending institutions";[2] but certain features of the National Housing Act were designed to eliminate the necessity for these limitations.

In December 1934 the President transmitted letters to the governors calling their attention to the need for facilitative legislation. All states with legislatures in session in 1935, save one, enacted the necessary legislation. After the session of 1937, "practically every principal lending institution in every State of the Union" was able to "make or purchase any mortgage insured under the provisions" of the National Housing Act.[3] In addition to this enabling legislation, the Federal Housing Administration has been interested in legislation making insured mortgages eligible as collateral for the deposit of public funds and eligible for the investment of public moneys or institutional funds, exempting insured mortgages from the operation of mortgage moratoria, and in other ways increasing the desirability of insured mortgages as investments. During the sessions of 1937 a total of 105 laws was passed by 42 legislatures to aid the Federal Housing Administration.[4]

Farm Credit Administration

The Farm Credit Administration is authorized to withhold farm loans if, from an examination of the laws of a state "relating to the conveying and recording of land titles, and the foreclosure of mortgages or other instruments securing loans . . . ," it appears that first mortgages furnish inadequate security.[5] Remedial legislation has been enacted where necessary, and proposals injurious to the interest of Farm Credit agencies have been checked in other instances. In 1937, for example, Idaho adopted legislation forbidding deficiency judgments in connection with mortgage foreclosures. Lending on real estate in Idaho was suspended until the act was repealed.[6]

---

[2] *Federal Housing Administration, Annual Report,* 1935, p. 27.

[3] *Federal Housing Administration, Annual Report,* 1937, p. 28.

[4] *Ibid.,* pp. 28–29. See pp. 107–10 for a tabulation of the state legislation enacted in 1937.

[5] 12 U. S. C. 971–73.

[6] W. Brooke Graves, "Influence of Congressional Legislation on Legislation in the States," 23 (1938) *Iowa Law Review* 526, n. 11.

In 1935 legislation was enacted in thirty-two states to facilitate short-term lending by newly created agencies of the Farm Credit Administration. Included in the legislation adopted were acts adding to the classes of agricultural personal property that might be offered as security for loans, acts simplifying and reducing the cost of ascertaining the status of title of property, and acts reducing charges for recording security instruments.[7]

FEDERAL HOME LOAN BANK BOARD

The Federal Home Loan Bank Board, like the Farm Credit Administration, is given authority to suspend lending operations if the land title and mortgage legislation of a state does not assure adequate security.[8] Circumstances have not necessitated extensive exercise of this power, but the Board has shown by an analysis of the lending operations of the Home Owners' Loan Corporation the added costs to the home owner because of archaic land title, mortgage, and foreclosure laws.[9] The preparation of model laws dealing with these subjects has been under way for some time. This work constitutes an important instance of pioneer research carried on in a field in which there has been no research leading to recommendations from state administrative agencies. The only source to which state legislatures can look for information is the Federal Government.

Under the supervision of the Board are the Federal savings and loan associations. The Board has sought legislation to permit the conversion of state-chartered building and loan associations into Federal associations. Forty states now permit conversion.[10] Most states have also authorized state-chartered associations to avail themselves of the benefits of share insurance through the Federal Savings and Loan Insurance Corporation, which is under the supervision of the Board.[11]

FEDERAL DEPOSIT INSURANCE CORPORATION

To permit the insurance of the deposits of state-chartered banks by the Federal Deposit Insurance Corporation, created in 1933, state legislation was required. Soon after the creation of the Corporation, the President directed a letter to each governor pointing out that if state banks were to receive the benefits of the act, additional legislation or amendments to existing statutes would be necessary in many states, and "in others, constitutional changes."[12] After the Corporation's legal staff was organized, "a legislative program for the various States was drafted and laid before the proper officials of each State for reference to and consideration by the State Legislature."[13]

Included in the program of suggested legislation of the Corporation have been bills specifically to authorize banks to take advantage of the benefits of deposit insurance, to authorize banks to rehabilitate their capital structures through the issuance of preferred stock without dou-

---

[7] Farm Credit Administration, *Annual Report,* 1935, pp. 101–3.

[8] 47 Stat. L. 725.

[9] See "Mortgages and Foreclosures," 4 (1937) *Federal Home Loan Bank Review* 40–45; and, in the same volume of the *Review,* "Costs of Title Examination and Proof," pp. 112–19; "Mechanics' Lien Laws as They Exist Today," pp. 232–36. The Federal Housing Administration has also been interested in the same general problem. See Frank Watson, "Flexible Foreclosures," 7 (1934) *State Government* 255–58.

[10] Earlier state legislation facilitating the conversion of state banks into national banks presents a parallel situation.

[11] For additional data, see Weintraub, *op. cit.,* 133–37. See also "State Legislation and the Insurance Program," 4 (1937) *Federal Home Loan Bank Review* 17.

[12] For a copy of the letter, see Comptroller of the Currency, *Annual Report,* 1933, p. 3.

[13] Federal Deposit Insurance Corporation, *Annual Report,* 1934, p. 25.

ble liability or to sell capital debentures to the Reconstruction Finance Corporation, and to authorize the appointment of the Federal Deposit Insurance Corporation as receiver of closed insured banks. In addition to these and other proposals of general application, which have been enacted by a large proportion of the state legislatures,[14] the Federal Deposit Insurance Corporation has been constantly interested in state legislation affecting the soundness of the banking structure to the end that deposit insurance risks might be reduced and that all banks created might be eligible for insurance. The assessment income of the Corporation is only one-third as great as would have been needed to meet the losses of depositors during the seventy years prior to the creation of the Corporation. To maintain the solvency of the insurance fund, sounder banking practices must prevail. Although state banks constitute only a small part of the banking business, their relatively high record of failures in the past has made them worthy of special attention.

Public Works Administration

To expedite the program of the Public Works Administration in aiding the construction activities of local governments through loans and grants, state legislation was frequently needed. Indeed, in some cases state legislation was requisite to proceed at all. In December 1934 the President transmitted letters to the governors pointing out the difficulties of the P.W.A. in dealing with municipalities under existing laws, informing them that the Public Works Legal Division was at their disposal for the drafting of corrective measures, and indicating the general types of legislation worthy of consideration. A total of 487 bills was soon furnished to meet requests following the letter.[15]

Over three hundred acts of P.W.A. parentage were passed.[16] An important type of legislation fostered was that authorizing the issuance of revenue bonds (to be retired from the earnings of the utility financed) as a means of avoiding constitutional debt limitations. That old institution, the special district, was dusted off and rechristened "authority," and promoted for the same purpose.[17] A careful administrative review by the Public Works Administration of the economic soundness of individual projects was substituted, in such cases, for the generally arbitrary state debt limits. Other legislation relaxed debt limitations, validated special procedures for bond issues, authorized municipalities to accept Federal grants, shortened and simplified the procedure for the award of contracts, and in other ways simplified the legal procedures concerning local public works.

Rural Electrification Administration

In making loans to finance the construction of rural electrification projects, the Rural Electrification Administration has been handicapped by the absence of appropriate state legislation. In many states inadequate legal basis has existed for the creation of farmers' co-operatives to construct and manage electric distributing systems, the existing corporation statutes being "uncongenial to such

---

[14] On the status of the legislative program, see Federal Deposit Insurance Corporation, *Annual Report*, 1935, pp. 27–28; 1936, p. 32; 1937, p. 24.

[15] H. L. Ickes, *Back to Work* (New York: Macmillan, 1935), pp. 220–24. For a list of bills enacted, see J. C. Pray, *Public Works Administration and Its Grant-in-Aid to Local Governments* (manuscript doctoral thesis, Harvard, 1938), pp. 256–66. See also J. F. Isakoff, *The Public Works Administration* (Illinois Studies in the Social Sciences, Vol. 23, No. 3, 1938), pp. 99–101.

[16] Pray, *op. cit.*, p. 107.

[17] See E. H. Foley, Jr., "Revenue Financing of Public Enterprises," 35 (1936) *Michigan Law Review* 1–43.

enterprise."[18] Acts following a model for the creation of electric membership corporations drafted by the Rural Electrification Administration legal staff have been enacted in fourteen states. Means for the creation of a suitable legal entity to deal with the Rural Electrification Administration are essential; the work has, however, been aided by other new state policies. Tax exemption is sometimes extended to co-operatives. Authority to use the highways for power lines is being granted, and, against considerable resistance from privately owned utilities, special regulatory policies to protect the co-operatives are being adopted.[19]

Other Legislation

The Public Works Administration and the Rural Electrification Administration have sought legislation to empower local agencies, public and semipublic, to deal with the Federal Government or to create special agencies for that purpose. The United States Housing Authority and the Soil Conservation Service have had somewhat similar objectives. The Housing Authority has continued the work of the Public Works Administration in securing state legislation authorizing the creation of local housing authorities empowered to deal with the Housing Authority, to exercise the power of eminent domain, to enjoy tax exemption, and to construct and operate housing projects.[20]

In its program for the control of soil erosion, the Soil Conservation Service has operated demonstration projects in selected areas, but it early recognized a need for special local governmental machinery through which farmers could work together as well as with the Soil Conservation Service. An act of 1935 provided that as a condition for the expenditure of funds for erosion control the Secretary of Agriculture could, if he deemed it necessary, require the enactment of suitable state and local laws for the restriction of soil erosion. A model soil-conservation-districts act was prepared, after consultation with state and local officials, and transmitted to the governors by the President in February 1935. By the end of 1937 about one-half of the states had adopted laws more or less along the lines of the model act, which permits the creation of special districts with power to make land-use regulations and to accept technical advice and other forms of assistance from the United States Department of Agriculture.[21]

Municipal Debt Adjustment

By an act of 1937 Congress, through an amendment of the bankruptcy act, provided for the composition of the debts of cities and political subdivisions unable to meet their obligations.[22] The act did not specifically require state consent to the exercise of Federal power, but the Attorney-General ruled that state legislation was essential, and more than one-third of the states adopted the necessary statutes. In the subsequent opinion of the Supreme Court upholding the act, the fact of state consent as expressed by legislation was pivotal. "The State acts in aid, and not in derogation, of its sovereign powers. It invites the intervention of the bankruptcy power to save its agency which the State itself is

---

[18] Rural Electrification Administration, *Report*, 1937, p. 52.

[19] "New Wisconsin Law Protects Co-ops from Encroachments of Utilities," *Rural Electrification News*, April 1937, pp. 14–15. See also R. D. Baum, "Power District Legislation," 26 (1937) *National Municipal Review* 28–30.

[20] See L. H. Keyserling, "Low Rent Housing," 11 (1938) *State Government* 83–84.

[21] See P. M. Glick, "State Legislation for Erosion Control," 3 (1937) *Soil Conservation* 120–25.

[22] 50 Stat. 653. Passed to replace the act of 1934 (48 Stat. 498) held void in Ashton v. Cameron County Water Improvement District No. 1, 298 U. S. 513 (1936).

powerless to rescue." [23] In this situation the Federal power is exercised not through an ordinary administrative agency but through the courts. Nevertheless, the linking of Federal and state power is in essence the same as that which occurs when an ordinary Federal administrative agency is involved.

Administrative Co-operation

The impression should not be conveyed that the Federal agencies under discussion rely solely on state legislation to aid them in achieving their objectives. While in some instances legislation alone is necessary, in other cases close co-operation is maintained with the appropriate state administrative agencies. The Federal Deposit Insurance Corporation, for example, exchanges information with state banking supervisors, at times conducts joint examinations of banks with them, and co-operates in other ways. The Rural Electrification Administration in some instances has cordial relationships with state utility commissions which may aid in the promotion of rural electrification through administrative orders. The Home Loan Bank Board has relationships of varying effectiveness with state supervisors of building and loan associations.[24]

Conclusions

The speed with which legislation was enacted by most of the states to facilitate Federal programs may be partly accounted for by the fact that most governors were in sympathy with the general aims of the National Administration. In 1935 and 1937, when most of the legislation was passed, the National Administration was at the peak of its prestige. Party forces tended to amalgamate Federal and state powers and to create, for the moment at any rate, an entirely different kind of federalism. The significance of agreement between President and governor on broad objectives in the legislative process is indicated by the situation in Georgia. Action in a number of the programs was held up until the anti-New Deal governor, Talmadge, retired from office. In some instances he was influential in preventing legislative action; in others, he vetoed bills passed by the legislature.

Another factor has probably been more fundamental than Federal-state political harmony in smoothing the way for state legislation. Individual citizens, state-chartered corporations, and political subdivisions have been desirous of taking advantage of the benefits of the various Federal programs. These interests have brought their point of view to bear upon the state legislatures. To these pressures was added the persuasion of Federal administrative units. While it cannot be accurately said that the state legislatures were ground between the upper and nether millstones, they were under varying degrees of compulsion through the combination of pressures from above and below.

The enactment of state legislation has to a degree been a condition precedent to the enjoyment within a state of the benefits of Federal legislation. That state action was at times a condition precedent was not due to deliberate Federal grasping for power, but was a product of legal circumstances. If, for example, state law operated to prevent state banks from participation in Federal deposit insurance, the requisite corrective amendment was generally desired by both state and Federal authorities and by the depositors. Most of the state legislation has not been absolutely necessary to permit the administration of a Federal act within a state, but has been enacted to make the work of the

---

[23] United States v. Bekins, 304 U. S. 27 (1938).

[24] On co-operation between state administrative agencies and Federal corporations, see Weintraub, *op. cit.*, Chap. VI.

Federal agencies concerned more effective or economical. Granting the desirability of the Federal policies, such concurrent action by the state legislatures seems an eminently sensible form of intergovernmental collaboration.

From the foregoing analysis it appears that there has been developed, more or less without design, a new method of linking Federal and state powers [25] through interrelated Federal and state action. In its most extreme form, the method makes the availability within a state of direct Federal services contingent upon the adoption of facilitative state policies. Although the utilization of the method has been restricted to a limited variety of situations, these uses suggest other potentialities. On a wide front there are governmental problems in which co-ordinated Federal and state action is indicated.[26] Especially when a complex, integrated program involving numerous Federal agencies and several states is elaborated jointly by Federal and state representatives, the Federal phases might well be made contingent upon state action in related fields as a spur to overcome the inertia of state legislatures. To follow this course would tend to pass from state legislation facilitative of direct Federal action to state legislation and administration complementary to Federal policy.

---

[25] This, of course, is what is accomplished through the Federal grant-in-aid, as has been pointed out by E. S. Corwin, "National-State Co-operation—Its Present Possibilities," 8 (1937) *American Law School Review* 687–707.

[26] See, for example, Great Plains Committee, *The Future of the Great Plains* (1937), Pt. III, for an integrated program of state and local action to deal with the problems of the Great Plains.

V. O. Key, Jr., Ph.D., is Associate in the Department of Political Science of The Johns Hopkins University, Baltimore, Maryland. He has served as instructor in political science at the University of California at Los Angeles, staff member of the Committee on Public Administration of the Social Science Research Council, and research technician for the National Resources Committee. He is author of "The Administration of Federal Grants to States" (1937).

The Future of Federal Grants-in-Aid

By Joseph P. Harris

FEDERAL aid has become one of the most important aspects of governmental finance in this country. During recent years it has greatly increased in size, and the prospect is for an even greater use of Federal aid in the future. It is time to examine critically the existing Federal aid policies and administration, the significant trends, and the defects indicated by experience, to see what changes are needed. Federal aid in this country has developed without a well-considered, consistent, national policy. It has been guided principally by the advocates of particular forms of aid to the states, with little attention to national interest.

Growth of Federal Aid

Prior to 1915 the total grants, not including those for the National Guard, amounted to less than $5,000,000 annually.[1] After the passage of the highway act in 1916, Federal aid rose to around $100,000,000 annually, at which point it remained fairly constant from 1918 through 1930. The annual expenditures for highways alone accounted for about $80,000,000. During the 1920's, when Federal aid was the subject of considerable controversy, the only substantial Federal aid was for highways. The other grants combined totaled only from ten to twenty million annually—less than 1 per cent of the national budget. Somewhat more than half of this went to the state agricultural colleges for experiment stations, extension work, and agricultural and scientific education; about a third went to vocational education; and the remainder, in annual appropriations of less than $1,000,000 each, to forest fire protection, vocational rehabilitation, public health, and maternal and child health. During these years state aid to local governments for highways and schools was several times larger than all Federal aid and was growing rapidly. By 1930 New York State alone was providing nearly $100,000,000 in state aid, or about the same amount as the total Federal aid to all the states.[2]

Since 1930 Federal aid has increased very rapidly, though it still constitutes only a small part of the national budget—less than 10 per cent. It has become in this country, as elsewhere in the world, an important aspect of governmental finance. In 1931 Federal aid increased to $180,000,000, largely because of an increase of highway aid to over $150,000,000, and at the close of the Hoover administration it had reached about $215,000,000 annually. Since 1933 it has greatly increased, amounting to $488,000,000 in 1938. This figure includes only the regular, permanent grants-in-aid to state and local governments, except the National Guard payments, and does not include work-relief expenditures, of which $122,000,000 was expended through emergency grants to the states for highways, and $176,000,000 in P.W.A. grants to states and local governments. The large expenditures for W.P.A., amounting to $1,414,708 in 1938, were disbursed for the most part under co-operative arrangements with state and local governments, but are not properly classified as Federal aid.

While the increase in Federal aid has

---

[1] The National Guard is omitted from these figures because it has become in reality a Federal rather than a state activity.

[2] See H. J. Bittermann, *State and Federal Grants-in-Aid* (Chicago: Mentzer, Bush & Co.), Chap. II; R. J. Hinckley, *State Grants in Aid* (Albany: New York State Tax Commission), p. 30.

been rapid since 1933, it is to be noted that such aid has accounted for only a relatively small part of the increase in national expenditures. Since 1935, when the present works program was instituted, the great bulk of expenditures for unemployment relief and public works has been disbursed directly by the Federal agencies in charge.

The increases in the regular, permanent Federal aid between 1931 and 1938 are to be accounted for largely by the new aids provided under the Social Security Act; but in addition, substantial increases have been made in other Federal aid, particularly vocational education and agricultural extension. Highway aid increased from $75,000,000 in 1930 to $186,000,000 in 1932. In 1938 it amounted to $138,000,000 under regular funds and $122,000,000 under emergency relief appropriations, making a total of $260,000,000. Subsidies to low-cost housing (not including loans for construction, which are to be repaid with interest) were added to the family of Federal aid by the Housing Act of 1937. This act authorizes loans of $800,000,000 to local housing authorities, and subsidies to reduce the rentals at $28,000,000 annually. Local authorities are required to make a contribution of at least 20 per cent of the Federal subsidy, which has usually been in the form of tax exemption.

Under the Social Security Act, Federal aid is provided for old-age assistance, aid to dependent children, aid to the blind, public health, child welfare, maternal and child health, vocational rehabilitation, and services for crippled children. Under this act the Federal Government is obligated to match state and local expenditures under approved plans for old-age assistance, aid to the blind, and aid to dependent children, without any limitation as to the total amount which any state may receive, though there are limitations as to the amount of grants per month to any individual which the Federal Government will match.[3]

The Federal aid payments to the states during the fiscal year 1938 for these three forms of public assistance amounted to $226,000,000, and are steadily increasing. Old-age assistance grants constitute the great bulk of this amount, totaling $196,000,000 in 1938, and it is expected that they will continue to increase for many years to come. The other grants to the states under the Social Security Act are much smaller and are definitely limited in amount. The aid for public health was originally fixed at $8,000,000 annually, but was increased to $11,000,000 by the last Congress and presumably will be increased substantially with the development of a broader public-health program in the future. The Social Security grants for the administration of unemployment compensation, including the operation of public employment offices, are really not grants-in-aid, for the states are not expected to match them, though they are required to match the funds appropriated for public employment offices under the Wagner-Peyser Act. The Social Security grants for this purpose, amounting to $53,000,000 in 1938, are, in effect, 100 per cent grants, the Federal Government bearing the entire cost of administration. This expenditure, it should be noted, is more than covered by the 10 per cent of the tax upon employers which is paid into the Federal treasury.

This brief review of the recent expansion of Federal aid indicates that: (1) the regular, permanent grants have now reached approximately one-half billion dollars annually, or about 6 per cent of the national budget; (2) substantial increases are to be expected, particularly

---

[3] Federal aid for dependent children was confined to one-third of the expenditures under the original act, but was raised in 1939 to 50 per cent.

for public-assistance grants under the Social Security Act, for public health, and for housing; (3) emergency grants to states and local governments for highways and public works under P.W.A. totaled $298,000,000 in 1938.

Future Growth

What are the future prospects for Federal aid? If no new aids are adopted and the present obligations and policies are carried out, there will be substantial increases of the present grants-in-aid; and it would be difficult to point to any aid which is likely to be curtailed in the future. It is very probable that new activities will be included within Federal aid. The dire straits of the schools in many states since the depression has brought about a great increase in state aid to education, and a growing demand for Federal aid as a means of assuring a reasonably adequate minimum standard of education throughout the country. Legislation providing for Federal aid has been considered at recent sessions of Congress, and in 1936 President Roosevelt created an Advisory Committee on Education, which made a report in 1938 recommending Federal aid for general education amounting to $72,000,000 for the first year and increasing annually to $200,000,000 by the fifth year. This amount is relatively small in proportion to the total cost of public education throughout the country, which in 1936 amounted to well over two billion dollars. Thus, the Federal aid proposed would have constituted less than 10 per cent of the total when the maximum proposed was reached. Legislation to carry this program into effect has met with considerable opposition in Congress, but it seems entirely probable that Federal aid will be provided sooner or later, and necessarily will be in large amounts.

It should also be noted that there is considerable sentiment in the country and in Congress for changing the present program for unemployment relief, turning it back to the states and localities to carry on with Federal aid. Legislation along these lines was strongly pressed at the last session of Congress as the most feasible means of reducing Federal expenditures for this purpose. If similar legislation is adopted in the future, which is rather probable, it will result in a very great increase in Federal aid, though probably a decrease in Federal appropriations.

World-Wide Movement

The expansion of Federal aid in this country is by no means exceptional to the trend in other countries. Every industrialized country has faced the problem of a growing disparity between local governmental tax resources and the demands for services, and has been forced to resort to central financial aid to local governments. The grant-in-aid is only one of several devices which may be used. Other means include the assumption by the central government of expensive activities formerly conducted by the local governments, the sharing of centrally collected taxes with the local units, and the use of "block" or unconditional subsidies, permitting the local governments to expend them for whatever purpose they may determine.

Although little attention has been paid to state aid to local units, it has greatly exceeded in amount Federal aid to the states (except emergency expenditures for unemployment relief), and within recent years has been increasing at a very fast rate, particularly for education and relief. Professor Newcomer estimated that state aid amounted to $340,000,000 in 1925.[4] By 1932, according to estimates by Professor Bittermann, it had increased to over $600,000,000, and by

[4] Mabel Newcomer, "Tendencies in State and Local Finance and Their Relation to State and Local Functions," *Political Science Quarterly*, Vol. XLIII (March 1928), p. 23.

1934 to over $900,000,000.[5] If current figures were available, they would undoubtedly show state aid amounting to well over a billion dollars annually, constituting nearly half of state expenditures, though probably amounting to only about one-sixth of the local governmental expenditures.

A few illustrations taken from the releases of the Bureau of the Census on *Financial Statistics of State Governments* for 1937 will indicate the very large part of the state budgets which state aid has become. New York in 1937 made grants to local authorities totaling $206,878,000 out of a total expenditure of $420,000,000; California, $88,000,000, while total state expenditures amounted to $224,000,000; Massachusetts, $31,000,000 out of total expenditures of $93,000,000. The growth of state aid is not confined to the more wealthy states. South Carolina, for example, provided nearly $10,000,000 of state aid while expending a total of about $33,000,000.

NATIONAL POLICY NEEDED

Because of the great increase in size of Federal aid, and the strong likelihood that it will continue as a major feature of our system of governmental financing, it is desirable to examine carefully the prevailing philosophy and policies. As long as Federal aid amounted to only a few million dollars annually, or even a hundred million, as was the case from 1918 to 1930—only about 3 per cent of the national budget—it was not so essential to develop a consistent and rational policy, or to consider carefully such matters as apportionment, measurement of the need of aided services, the financial abilities of the states, and the many problems of Federal and state administration of grants. Heretofore, national policies on the subject have been dictated largely by those who were interested in securing legislation, with little attention to consistency or national interest. Now there are commanding reasons why our whole grant-in-aid program should be broadly considered and policies developed which will safeguard national interest.

Opposition to Federal aid has been raised upon a number of grounds. It has been said: (1) that it is unsound to separate the pleasure of spending from the pain of levying taxes; (2) that grants-in-aid are a form of bribery to state and local officials, inducing them to spend public funds and to carry on activities beyond their need under the inducement of securing easy money from the Federal Government; (3) that Federal aid is an insidious means whereby the Federal Government may encroach upon the sovereign rights of the states, using Federal funds to secure state acquiescence to dictation, supervision, and control from Federal officials unacquainted with local problems and not responsible to local voters; and finally, (4) that it is unfair to tax the wealthier states to support governmental services in the poorer.

On the other hand, it has been maintained by advocates of Federal aid: (1) that it is a useful device by which the Federal Government and the states and local governments may join together in the financing of services of national as well as state and local interest, and as such, is an effective device whereby the National Government may carry out a national policy without duplicating and competing with similar services rendered locally; (2) that it lends flexibility which is sorely needed in our rigid constitutional system; (3) that it is a valuable means of financing governmental services beyond the means of state and local authorities; (4) that it constitutes an important aspect of tax reform, per-

---

[5] H. J. Bittermann, *State and Federal Grants-in-Aid, op. cit.*, p. 50. See, however, other and smaller estimates on p. 54.

mitting the taxing of income concentrated in wealthier states, and derived from nationwide operations, to support important governmental services of national concern; (5) that it is an important means for the preservation of state and local governments by providing them with the means to carry on the functions assigned to them; and (6) that Federal supervision has been an important element in improving state and local standards of administration.

During the period from 1920 to 1930, Federal aid aroused considerable opposition and was denounced by leaders of both of the major political parties. Despite these oratorical fulminations of Democrats and Republicans alike, there was no falling off of Federal aid, and except for aid for maternal and child health, no attempt was made to curtail individual grants. Political leaders charged that Federal bureaucrats were dictating to the officials of the sovereign states, but the officials themselves reported the most amicable and helpful relations.

On the other hand, the great increase in Federal aid during the New Deal administration has occasioned relatively little opposition. The greatest increase has come through the Social Security Act, but opposition to this act was centered on the social insurance features rather than upon the Federal aid for public assistance. The movement for old-age pensions—by far the largest of these aids—had become so strong by 1935 that there was no opposition to Federal aid for this purpose. Opposition came rather from those who would have the Federal Government take over the entire cost and pay substantially larger pensions. Federal aid was utilized because the Administration and a majority of members of Congress believed that old-age assistance should be left to the states and localities to administer. They believed that if half of the cost were borne locally, this would provide needed protection against raids on the Federal treasury. Thus Federal aid was provided as a means of keeping the costs down. The same reasoning will probably operate with respect to other functions in the future, and strange as it may seem, Federal aid will probably be expanded as a means of balancing the national budget.

Federal aid is neither wholly good nor wholly bad, and a discussion of its merits and faults without attention to the provisions and the operation of individual grants is of little merit. The formulation of a rational, consistent national policy must await a more discriminating consideration of the practical operation and problems which experience has indicated. The remainder of this article is devoted to a consideration of some of these problems in an attempt to state some of the essentials of a sound national policy. Federal aid should not be adopted indiscriminately for any state and local service which can command a powerful enough lobby to force through the necessary legislation. It is by no means clear that it is suitable to all activities alike. In some instances Federal aid ought to be denied because the service is essentially local; in other instances it should be refused because the service can be rendered effectively and economically only by the Federal Government. If new Federal aid is provided, careful consideration should be given to the provisions of the law which govern it, the allocation of aid to the several states, and the administration of the grants. Some of the important older grants need to be reconsidered in the light of actual experience, and defects corrected as far as possible.

Effect of Federal Aid on Unaided Services

A major problem in Federal aid is its effect upon unaided government services. As long as Federal aid was relatively small in amount, the effect of singling out a few governmental functions or parts of functions for Federal aid, thus placing them in a preferred position in securing state and local appropriations, was not particularly serious. But now that Federal aid has reached large proportions and is provided for many important activities, it is having serious effects in inducing state and local legislative bodies to favor these activities at the expense of others equally meritorious. Consider, for example, the effect of Federal aid upon expenditures for highways and old-age assistance. An impartial student of public finance would be forced to admit that these activities have been placed in a highly preferred position, and that other governmental functions equally important have suffered because of the diversion of available state and local funds into these and other activities which are Federally aided. Who can maintain today that general education is less deserving of Federal aid than the special types of education which are aided?

That general welfare services have been neglected and have actually suffered because of the drain upon public resources caused by old-age assistance, no one can deny. In May 1939 the general relief expenditures by states and local governments in this country amounted to $39,000,000 while the expenditures for old-age assistance alone from all sources amounted to over $35,000,000.[6] It will hardly be maintained that this is a reasonable distribution of public funds, nor can it be denied that persons cared for under general relief have been neglected.

An examination of the payments by individual states affords some striking contrasts. New York State, which has attempted to maintain a reasonable balance between general relief and old-age assistance, paid out four times as much for general relief as the total payments from all sources for old-age assistance, and New Jersey expended nearly three times as much for general relief as for old-age assistance. Massachusetts, Wisconsin, Minnesota, California, and a number of other states spent roughly the same amount for each. In a number of poorer states where the old-age movement has been strong, the comparison is extremely significant. Oklahoma spent during May, with Federal aid, $1,190,000 for old-age assistance, but only $59,000—one-twentieth the former amount—for general relief. Texas spent $1,640,000 for old-age assistance, but only $127,000, or less than one-twelfth, for general relief. Colorado spent $1,013,000 for old-age assistance, but only $187,000 for general relief.

Further comparisons of expenditures for Federally aided with unaided activities would, it is believed, afford striking evidence of the distortion of state and local expenditures induced by Federal aid at present. The effects are already serious, and may become even more so in the future. All other governmental services suffer when a disproportionate part of state and local funds, which are necessarily limited in amount, are spent on Federally aided activities.

Budgeting is essentially a process of balancing the needs for all governmental services, weighing one against the other, and considering the needs of all in relation to the funds which are available. A basic fault of any form of outside aid with a matching requirement is that it may induce local authorities to make an unwise distribution of available local funds. During the first few years of any new Federal aid, it is to be expected that its influence will be that of stimulating local appropriations; but after the service is established and the state and local authorities are in a position to appraise

[6] These figures are taken from *Social Security Bulletin*, July 1939.

its value to the community, the effect of Federal aid should be limited largely to support rather than further stimulation of the particular service. It is to be expected, of course, that Federal aid will enable state and local authorities to render more effective governmental services than would otherwise be possible, but it is of doubtful wisdom to give a preferred position permanently to particular activities at the expense of others.

Federal Aid without Distortion

The question will immediately be raised, How may Federal aid be provided without resulting in a distortion of state and local budgets? Will not local officials inevitably favor those activities which receive outside aid, and be tempted to make appropriations, not on the basis of need for the service, but in order to secure the "free" Federal money? One solution is to provide Federal aid without any strings attached, permitting its use for any purpose the local authorities may decide. The "block" or unconditional subsidy has the merit of leaving the local authorities free to weigh the relative claims of the several governmental services, but experience in this country and abroad with this form of aid has been, on the whole, unsatisfactory. It has led to extravagance, and has not permitted the establishment of a national minimum standard of either service or administration.

Another solution would be to relax the matching requirement, and there is a trend in this direction. If satisfactory administrative supervision can be secured, thus assuring reasonably good administration, the matching requirement, which is designed to afford protection against improvident spending, might be relaxed. So far, however, there has been considerable reluctance on the part of Congress to grant adequate authority to the Federal agency in charge, permitting the supervision which would be needed if matching were waived. It is significant that the matching requirements have been relaxed with respect to emergency highway aid, and the Federal supervision and standards were adequate to assure satisfactory expenditure of these unmatched funds. On the other hand, the Federal grants for unemployment compensation administration, which do not require matching, have given rise to considerable difficulties which both Federal and state administrators believe would be avoided if there were matching provisions.

A third solution would be to provide Federal aid for most of the expensive state and local functions, thus avoiding the favoring of a few. This is the solution which England has followed. An examination of the list of central grants to the municipalities in England indicates that practically all municipal services of any size receive central aid. A similar policy in this country would mean that Federal aid would be provided for welfare activities generally instead of for particular forms of public assistance, for education generally instead of for a few specialized aspects, and for law enforcement, recreation, and a few other state and local services not aided at present. Regulatory functions of government are relatively inexpensive and do not require outside aid. It will be objected, of course, that to extend Federal aid to these additional state and local services would result in further unbalancing of the Federal budget. This by no means follows. The total grants-in-aid are small in comparison with the expenditures for the emergency public works, for national defense, and for payments to veterans. As indicated above, Federal aid for general welfare and relief would probably result in a reduction rather than an increase of the Federal expenditures.

The present policy of Federal aids for favored functions and segments of these functions is indefensible. It would be better to appropriate the same amount of money under broader grants, permitting it to be used for all aspects of these services, thus avoiding the splintering effect of existing Federal aid.

It is significant to note that Federal and state aids to local governments in this country now amount to only about one-sixth of the total local expenditures, while in England central grants to the municipalities nearly equal the local tax revenues, the central government thus bearing approximately half the cost of local government. We have not reached the limit of Federal and state aid, but before they are expanded further, a more rational and consistent policy and better administration are needed.

Fixing and Apportioning Appropriations

Another major problem is that of determining the total amount of Federal aid to be appropriated for each purpose. Heretofore little attempt has been made to meet this problem in a scientific way. The total appropriation has been fixed in an offhand manner, without much attention to the total need for the particular service throughout the country. The pressure groups supporting the legislation or appropriation have tried to secure whatever amount they thought would be possible, and Congress and administrators have been inadequately armed with the facts to pass upon these claims. The time has come when the Federal appropriation ought to be considered much more carefully with relation to the estimated cost of the service and the need for Federal aid.

The method of apportionment among the states has, in the main, been decided in the same offhand manner. Some of the earliest grants apportioned an identical amount to every state, large and small. The only justification for this practice is the fact that every state has two Senators. It is still retained in a few Federal aids, though relatively small amounts are so apportioned. Many of the Federal aids provide for apportionment on the basis of population, either total population or the population served by the particular service. This formula has not worked badly for minor grants. Although population is only a very rough indication of the need for any governmental service, and the inevitable result of such apportionment is that some states receive more and others much less Federal aid than they need, nevertheless, for minor grants such inequities may be tolerated. The highway grants, being based in equal proportion upon population, area, and mileage of post roads, has worked with a fair degree of satisfaction. The poorer and more sparsely settled states have received relatively larger amounts. The method of distribution of forestry aid is particularly significant. The United States Forest Service, in conjunction with the states, determines upon what the cost of adequate protection would be for each state, and this estimate is made the basis for the distribution of part of the Federal aid. The remainder is apportioned in proportion to the total expenditures for this purpose by the states.

Much more refined methods of apportionment are needed, though it is also desirable to keep the method as simple and understandable as possible. Ideally, Federal aid should be apportioned among the states upon two principal bases, namely, the need for the particular service and, if a national minimum standard is desired, the relative financial abilities of the states to render this minimum service. At present little attention is given to either factor. During 1933–35 the Federal Emergency Relief Administration grants for relief were apportioned by the administrative agency, and Administrator Hopkins attempted to require each state to bear a "fair" share of the cost of relief; but there was no agreed method of determining what was a "fair" proportion, and the division led to many serious disputes between the states and the Federal authorities, with curtailment of relief in several states for a period. This experience has increased the reluctance of Congress to permit any administrative discretion in the distribution of Federal aid. The Surgeon General is authorized to determine the method of allocation of Federal aid for public health services, in consultation with state health officers, the act providing that three factors shall be taken into account, namely: population, special health problems, and relative financial need of the several states. This aid, it should be noted, is relatively small in size.

Need for Equalization

Except for a small part of the Federal aid for public health, and the unemployment relief grants from 1933 to 1935, there has been little effort in the distribution of Federal aid to take into account the financial abilities of the states, though the desirability of doing so is generally recognized. Most of the states have introduced some "equalizing" factor in the allotment of state aid for education. The public assistance grants under the Social Security Act, being based upon the expenditures of the state and local governments, operate with just the opposite effect; to the wealthiest states the largest Federal aid is provided, for it is these states that are able to make the most adequate payments. In the poorest states the old-age assistance grants average less than ten dollars per month, while the national average is $19.20, and many wealthier states are paying around twenty-five dollars per month on the average. To the needy aged person in Arkansas the Federal Government pays three dollars per month, but to the aged recipient in Massachusetts it pays over fourteen dollars. The five states which are paying average pensions of less than ten dollars per month—Arkansas, Alabama, Georgia, Mississippi, and South Carolina—with a combined population of 11,158,000, received in Federal aid $4,987,000 for old-age pensions in 1938; while Massachusetts, Colorado, and California, having a combined population of 10,963,000, or slightly less than that of the former five states, received $38,951,000, or seven and one-half times as much. These, of course, are the states standing at the ends of the scale. It is of interest that these five southern states received $14,229,000 in Federal aid for highways from the regular appropriation, while the corresponding highway aid to California, Colorado, and Massachusetts totaled $10,118,000.

The inequity of the percentage grants for public assistance under the Social Security Act is widely recognized, and at the last session of Congress the Social Security Board advocated legislation which would permit larger proportionate grants to the poorer states, to be varied in inverse proportion to the average per capita income in the several states. Legislation along this line was proposed by Senator Byrnes and others, but this feature encountered opposition from representatives from the wealthier states, and was not incorporated in the amendments to the act which were passed. Many members of Congress, even from the poorer states, thought that it would be unsafe to relax in any way the 50 per cent matching requirement, for once this principle were abandoned, there would be constant efforts for further modifications, and Congress would not be able to withstand the pressure.

There is much to be said for this position, particularly as long as percentage grants are continued without any limitation upon the amount of Federal aid to each state. The solution of the problem is not to be found in merely authorizing larger grants to the poorer states, but rather in the allocation of Federal aid among the states on the basis of the need within each state for old-age assistance, determined in a uniform manner, plus some adjustment whereby the poorer states may receive a relatively larger proportion of Federal aid than the wealthy states. Unless the unlimited percentage grants for old-age assistance are modified so as to correct the existing defects, it will be necessary sooner or later for Congress to grant to the Federal agency more adequate authority whereby a greater degree of uniformity in policies and administration may be secured, or it may become necessary for the Federal Government to take over the entire cost and provide direct Federal administration.

The change most to be desired is to provide Federal aid generally for welfare and relief, instead of singling out a few activities for preferred treatment. The old-age assistance forces in this country are strong enough to secure adequate appropriations without the added inducement of unlimited Federal aid, while other related welfare activities receive no Federal aid.

The proposal for Federal aid to education made by the Advisory Committee on Education called for allocation in proportion to the financial abilities of the states. The committee reasoned that since the primary objective was to bring up the standard of educational opportunity in the poorest states, and since the amount of Federal aid recommended was small in proportion to the total cost, the objective could be achieved only by allocating the bulk of Federal aid to the poorer states, with little aid to the wealthier states.

This position would appear to be eminently sound, but heretofore it has been necessary for proposed Federal aids to provide substantial sums to all the states in order to win Congressional support.

Greater attention should be given to the financial abilities of these several states in the distribution of Federal aid, but it does not follow that merely because a state is poor it should receive proportionately larger Federal aid. There are said to be many counties in the country which are now being supported in substantial degree by state aid. Communities which cannot economically support themselves should not be artificially maintained by government subsidy. The principal of distribution in proportion to financial abilities should never go to the length of retarding the normal and necessary readjustments in population.

It is significant to note that in 1938 the Federal Government expended in North Dakota for Federal aid, work relief, Civilian Conservation Corps, National Guard, and agricultural adjustment payments, a total of $39,900,000, while the total expenditures of the state and all local governments for all governmental services, capital outlays, and interest charges in 1932, less Federal aid, amounted to only $41,000,000! In South Dakota these Federal payments in 1938 amounted to $43,000,000, while all governmental costs in 1932, less Federal aid, totaled $46,000,000. In New York State the same Federal payments in 1938 amounted to only 18.2 per cent of the 1932 governmental costs, less Federal aid; in Massachusetts, 25 per cent; and in Illinois and Wisconsin, 30 per cent.[7] It should be noted, however, that Federal aid to the state constitutes only a very small part of the total Federal expenditures included in these figures.

[7] The statistics are taken from the 1938 *Annual Report* of the Secretary of the Treasury, and the report of the U. S. Bureau of the Census on the *Financial Statistics of State and Local Governments, 1932.*

Federal Aid Pressure Groups

Another important aspect of Federal aid is the ability of powerful and organized lobbies for particular functions to force through legislation or appropriations in Congress. The strength of these pressure groups, rather than any rational consideration or governmental finance, has been the controlling factor behind Federal and state aid. This fact constitutes one of the greatest dangers to the future. State officials receiving Federal aid are not subject to the same responsibility and restrictions which apply to Federal officials in lobbying for appropriations before Congress, and they are able to reach the ear of Congressmen in a much more direct and effective manner.

The ability of the lobby for vocational education in 1937 to force through a great increase in the Federal appropriation over the opposition of the Administration, the inability of the President to secure even a consideration by Congress of his proposal the same year to reduce highway appropriations, and the liberalization of the provisions for old-age assistance by the last Congress, are straws indicating the effectiveness with which these lobbies operate. In Canada, the Dominion has discontinued a number of important aids to the provinces, including that for highways; but in this country, when the President proposed as an economy measure a reduction of highway aid, the Chairman of the House Committee refused even to call his committee to consider the recommendation.

If Federal aid is to be utilized extensively in the future, it is imperative that steps be taken to curtail the strength of powerful lobbies and to enable the Government to adopt a well-considered and balanced program. The responsibility for the formulation of such a program in the light of the financial ability of the Federal Government itself will necessarily have to be placed more definitely upon the administration—regardless of which party is in power—and Congress will be forced to follow the practice of refusing to raise the budget estimates.

Administration

A final consideration in the future of Federal aids, and one of which space does not permit more than brief mention here, is their administration.[8] Unless satisfactory administration can be developed whereby the central government is assured that its funds are being wisely, economically, and efficiently expended, Federal aid is unsound.

The general experience with grant-in-aid administration in this country has been that the standards of state administration have been improved through the influence and the requirements made of the states by the Federal agency. A number of years ago Sidney Webb said of grant-in-aid in England,

> ... if we examine, one by one, the different branches of public administration ... we shall find that, so far as they are entrusted to our local governing bodies and disregarding particular cases, they vary in efficiency according to the extent to which use has been intelligently made of the grant-in-aid.

This has been equally true of this country, though Congress has been little interested in administration, and has been reluctant to grant adequate authority to the Federal agency to require reasonable standards.

Who would question the salutary influence of the United States Bureau of Public Roads upon state highway construction and planning? Many would like to have seen even more vigorous Federal supervision, particularly the re-

---

[8] See the able study by V. O. Key, Jr., *The Administration of Federal Grants to States*, Public Administration Service, 1937.

quirement of nonpolitical administration of highways by the states.

No one would question that the Social Security Board has worked constantly and effectively for efficient and nonpolitical administration of the public assistance and social insurance activities under its supervision, and has required many states to correct bad situations when public opinion in the state seemed powerless to bring about any improvement. The requirement of the Social Security Board that the co-operating states shall establish merits systems—a requirement which was questionable under the original provisions of the act, but now specifically authorized by law—should be extended to all Federally aided activities. Similarly, the earlier requirement of the United States Employment Service that appointments should be made on the basis of competitive examinations is to be commended. Little defense can be made of Federal or state aid if the local administration is conducted under a system of political spoils.

The essentials for sound administration of Federal aid by the Federal agency in charge include the following: (1) adequate grant of authority to the Federal agency, not merely to see that the Federal law is observed, but to require a reasonable standard of administration by the states; (2) an adequate Federal staff of persons with technical competence and practical experience; (3) the rendering of various kinds of technical service and assistance to the state agencies, particularly in the conduct of research; (4) the adoption of a policy of developing strong administration by the states, with a minimum of Federal dictation and interference as long as the state administration is reasonably satisfactory.

Summary

Federal aid may be said to be at a midway point. Prior to 1930 it was relatively small in amount (except the highway grants), and was limited to a few major functions regarded for some reason as objects of national interest; now it has become very large in amount, totaling over one-half billion dollars from regular appropriations, and has been expanded to a wider range of governmental services. It is destined to become even larger. Formerly it was utilized largely as a device for stimulating the states to undertake a few favored activities; now the emphasis has shifted from stimulation to support, and the Federal Government shares with the states and the localities the cost of an increasing number of expensive functions. Formerly the Federal Government might disregard the effects of Federal aid in stimulating the aided activities at the expense of other functions, and, indeed, regard the stimulating effect with satisfaction as carrying out the purpose of the Federal legislation; now the serious effects of Federal aid in distorting state and local budgets need to be taken into account.

In view of the size and importance of Federal aid, and its probable increasing future role, the time has come for the Federal Government to adopt a more consistent, rational policy, and to correct some of the existing defects which experience has indicated in existing policies and administration. It is suggested that some of the important elements of such a national policy on Federal aid include the following:

1. Greater attention should be given to the effects of Federal aid on the whole structure of state and local finance, with particular attention to how it affects unaided activities, and steps should be taken to lessen the undue, permanent preference now given to particular functions or parts of functions which receive Federal aid. The steps to be taken might include a broadening of the purposes of Federal aid, thus avoid-

ing the favoring of certain functions; and revision of the terms of Federal aid. The unlimited percentage grants for expensive governmental services should be abandoned.

2. More careful consideration should be given to the amount of Federal aid to be provided for each aided function, based upon better factual data of the need for the service throughout the country. It is highly desirable to curtail the power of special interest groups to lobby through appropriations for Federal aid, and to establish more definite responsibility for the passing upon appropriations with a view to national rather than special interests.

3. The method of distribution of Federal aid should be given more careful attention in the future, with less use of rule-of-thumb methods of allocation. Total population is too rough a measure of the need for a particular service to serve as a basis of distribution, particularly for expensive services, and simple percentage grants are undesirable. One solution would be to authorize the administrative agency in charge, under suitable statutory provisions, to determine the need for the service in each state, to be used as the basis for distribution. Greater attention will also need to be given to the financial abilities of the several states, particularly where a minimum national standard of service is desired.

4. The maintenance of reasonable standards of administration is of the utmost concern to the Federal Government as a protection against unwise and improvident expenditure of Federal aid. The simple faith in the efficacy of the matching requirement as a means of assuring satisfactory administration is not supported by actual experience. The standards of administration of state and local governments are, unfortunately, frequently low. Experience indicates that the Federal agency administering Federal aid may exert considerable influence in improving state and local administration by the insistence upon a merit system in personnel and nonpolitical administration, the provision of technical services and research, the building up of professional standards and techniques, the interchange of information and experience among the administrative officials of the several states, and in other ways. Congress should hold the administrative agencies in charge responsible for insistence upon satisfactory administrative standards—many of which might well be specified in the statute—without undue interference or dictation in routine matters, and should grant adequate authority to enable the agency to carry out that responsibility.

Joseph P. Harris, Ph.D., is professor of political science at the University of California, Berkeley. He has also served in the departments of political science at the universities of Wisconsin and Washington; as assistant executive director of the President's Committee on Economic Security; and as director of research of the President's Committee on Administrative Management and of the Committee on Public Administration of the Social Science Research Council. He is author of "Registration of Voters in the United States" (1927), "Administration of Elections in the United States" (1934), and "County Finances in the State of Washington" (1935).

Intergovernmental Taxation Today

By David Fellman

ONE of the important by-products of the American federal system has been the problem of intergovernmental taxation. The courts have been wrestling with the problem ever since John Marshall ruled that, even in the absence of any definite constitutional provision, Maryland could not tax the notes of the United States Bank, on the general theory that the states may not interfere by taxation with the execution by the National Government of its valid powers.[1] The immunity was made reciprocal some fifty years later when state instrumentalities were put beyond the national taxing power, the Court proclaiming that either way "the exemption rests upon necessary implication, and is upheld by the great law of self-preservation."[2] The proposition that neither the national nor the state governments may tax each other's instrumentalities and employees grew, in the course of litigation, into a confusing body of legal principles. Rules were announced in terms of sweeping absolutes, only to suffer the corrosion of limitation, distinction, exception, and occasional overruling. During the past two years all three branches of the National Government have cooperated in reducing the area of tax immunity. The law of intergovernmental taxation is now beginning to square with the necessities of legal logic and social justice.

Federal Taxation of State Instrumentalities

The gradual whittling down of ancient doctrine may be seen in considering the cases dealing with the Federal taxation of state instrumentalities. In *Collector* v. *Day*[3] the Court decided that the National Government could not constitutionally tax the salary of a state official, and in the *Pollock* case[4] immunity was extended to the interest derived from state and local bonds. The rule of immunity, however, was steadily narrowed in scope in subsequent decisions. One important exception was developed where the state engaged in nongovernmental or proprietary activities. In *South Carolina* v. *United States*[5] the Supreme Court held that a state-owned and state-operated liquor dispensary system was taxable, on the theory that there can be no immunity when the state enters "an ordinary private business." Such functions as the courts, police, administration of the law,[6] schools, hospitals and parks,[7] public ferries,[8] and water works[9] were considered governmental in character. On the other hand the courts ruled that a state-owned liquor business,[10] college football contests,[11] a public wharf,[12] a street railway sys-

---

[1] McCulloch v. Maryland, 4 Wheat. 316 (1819).
[2] Collector v. Day, 11 Wall. 113, 127 (1870).
[3] *Ibid.*
[4] Pollock v. Farmers' Loan & Trust Co., 157 U. S. 429, 158 U. S. 601 (1895).
[5] 199 U. S. 437 (1905).
[6] Collector v. Day, *supra*, note 2; Indian Motocycle Co. v. United States, 283 U. S. 570 (1931); Ambrosini v. United States, 187 U. S. 1 (1922).
[7] Hoskins v. Comm'r, 84 F. (2d) 627 (C. C. A. 5th, 1936); Mallory v. White, 8 F. Supp. 989 (D. C. Mass. 1934); Comm'r v. Schnackenberg, 90 F. (2d) 175 (C. C. A. 7th, 1937).
[8] Jamestown & Newport Ferry Co. v. Comm'r, 41 F. (2d) 920 (C. C. A. 1st, 1930).
[9] Brush v. Comm'r, 300 U. S. 352 (1937).
[10] South Carolina v. United States, *supra*, note 5; Ohio v. Helvering, 292 U. S. 360 (1934).
[11] Allen v. Regents, 304 U. S. 439 (1938).
[12] Galveston v. United States, 10 F. Supp. 810 (Ct. Cl. 1935), *cert. denied*, 297 U. S. 712 (1936).

tem,[13] and a bank[14] were not governmental activities.

It was always difficult to rationalize these cases. It is not at all apparent that a municipally owned street car system is any less governmental in character than a water works. The courts tried without much success to work out a definition of what constituted a governmental activity. It was suggested that tax-exempt functions were only those which were "strictly" governmental, or functions which were "traditional," "usual," "indispensable," or "essential."[15] Manifestly, these were extremely vague terms with which to describe the limits of an immunity from the national taxing power which at best was based upon an inference of doubtful validity.

An even more significant exception was developed by the courts in the elaboration of the burden theory, according to which immunity was refused where it was shown that the tax did not really burden the state. Under the weight of this exception the rule ultimately collapsed. An important application of the burden theory is found in numerous cases denying tax immunity to persons whose incomes were derived from some contractual relationship with a local government, or whose compensation was paid from other than public funds. In the leading case, *Metcalf & Eddy* v. *Mitchell*,[16] the Supreme Court held that consulting engineers who were employed by several local governments for work on public water supply and sewage disposal systems, whose duties were prescribed by contract and were not permanent or continuous, and who were free to accept other employment concurrently, were not tax-exempt state officials or employees. The Court asserted that the principle of immunity must be given a practical construction to avoid the serious impairment of the national taxing power. In the most recent case on this point, exemption was denied to persons employed by several states to liquidate insolvent banks and other corporations, their compensation being paid from the assets of the insolvent enterprises, the Court stating "that the inferred exemption from Federal taxation does not extend to every instrumentality which a State may see fit to employ," and that "it is cabined by the reason which underlies the inference."[17]

Accordingly, many persons having the status of independent contractors were denied tax exemption: attorneys engaged by state governments to conduct particular investigations, criminal prosecutions, or civil litigation,[18] attorneys engaged contractually by special local districts,[19] engineers, architects, real estate experts, consulting actuaries, and collectors of delinquent taxes employed by various units of local government.[20] Similarly, immunity was denied to persons who contracted for the performance of such services as the paving of streets or the collection and disposition of waste.[21]

[13] Helvering v. Powers, 293 U. S. 214 (1934).
[14] North Dakota v. Olson, 33 F. (2d) 848 (C. C. A. 8th, 1929), *dismissed*, 280 U. S. 528 (1929).
[15] Brush v. Comm'r, 300 U. S. at 361–62.
[16] 269 U. S. 514 (1926).
[17] Helvering v. Therrell, 303 U. S. 218, 223 (1938).
[18] Lucas v. Reed, 281 U. S. 699 (1930); Lucas v. Howard, 280 U. S. 526 (1929); Comm'r v. Murphy, 70 F. (2d) 790 (C. C. A. 2d, 1934), *cert. denied*, 293 U. S. 596 (1934); Ewart v. Comm'r, 98 F. (2d) 649 (C. C. A. 3d, 1938).
[19] Haight v. Comm'r, 52 F. (2d) 779 (C. C. A. 7th, 1931), *cert. denied*, 285 U. S. 537 (1932); Devlin v. Comm'r, 82 F. (2d) 731 (C. C. A. 9th, 1936).
[20] Pease v. Comm'r, 83 F. (2d) 122 (C. C. A. 6th, 1936), *cert. denied*, 299 U. S. 562 (1936); Mesce v. United States, 64 Ct. Cl. 481 (1928), *cert. denied*, 278 U. S. 612 (1928); Campbell v. Comm'r, 87 F. (2d) 128 (C. C. A. 7th, 1936), *cert. denied*, 301 U. S. 688 (1937); Pickett v. United States, 100 F. (2d) 909 (C. C. A. 8th, 1938).
[21] Sackley Co. v. United States, 65 Ct. Cl.

Auditors appointed by courts to report on the financial standing of surety companies, executors of estates, court-appointed referees and special guardians, and pilots appointed by a public authority, whose compensations were not paid from public sources, were also held taxable.[22] The distinction between the bona fide officer or employee and the independent contractor, though never clearly defined, was an important factor in undermining the idea of tax immunity.

Lessees of public lands

Another illustration of the drift away from tax exemption is found in a series of cases dealing with the taxability of lessees of public lands. In *Gillespie* v. *Oklahoma*[23] the Court held the income of a lessee of restricted Indian lands exempt from state taxation, and a few years later ruled, in *Burnet* v. *Coronado Oil & Gas Co.*,[24] that a lessee of state school lands was likewise immune from Federal taxation. The exemption of private corporations engaged in business for profit, where the burden on government was wholly speculative, was obviously unjustified, and the process of distinction and limitation soon began. The profits of a lessee of Texas oil lands were held taxable on the tenuous ground that under Texas law title to oil and gas in place passed to lessees before extraction.[25] A lessee of city-owned lands, under which the oil and gas recovered were sold by the parties jointly and the proceeds divided in stated proportions, had to pay Federal taxes, the effect being "inconsiderable as respects the activities of the city."[26] Buildings erected by lessees on school lands, under long-term leases, were held taxable, the rental being based upon the value of the land and not upon the improvements.[27] Profits derived from the sale of such a lease were also considered taxable.[28] Furthermore, sublessees were excluded, with little logic, from the rule of tax immunity.[29] What little was now left of the original doctrine was finally swept aside in *Helvering* v. *Mountain Producers Corp.*,[30] the Court flatly overruling the *Gillespie* and *Coronado* cases in upholding a tax on the income of a lessee of state school lands, even though the state reserved a considerable royalty to itself. Speaking for the Court, the Chief Justice wrote:

Immunity from nondiscriminatory taxation sought by a private person for his property or gains because he is engaged in operations under a government contract or lease cannot be supported by merely theo-

---

304 (1928), *cert. denied*, 278 U. S. 609 (1928); Brooklyn Ash Removal Co. v. United States, 10 F. Supp. 152 (Ct. Cl. 1935), *cert. denied*, 295 U. S. 752 (1935).

[22] Miller v. McCaughn, 22 F. (2d) 165 (E. D. Penna. 1927), *aff'd*, 27 F. (2d) 128 (C. C. A. 3d, 1928); N. Y. Trust Co. v. United States, 63 Ct. Cl. 100 (1927), *cert. denied*, 274 U. S. 756 (1927); Saxe v. Anderson, 19 F. Supp. 21 (S. D. N. Y. 1937), *aff'd sub nom.* Saxe v. Shea, 98 F. (2d) 83 (C. C. A. 2d, 1938), *dismissed*, 83 Law. Ed. Adv. Op. 338 (1939); Bew v. United States, 35 F. (2d) 977 (Ct. Cl. 1929), *cert. denied*, 281 U. S. 750 (1930).

[23] 257 U. S. 501 (1922).

[24] 285 U. S. 393 (1932).

[25] Group No. 1 Oil Corp. v. Bass, 283 U. S. 279 (1931).

[26] Burnet v. A. T. Jergins Trust, 288 U. S. 508, 516 (1933).

[27] Eckstein v. United States, 10 F. Supp. 231 (Ct. Cl. 1935), *cert. denied*, 296 U. S. 582 (1935); Metropolitan Bldg. Co. v. United States, 12 F. Supp. 537 (Ct. Cl. 1935), *cert. denied*, 297 U. S. 713 (1936); Helvering v. Atlas Life Ins. Co., 78 F. (2d) 166 (C. C. A. 10th, 1935).

[28] Marland v. United States, 53 F. (2d) 907 (Ct. Cl. 1931), *aff'd on rehearing*, 3 F. Supp. 611 (Ct. Cl. 1933), *cert. denied*, 290 U. S. 658 (1933).

[29] Wanless Iron Co. v. Comm'r, 75 F. (2d) 779 (C. C. A. 8th, 1935), *cert. denied*, 295 U. S. 765 (1935); Hobart Iron Co. v. Comm'r, 83 F. (2d) 25 (C. C. A. 6th, 1936), *cert. denied*, 299 U. S. 543 (1936).

[30] 303 U. S. 376 (1938). Accord: Helvering v. Bankline Oil Co., 303 U. S. 362 (1938).

retical conceptions of interference with the functions of government. Regard must be had to substance and direct effects. And where it merely appears that one operating under a government contract or lease is subjected to a tax with respect to his profits on the same basis as others, who are engaged in similar businesses, there is no sufficient ground for holding that the effect upon the government is other than indirect and remote.

In many other comparable situations immunity from Federal taxation has been refused. Thus, the mere fact that a corporation receives its charter from a state government does not make it a nontaxable state instrumentality.[31] While it is improper to impose a sales tax directly upon sales to local governments, Federal taxes levied on the transportation or manufacture of goods sold to them, with the seller paying the taxes, are valid, since the burden falls upon the transportation or manufacture, which is not part of the sale, but preliminary to it.[32] Income derived from the purchase of delinquent tax sale certificates,[33] or from the sale of land to a city for a public use,[34] or from a compensation or condemnation award by a city,[35] has been held subject to national taxation.

Salaries of state employees

Finally, in the case of *Helvering* v. *Gerhardt*,[36] decided in 1938, the Supreme Court held taxable the salaries of a construction engineer and two assistant managers employed by the Port of New York Authority, a corporation established by compact between New York and New Jersey to build and operate essential transportation facilities. The Court stated that the exemption from national taxation established in *Collector* v. *Day* should be narrowly limited because of the importance of preserving in its vigor the taxing power of a government in which all the people are represented, particularly when exemptions are demanded for the benefit of privileged classes of taxpayers without compensating advantage to the state. A nondiscriminatory tax on the net income of employees, "derived from their employment in common occupations not shown to be different in their methods or their duties from similar employees in private industry," does not burden the state, whose continued existence does not require a competitive advantage over private industry. Thus, the nature of the activity, whether governmental or proprietary, was not considered, since, whatever its character, the burden on the state was "wholly conjectural," but even if there was some charge on the state, "such burdens are but normal incidents of the organization within the same territory of two governments, each possessed of the taxing power." The last step was taken in 1939, in *Graves* v. *New York ex rel. O'Keefe*,[37] wherein *Collector* v. *Day* was specifically overruled. In refusing an employee of the Home Owners' Loan Corporation exemption from state taxation, the Court held that in the light of this and other recent decisions, nothing was left of the original immunity doctrine, so far, at least, as local employees are concerned.

The Court has not ruled squarely on

---

[31] Flint v. Stone Tracy Co., 220 U. S. 107 (1911).

[32] Wheeler Lumber Co. v. United States, 281 U. S. 572 (1930); Liggett & Myers Co. v. United States, 299 U. S. 383 (1937).

[33] Wiltsie v. United States, 3 F. Supp. 743 (Ct. Cl. 1933), *cert. denied*, 291 U. S. 664 (1934).

[34] Fullilove v. United States, 7 F. Supp. 468 (W. D. La. 1934), *aff'd*, 71 F. (2d) 852 (C. C. A. 5th, 1934), *cert. denied*, 293 U. S. 586 (1934); B. & O. R. Co. v. Comm'r, 78 F. (2d) 460 (C. C. A. 4th, 1935).

[35] Acme Land & Fur Co. v. Comm'r, 84 F. (2d) 441 (C. C. A. 5th, 1936); U. S. Trust Co. v. Anderson, 65 F. (2d) 575 (C. C. A. 2d, 1933), *cert. denied*, 290 U. S. 683 (1933).

[36] 304 U. S. 405.

[37] 83 Law. Ed. Adv. Op. 577.

the question of taxing state and local securities since its original decision in 1895, and Congress has not yet attempted to tax them. Here again, however, the tendency has been to narrow the range of immunity from Federal taxation, in the adjudication of various collateral issues. Thus, it has been decided that profits derived from the sale of state bonds are taxable,[38] and that the interest paid on money borrowed to buy tax-exempt municipal bonds may not be deducted from the income tax returns.[39] An inheritance tax on an estate which includes tax-exempt securities is valid,[40] as well as a succession tax upon a bequest to a municipal corporation.[41] A Federal corporate excise tax may be computed on a basis which includes income from local bonds.[42] A Federal tax on the average amount of deposits in banks may include deposits of a state government, since the tax is on the bank not as an agent of the state, but as a bank receiving deposits.[43]

These cases are in accord with the trend of tax decisions in other fields, which make a distinction between income and its source. Thus, a state may tax the securities of another state,[44] and one state may tax a resident on income received from rents on land in another state, the Court asserting that "income is not necessarily clothed with the tax immunity enjoyed by its source."[45] In upholding a recent state gross income tax as applied to the interest on local bonds issued tax-exempt, the Court argued that it was not unreasonable for the state to make a distinction between taxing the bonds and taxing the interest on the bonds, for the tax "is not laid upon the obligation," but rather "upon the net results of a bundle or aggregate of occupations and investments."[46] The well-established doctrine that the states may tax net income derived from interstate commerce and exportation, although a direct burden upon such commerce would be invalid, is also in point.[47] If a tax on income is not necessarily a tax on its source, then, in the light of the present interpretation of the range of state immunity from Federal taxation, national taxation of state bonds may very well receive the Court's blessing without benefit of constitutional amendment.

STATE TAXATION OF FEDERAL INSTRUMENTALITIES

The taxability of Federal instrumentalities and employees by the states presents an altogether different legal problem. As the court decisions now stand, several propositions are clearly indicated. First of all, there is no doubt of the fact that the states may tax any Federal instrumentality with the consent of Congress. No question of constitutional right exists where Congress has removed all doubt by expressly permitting its agencies to be taxed by the states. Thus, the Act of Congress permitting the nondiscriminatory taxation of national bank shares was upheld.[48] It is also clear that where Congress has stipulated exemption from local taxation, local taxation is precluded. The first issue to be determined in any specific instance,

[38] Willcuts v. Bunn, 282 U. S. 216 (1931).
[39] Denman v. Slayton, 282 U. S. 514 (1931).
[40] Greiner v. Llewellyn, 258 U. S. 384 (1922).
[41] Snyder v. Bettman, 190 U. S. 249 (1903).
[42] Flint v. Stone Tracy Co., *supra*, note 31.
[43] Manhattan Co. v. Blake, 148 U. S. 412 (1893).
[44] Bonaparte v. Tax Court, 14 Otto 592 (1881).
[45] People ex rel. Cohn v. Graves, 300 U. S. 308, 313 (1938).

[46] Hale v. State Board, 302 U. S. 95, 108 (1937). Accord: Adams Manufacturing Co. v. Storen, 304 U. S. 307 (1938).
[47] United States Glue Co. v. Oak Creek, 247 U. S. 321 (1918); Peck & Co. v. Lowe, 247 U. S. 165 (1918).
[48] Van Allen v. Assessors, 3 Wall. 573 (1866); First Natl. Bank v. Anderson, 269 U. S. 341 (1926).

therefore, is whether Congress has actually expressed an intent, one way or the other.[49] There is no case where local taxation of national agencies has been permitted in the face of a specific exemption by Congress.

Furthermore, the distinction between governmental and proprietary activities does not apply to the activities of the National Government. None of its functions has ever been judicially held to be other than governmental, even though comparable state functions have been construed to be nongovernmental in character. For example, a state-owned bank and a municipally owned trolley system are proprietary activities, while on the other hand a Federally chartered bank [50] and the government-owned Panama Railroad Company [51] are not. The Supreme Court has explicitly accepted the theory, long urged, that since the Federal Government

derives its authority wholly from powers delegated to it by the Constitution, its every action within its constitutional power is governmental action, and since Congress is made the sole judge of what powers within the constitutional grant are to be exercised, all activities of government constitutionally authorized by Congress must stand on a parity with respect to their constitutional immunity from taxation.[52]

The principle of national supremacy insures that the will of Congress will prevail. In this as in other fields of public law, the federal principle has not been a reciprocal principle. Chief Justice Marshall explained the difference between the whole and its parts in the very first intergovernmental tax case:

The people of all the States, and the States themselves, are represented in Congress, and, by their representatives, exercise this power. When they tax the chartered institutions of the States, they tax their constituents. . . . But, when a State taxes the operations of the government of the United States, it acts upon institutions created, not by their own constituents, but by people over whom they claim no control.[53]

The sole area of controversy is found, therefore, in the large number of instances where Congress has been silent on the subject of taxation. It is now clear that the silence of Congress is not necessarily either an invitation to tax or a prohibition of taxation. Justice Stone recently stated the rule as follows:

Silence of Congress implies immunity no more than does the silence of the Constitution. It follows that when exemption from state taxation is claimed on the ground that the Federal Government is burdened by the tax, and Congress has disclosed no intention with respect to the claimed immunity, it is in order to consider the nature and effect of the alleged burden, and if it appears that there is no ground for implying a constitutional immunity, there is equally a want of any ground for assuming any purpose on the part of Congress to create an immunity.[54]

Burdening Federal functions

Whether or not particular state taxes burden Federal functions has been the subject of prolonged controversy, and while it is true, as Justice Frankfurter has remarked, that the doctrines of *McCulloch* v. *Maryland* "have been distorted by sterile refinements unrelated to affairs," [55] the tendency of interpretation in recent years has been increasingly realistic.

An examination of a few important fields of Federal activity will illustrate

---

[49] Baltimore Natl. Bank v. State Tax Comm., 297 U. S. 209 (1936). Cf. 49 Stat. 1185 (1936).
[50] McCulloch v. Maryland, 4 Wheat. 316 (1819); Osborn v. Bank, 9 Wheat. 738 (1824).
[51] New York ex rel. Rogers v. Graves, 299 U. S. 401 (1937).
[52] Graves v. New York ex rel. O'Keefe, 83 Law. Ed. Adv. Op. 577, 579 (1939).

[53] McCulloch v. Maryland, 4 Wheat. at 435.
[54] *Supra*, note 52, at 581.
[55] *Ibid.*, at 585.

the present scope of Federal immunity. It is well established that the states may not tax Federal securities or their income directly, on the theory that this is a burden upon the national borrowing power,[56] nor may the states tax the income of Federal securities by an otherwise valid tax which singles out Federal securities for discriminatory treatment.[57] It is not improper, however, for a state to levy a franchise tax measured by net property or income which includes tax-exempt bonds of the United States or their income.[58] A stockholder may be taxed on the full value of his shares, even if the corporation's assets include tax-exempt Federal paper.[59] The states may also tax a bequest of Federal securities.[60]

May the states tax the salaries of Federal employees? In the *Dobbins* case,[61] decided in 1842, the Supreme Court held that the salary of the captain of a Federal revenue cutter was exempt from a nondiscriminatory local tax, and this holding was reaffirmed as late as 1937, in *New York ex rel. Rogers* v. *Graves*,[62] where it was held that a state could not tax the salary of the general counsel of the government-owned Panama Railroad Company. But in the last term of court, the *Rogers* case was specifically overruled when it was decided that an attorney employed at a fixed annual salary by the Home Owners' Loan Corporation to examine titles was not free from the obligation of paying a state income tax; since the statute setting up this agency did not specify immunity, the Court ruled that none should be granted, for the tax imposed no economic burden on the government.[63] "The theory which once won a qualified approval," it was asserted, "that a tax on income is legally or economically a tax on its source, is no longer tenable."

Lessees of Indian lands

The evolution of the doctrine of immunity with respect to lessees of Indian lands presents a parallel situation. In several cases the Supreme Court established the immunity of lessees of mines or oil wells on restricted Indian lands from local occupation, capital stock, ad valorem, and income taxes, on the theory that they were Federal instrumentalities.[64] But this immunity was soon subjected to one limitation after another. A railroad whose right of way and station grounds were granted by Congress to serve mines situated on Indian lands was denied exemption.[65] The shift from the old policy of restricted allotments to the new policy of permitting and encouraging Indians to assume the responsibilities of citizenship was also taken into consideration.[66] Furthermore, taxation was allowed where the oil had been removed from the land and stored in the

---

[56] Weston v. Charleston, 2 Pet. 449 (1829); Bank of Commerce v. New York City, 2 Black 620 (1862); Smith v. K. C. Title & Trust Co., 255 U. S. 180 (1922).

[57] Miller v. Milwaukee, 272 U. S. 713 (1927); Macallen v. Massachusetts, 279 U. S. 620 (1929); Schuylkill Trust Co. v. Philadelphia, 296 U. S. 113 (1936).

[58] Society for Savings v. Coite, 6 Wall. 594 (1868); Provident Institution v. Massachusetts, 6 Wall. 611 (1868); Home Ins. Co. v. New York, 134 U. S. 594 (1890).

[59] Van Allen v. Assessors, 3 Wall. 573 (1866); Cleveland Trust Co. v. Lander, 184 U. S. 111 (1902); Des Moines Natl. Bank v. Fairweather, 263 U. S. 103 (1926); Schuylkill Trust Co. v. Pennsylvania, 302 U. S. 506 (1938).

[60] Plummer v. Coler, 178 U. S. 115 (1900).

[61] Dobbins v. Comm'r, 16 Pet. 435.

[62] 299 U. S. 401.

[63] Graves v. New York ex rel. O'Keefe, *supra*, note 52.

[64] Choctaw R. Co. v. Harrison, 235 U. S. 292 (1914); Jaybird Mining Co. v. Weir, 271 U. S. 609 (1926); Indian Territory Oil Co. v. Oklahoma, 240 U. S. 522 (1916); Gillespie v. Oklahoma, 257 U. S. 501 (1922).

[65] Choctaw R. Co. v. Mackey, 256 U. S. 531 (1921).

[66] Shaw v. Oil Corp., 276 U. S. 575 (1928); Leahy v. State Treasurer, 297 U. S. 420 (1936).

lessee's tanks,[67] and where the tax was on the lessee's buildings and machinery.[68]

Finally, in 1938, the Court overthrew the whole doctrine of immunity by ruling that lessees of government lands may be compelled to pay state income taxes on incomes derived from the land, since the Federal Government is not burdened.[69] Similarly, while it is well established that lands owned by the United States are not subject to state taxation,[70] even though leased to private parties,[71] tax exemption disappears after the land passes to private ownership,[72] even though title has not been formally transferred.[73] A state may also tax land purchased from a Federal housing corporation, even though the government retains the right of foreclosure, at least to the extent of the equitable interest of the buyer.[74]

Those doing business with government

The Court has been increasingly critical of the claim to immunity from local taxation advanced by persons or corporations having business dealings with the government. A state may not levy a tax directly on sales to government agencies,[75] or on the withdrawal from storage of gasoline sold to the United States, a necessary step in the sale itself,[76] or on telegraph messages sent by officers of the United States on public business.[77] On the other hand, a state may tax the interest of a company owning a dry dock on land conveyed to it by the United States, notwithstanding the fact that in case of the nonfulfillment of a subsequent condition the land would be forfeited to the United States, and the government retained a continuing right to use the dock, the tax being only on the company's interest.[78] Similarly, a state may tax premiums collected by insurance companies on surety bonds of United States officials.[79] The machinery and boats of a dredging company engaged in work in pursuance of a contract with the United States may be taxed,[80] as well as property used to perform a contract to carry the mails, even though the tax is measured by gross receipts.[81] A state excise tax on gasoline used by a contractor with the Federal Government for the construction of river levees is valid.[82]

Recently the Court upheld a nondiscriminatory state privilege tax on gross receipts,[83] an occupation tax on gross income,[84] and a personal income tax on net income [85] of contractors with the government. In these cases the idea was developed that the burden of such

[67] Indian Territory Illuminating Oil Co. v. Brd. of Equalization, 288 U. S. 325 (1933).
[68] Taber v. Indian Territory Illuminating Oil Co., 300 U. S. 1 (1937).
[69] Helvering v. Mountain Producers Corp., 303 U. S. 376.
[70] Van Brocklin v. Tennessee, 117 U. S. 151 (1886); Irwin v. Wright, 258 U. S. 219 (1922).
[71] Springfield v. United States, 99 F. (2d) 860 (C. C. A. 1st, 1938).
[72] Exchange Trust Co. v. Drainage Dist., 278 U. S. 421 (1929).
[73] Bothwell v. Bingham County, 237 U. S. 642 (1915).
[74] New Brunswick v. United States, 276 U. S. 547 (1928).
[75] Panhandle Oil Co. v. Mississippi, 277 U. S. 218 (1928); West Co. v. Johnson, 20 Cal. App. (2d) 95, 66 Pac. (2d) 1211 (1937), *cert. denied,* 302 U. S. 638 (1937).

[76] Graves v. Texas Co., 298 U. S. 393 (1936).
[77] Western Union Co. v. Texas, 105 U. S. 460 (1882); Williams v. Talladega, 226 U. S. 404 (1912).
[78] Baltimore Shipbuilding Co. v. Baltimore, 195 U. S. 375 (1904).
[79] Fidelity & Deposit Co. v. Pennsylvania, 240 U. S. 319 (1916).
[80] Gromer v. Standard Dredging Co., 224 U. S. 362 (1912).
[81] Alward v. Johnson, 282 U. S. 509 (1931).
[82] Trinityfarm Construction Co. v. Grosjean, 291 U. S. 466 (1934).
[83] James v. Dravo Contracting Co., 302 U. S. 134 (1937).
[84] Silas Mason Co. v. Tax Comm., 302 U. S. 186 (1937).
[85] Atkinson v. Tax Comm., 303 U. S. 20 (1938).

taxation upon the Federal Government, if any at all, is remote and indirect, that the cost to the government is not inevitably increased since the contractor may absorb the tax, and that in any event, taxes should be regarded as a normal part of the expense of getting the work done. The Court did not believe that this opened the door to destructive state taxation, since this argument "ignores the power of Congress to protect the functions of the National Government and to prevent interference therewith through any attempted state action."[86] After all, it is rather well established today that the power to tax is not necessarily the power to destroy.

Federal incorporation

The same view prevails with respect to corporations which the government has chartered but which are privately owned and operated for profit, for it is now settled doctrine that the mere fact of Federal incorporation does not render the corporation tax-exempt if Congress has not stipulated exemption by law. Of course, this does not mean that the states may tax the franchise itself, for that would be a burden upon the power to create it.[87] Thus, railroads having Federal charters are subject to local taxation of their property, for in giving the Constitution a "practical construction" the Court saw no point in needlessly embarrassing the states in the collection of their necessary revenues without any corresponding advantage to the United States.[88] Similarly, immunity from local taxation does not follow from the fact that the Federal Government has given franchises or licenses to companies engaged in the telegraph, bridge-building, electric power, or warehouse business,[89] for "the mere extension of control over a business by the National Government does not withdraw it from a local tax which presents no obstacle to the execution of the national policy."[90] Thus also, the astounding rule once announced by the Court that royalties derived from patents issued by the government were not subject to state taxation[91] was soon limited in scope,[92] and then squarely overruled four years later when the Court upheld a state privilege tax on the business of licensing copyrighted motion pictures, measured by gross receipts, since the United States has no interest aside from the general benefits derived by the public from the labor of authors.[93]

Congress has also created corporations of its own, most of them to meet the emergencies of the war and the depression, of which it maintains direct ownership, and many of which produce revenue. Most of these corporations are specifically exempted from direct taxation by the states except as to their realty, and as a matter of constitutional law they may not be taxed directly by the states if the tax is burdensome. Thus, it was held that the states could not tax the physical property of corporations chartered by the government for war purposes.[94] Mortgages held by a

[86] James v. Dravo Contracting Co., 302 U. S. at 160.
[87] California v. Central Pac. R. Co., 127 U. S. 1 (1888).
[88] Railroad Co. v. Peniston, 18 Wall. 5, 31 (1873); Thomson v. U. P. R. Co., 9 Wall. 579 (1869); Central Pac. R. Co. v. California, 162 U. S. 91 (1896).
[89] Western Union Co. v. Gottlieb, 190 U. S. 412 (1903); Keokuk Bridge Co. v. Illinois, 175 U. S. 626 (1900); Susquehanna Power Co. v. State Tax Comm., 283 U. S. 291 (1931); Broad River Power Co. v. Query, 288 U. S. 178 (1933); Federal Compress & Warehouse Co. v. McLean, 291 U. S. 17 (1934).
[90] Federal Compress & Warehouse Co. v. McLean, 291 U. S. at 23.
[91] Long v. Rockwood, 277 U. S. 142 (1928).
[92] Educational Film Corp. v. Ward, 282 U. S. 379 (1930).
[93] Fox Film Corp. v. Doyal, 286 U. S. 123 (1932).
[94] Clallam County v. U. S. Spruce Prod. Corp., 263 U. S. 341 (1923); Brunswick v.

Federal agency, which are declared by law to be governmental instrumentalities, are not subject to a state mortgage recordation tax.[95] Nor is a Federal corporation required to pay an entrance fee to do business within a state,[96] or local motor vehicle license taxes.[97] In the absence of any grant of immunity by Congress, however, the Court recently ruled that attorneys employed by the Home Owners' Loan Corporation, the Reconstruction Finance Corporation, and the Regional Agricultural Credit Corporation were no longer immune from nondiscriminatory state income taxes.[98] Various state courts are beginning to follow suit by refusing exemption to employees of various Federal farm credit agencies.[99]

Differential Factors

The essence of the prevailing view with respect to intergovernmental taxation is found in the separation of income from its source and in the distinction between a nondiscriminatory tax and a discriminatory one. Congress may ask state employees to pay an income tax which all persons in the country are required to pay, but it would be a burden on the state to single out its employees for special treatment. Indeed, the tax which was condemned in the *McCulloch* case was directed specifically against the Bank of the United States, and could have been set aside merely on grounds of discrimination.[100] But the nationalistic Marshall, speaking in terms of the sweeping absolutes of the age of rationalism, was anxious to establish the supremacy of the Federal Government when he announced that the power to tax is the power to destroy. As Justice Holmes remarked, "In those days, it was not recognized as it is today, that most of the distinctions of the law are distinctions of degree. . . . The power to tax is not the power to destroy as long as this court sits." [101]

That these tax immunities are undesirable from the social and economic points of view is agreed by most students of the subject. Says Professor Paul Studenski:

It is conceded generally that tax exemption results in heavy losses of revenue to the Federal Government, that it diverts the flow of capital from private industry and hence retards industrial growth, that it permits some citizens to escape their proper share of the costs of government, and that it invalidates the ability-to-pay principle of taxation to which we, as a democratic people, are presumably committed.[102]

Furthermore, it may be added that a special inequity results from the fact that under a system of progressive taxation the relative advantages of tax exemption are greater for those who have large incomes.

Abolition of Tax Exemptions

President Roosevelt took an impor-

United States, 276 U. S. 547 (1928); U. S. Shipping Brd. Emergency Fleet Corp. v. Delaware County, 17, 25 F. (2d) 40, 722 (C. C. A. 3d, 1928), *dismissed*, 275 U. S. 483 (1927), *cert. denied*, 278 U. S. 607 (1928).

[95] Federal Land Bank v. Crosland, 261 U. S. 374 (1923); H.O.L.C. v. Anderson, 145 Kan. 209, 64 P. (2d) 14 (1937); Pittman v. H.O.L.C., 2 A. (2d) 689 (Md. 1938), *affirmed*, Nov. 6, 1939, 7 U. S. Law Week, 503.

[96] Federal Land Bank v. Statelen, 191 Wash. 155, 70 P. (2d) 1053 (1937).

[97] Federal Land Bank v. Highway Dept., 172 S. C. 174, 173 S. E. 284 (1934).

[98] Graves v. New York ex rel. O'Keefe, *supra*, note 52; State Tax Comm. v. Van Cott, 83 Law. Ed. Adv. Op. 588 (1939).

[99] Parker v. Tax Comm., 178 Miss. 680, 174 So. 567 (1937), *cert. denied*, 302 U. S. 742 (1937); State ex rel. Baumann v. Bowles, 342 Mo. 357, 115 S. W. (2d) 805 (1938); Clinton v. Tax Comm., 146 Kan. 407, 71 P. (2d) 857 (1937).

[100] See the remarks of Justice Stone in Helvering v. Gerhardt, 304 U. S. at 413.

[101] Dissenting in Panhandle Oil Co. v. Mississippi, 277 U. S. at 223.

[102] 17 *Tax Mag.* 5, 6 (1939).

tant step in the direction of a more equitable tax system when he sent a special message to Congress, on April 25, 1938, asking for the enactment of "a short and simple statute" abolishing all tax exemptions of both Federal and state instrumentalities.[103] Congress responded with the passage of the Public Salary Act of 1939,[104] which brought the salaries of state officers and employees within the ambit of the Federal taxing power, and expressly permitted the non-discriminatory taxation of the salary of any officer or employee of the United States by the states. No action has yet been taken with respect to the taxation of securities, although hearings have been held on the subject by a special Senate committee. It should be noted that there is no inclination on the part of either the President or Congress to make any tax in this field retroactive.

The yield to the Federal Government alone which would result from abolishing tax exemptions would be considerable. The Treasury found that state and local interest-bearing securities outstanding on June 30, 1938 amounted to $19,170,-000,000, and that the value of all securities of the Federal Government and its agencies was $44,568,000,000, of which securities about one-third were wholly tax-exempt and two-thirds partially exempt.[105] Under-Secretary of the Treasury Hanes recently estimated that the annual increase in revenue to the United States from abolishing the exemption of all bonds would be from $179,000,000 to $337,000,000, and that the annual increase in interest costs to the government would be from $19,000,000 to $50,000,000. The yield to the government from taxing state and local employees was estimated at but $16,000,000, for, although there are some 2,600,000 state and local employees, their average salary is but $1,400, and only a fourth of them receive more than $2,500.[106] In addition, one may say that the abolition of these tax immunities would have beneficial moral results, for government has an obligation to be just and fair to all.

[105] *Annual Report,* Secretary of the Treasury, June 30, 1938, p. 543.
[106] Special Committee on Taxation of Governmental Securities and Salaries, *Hearings,* United States Senate, 76th Cong., 1st sess., Jan. 18–Feb. 16, 1939, Part I, pp. 10–11.

[103] 83 *Cong. Rec.* 5683.
[104] *Pub. Laws,* 76th Cong., 1st sess., c. 59.

David Fellman, Ph.D., is instructor in political science at the University of Nebraska, Lincoln. He is the author of a number of articles on related topics, that have been published in the professional journals.

Federal-State Personnel Relations

By George C. S. Benson

THE rapidly expanding literature of public administration has wisely ignored much of the old-line political science which was one of its several parents. It has not worried itself greatly about sovereignty or pluralism or academic distinctions between types of states, and has thus avoided much confused metaphysical thinking, all unrelated to reality.

At the same time, however, public administration should be alert to pick up any political science viewpoints which may affect the basic goals of our administrative institutions. Recent treatments of administrative aspects of American federalism have been unfortunately devoid of careful analysis of the manner in which the fundamental goals of our American federal system are affected by the administrative institutions described.

For example, Professor V. O. Key's otherwise brilliant study of *The Administration of Federal Grants to States*[1] omits the most fundamental reason for operating governmental services through grants to the states rather than through a Federal agency—the value of political decentralization for the maintenance of constitutional, democratic government. Moreover, although the book mentions such other important purposes of a grants-in-aid system as the desirability of flexibility, it consistently omits mention of instances in which an excess of Federal administrative zeal has defeated these purposes. Similarly, Professor Jane Perry Clark portrays *The Rise of a New Federalism*[2] in a volume which, however stimulating, makes almost no attempt to define the goals of our federal system or to appraise any of the various devices of the new federalism in the light of these objectives. The editor of this issue of THE ANNALS displays a broader viewpoint in his *Uniform State Action*,[3] but even he fails to evaluate the techniques which he portrays in the light of their effect on the ultimate aims of the federal system.

This brief article cannot hope to achieve what these learned authors have failed to accomplish. It aims merely to suggest a method of analysis which, applied to certain Federal administrative institutions, will not ignore all that comparative and historical political science has taught about federalism. Particular application will be made to the field of Federal-state personnel relations, since the writer has had both official connections and research relationships with Federal and state agencies in that sphere. In fairness to the reader, however, it should be noted that these reflections are only offshoots of these experiences, and that the writer might express very different viewpoints if he had conducted researches as extensive as those noted above.

Values and Criticisms of Federalism

What advantages do we feel that our federal system possesses as contrasted with a unitary system? The following distinctive features are certainly fundamental:

1. The prevention, by division of the agencies possessing political power, of the acquisition by any one agency of power sufficient to overthrow democratic, constitutional government;

---

[1] Chicago: Public Administration Service, 1937.
[2] New York: Columbia University Press, 1938.
[3] Chapel Hill: University of North Carolina Press, 1934.

2. An opportunity for experimentation in governmental matters;

3. An opportunity to adapt governmental programs to needs of different localities;

4. An opportunity to train our citizenry in state institutions before selecting them for national responsibilities;

5. The administrative advantages attendant upon a forced administrative decentralization.

Recognition of the desirability of these goals does not, however, deny the validity of certain basic criticisms of a federal form of government. The most obvious disadvantages are:

1. The tendency of freedom of commerce—almost universal within federal systems—to place economic handicaps on progressive social legislation by members of the system. These handicaps frequently operate to prevent establishment of even minimum nationwide standards.

2. The great variations in financially feasible governmental programs of member states which result from the unequal economic resources of different members of federal systems. These variations adversely affect establishment of nationwide minimum levels of government personnel.

3. The central government almost inevitably possesses a predominance in financial resources over most of the member units, simply because most taxes can be collected more effectively over an entire economic area than over portions of such an area.

A problem, if not a disadvantage, arises from the fact that the financial strength of the federal government often exceeds its responsibilities. Federal financial supremacy often results in higher-salaried personnel and hence better administrative standards. Some system is needed whereby not only some of the money may be passed on to member units, but also some of these higher administrative standards may be established within the states.[4]

FIELDS OF GRANTS-IN-AID

One of the natural results of the desire to maintain the basic values of federalism and yet to overcome its basic disadvantages has been the grants-in-aid system. Such systems are now in effect in connection with several aspects of public welfare—including public health, public assistance, and one form of social insurance—with roads, with limited aspects of education and conservation, with military affairs, with agricultural research and education, and with employment offices. At present, indications point to the extension of grants-in-aid to other fields. A discussion as to what fields of governmental activity are, in view of the underlying purposes of our federal system, most appropriate for grants-in-aid, although beyond the scope of this article, would prove useful and interesting.

Within the fields of grants-in-aid activity, one of the most crucial problems of Federal-state relations is that of selection and tenure of personnel. Personnel standards are the key to successful administration—a fact which most Federal agencies realize. On the other hand, an unhealthy majority of the states have been operating their administrative machinery without any true personnel standards. Although glad to receive Federal funds to hire more friends or political allies, many state administrations object to Federal "interference" in selection of personnel for the Federally aided activities. This dualism of viewpoint makes the personnel field a particularly interesting one from the stand-

[4] All these points could be expanded upon and other points which arise in particular federal systems could be discussed far beyond the scope of this article. It is hoped, however, that this too succinct statement will serve the purpose of illustrating the technique needed in critical literature in this field.

point of Federal-state relations and also an excellent one in which to analyze new administrative developments in the light of the objectives of federalism.

Federal Policy toward State Personnel

Three major methods of approach characterize Federal policy towards state personnel in aided activities. The first, exemplified by the Federal Bureau of Public Roads, leaves personnel problems almost entirely to the states and attempts to judge whether or not the state performance is up to the nationwide standard by measuring the administrative performance on the job. This laissez faire attitude towards personnel does not interfere with three of the five purposes of federalism outlined above—i.e., division of power, chance for experiment, and opportunity for localized adaptation. It has, however, resulted in extensive political machinations in state highway departments which, it might be claimed, "mistrain" citizens for national responsibility. A more definite charge grows out of the fact that frequent political overturns in state highway departments result in a financial wastage which escapes the spotlight under the Bureau's system of measuring administrative performance. Thus, the fullest attainment of two of the goals of grants-in-aid—a nationwide level of governmental performance and an improvement of administrative standards—is less likely to be secured by this method.

The second method may be characterized as one of occasional interference with state personnel decisions. This approach, which usually takes the form of withholding approval of appointments, Professor Key has described as "an unsystematic effort to deal with aggravated situations on the basis of no explicit Federal policy." [5] This policy has been followed—with a minimum of pressure—by the Co-operative Extension Office of the United States Department of Agriculture in connection with agricultural extension work, and by the Office of Experiment Stations in connection with state agricultural experiment stations. Like the first method noted above, it does not seem to obstruct the accomplishment of any of the goals of federalism. And, especially in the case of the experiment stations, which usually enjoy college or university immunity from state politics, it has been possible to steer clear of the rocks of politics. In the case of the extension service, however, the establishment of a national minimum standard of aid to farmers has not been achieved.[6]

The same method was followed much more aggressively by the Federal Emergency Relief Administration. The writer is not in a position to say whether F.E.R.A. policies did violence to any of the fundamentals of American federalism. The political reactions which resulted from these policies, however, certainly hindered subsequent development of nationwide administrative standards by other granting agencies, and it is generally supposed that they were not unrelated to the insertion of the parenthetical clause in the original Social Security Act which prohibited control of personnel methods by most of the granting agencies operating under that act.[7] The way in which the Federal Emergency Relief Administration used its power to approve state appointments also pointed towards a type of political centralization which federalism aims to to avoid.

Federal control of state personnel is

[5] *The Administration of Federal Grants to States*, p. 315.

[6] See Gladys Baker, *The County Agent* (Chicago: University of Chicago Press, 1939), *passim*, but especially Chaps. V and VII.

[7] In this connection see Lewis Meriam, "Personnel Administration under the Social Security Act," The Annals, March 1939, pp. 159–64.

also frequently achieved by setting up minimum education and experience qualifications for personnel. The Rehabilitation Service, the Vocational Education Service, and the United States Public Health Service have used this technique. While further study would be necessary to demonstrate the point, the writer is inclined to believe that this technique often fails to secure nationwide administrative standards, since it sometimes creates an opportunity to appoint incompetent people. Occasionally, only incompetent people meet the specifications. "Standards" thus become barriers to good selection. Worse than that, however, it sometimes ties a program down to some narrow professional viewpoint, and thus the chance for experimentation in the different states—one of the goals of a federal system—is curtailed. In so far as nationwide standards are not applicable in certain states, it prevents adaptation to the needs of different areas.

The requirement of merit systems in the services aided seems to be the most promising Federal method thus far attempted. Of course this is true only if the merit systems are under state auspices. The United States Employment Service has required merit systems—admittedly too Federal in their original administration, but now somewhat more under state control. The revised Social Security Act will enable the Social Security Board to prescribe the state merit systems which it has previously only been able urgently to recommend. If the Board in its administration of this new power keeps in mind the fundamental aims of a federal system, the results of the experiment should be highly desirable.

To keep in mind the aims of a federal system is, however, a task more easily said than done. The merit-system requirements should be sufficiently rigid to insure that appointments will be made only from eligible registers, that persons shall not be removed for political reasons, and that the process of examination and appointment shall be free from factors tending to favor particular individuals or factions. At the same time, it should definitely leave room for variations from state to state, according to different local conditions, and should provide opportunity for experimentation. The middle way which combines all these advantages will be hard to discover.

Dangers of Federal Requirements

A few suggestions may be made, however. The Federal agencies should be extremely cautious about requiring or even strongly suggesting years of certain experience or certain education as minimum qualifications. This is especially true in the various fields of activity for which professional requirements are not yet universally agreed upon, or for which professional schools are only training in part (since they often have not yet adjusted themselves to public needs). There is a growing danger from professional overspecialization in American society. It would be extremely unfortunate if grants-in-aid should serve to let narrow professional groups in the Federal Government dictate the establishment of similar narrow professional groups in state services. Professor Key repeatedly points out as an advantage of grants-in-aid that they enable professional administrators to have their own way on matters of appointment. In doing so he ignores the dangers both of narrow professionalism and of loss of state political responsibility. The writer in saying this does not lose sight of the necessity for Federal standards for state personnel.

On the matter of experience requirements, there is the further danger, noted above, that Federal standards may become barriers to more competent personnel. Experience requirements may handicap a departmental personnel. Unemployment compensation is now facing this situation to some extent as a result of a Federal "suggestion" of experience for claims examiners. In one southern state, able, likable school teachers had to be turned away from a $1,000-a-year receptionist job because they had no clerical experience. The Federal staff was not aware of the low level of salaries and the high quality of applicant personnel in that state. Experience requirements may also assume political significance if there is a battle of ins against outs, and the control of this weapon by one agency would violate a basic purpose of the federal system.

Residence requirements raise a rather knotty problem. In themselves, they often operate against selection of the best personnel. On the other hand, if a grants-in-aid system is designed to admit of adaptation to regional or state needs, perhaps residence requirements may serve a useful purpose. Thus far Federal agencies have not displayed marked tendency to eliminate them, and where such efforts have been made—as in the attitude of the Department of Agriculture toward having county agents work in the county where they were reared—the position is not unreasonable.

The Federal requirement of a merit system is likely to have as an important by-product advantage the encouragement of general state merit systems which include departments not receiving Federal aid. Thus one of the basic goals of grants-in-aid—the improvement of state administrative standards—can be achieved without any danger to the federal system. It will be interesting to see whether the Social Security Board's power to require merit systems will continue to have the good influence in this direction which is said to have accompanied its recommendations of such systems. It has also been said that the Federal Government requirements have taught the states to dislike or to evade merit systems. Both statements need investigation.[8] The Federal staff needs also to be alert to the possibility of passing information from state to state—a legitimate but often overlooked goal of the federal system.

Joint Examinations and Appointments

Turning from the subject of grants-in-aid to other types of Federal-state personnel relations, we may note the interesting possibilities inherent in the use of joint Federal-state examinations in cases where uniform class specifications have been worked out for state and Federal positions. For a number of years the United States Civil Service Commission has offered to state governments lists of persons from their respective states on Federal eligible registers. If Federal-state examinations could be offered jointly, there might be real economy and greater opportunity for study of statistical validity and perhaps even reliability of examinations.

Several difficulties are apparent, however. The United States Civil Service Commission examining unit, although improving, is not financed on a scale to permit better performance than that of a number of the best state and local staffs. Hence, it is hardly fitted to assume leadership in any movement for joint examinations. A number of Federal personnel practices also do not appeal to the best state and local jurisdictions. The device of selective certification in the Federal system, while having real administrative utility, is susceptible to great political pressure. The complicated statutory classification system of the Federal Government is

[8] One of the best sources of information is an unpublished manuscript by Elmer B. Staats of the staff of the United States Budget Bureau.

frequently criticized by state and local technicians. It would be particularly difficult in the case of posts involving administrative responsibility to devise uniform class specifications as a basis for joint Federal-state examinations. Only when our personnel people begin to plan recruitment in terms of careers in public service will joint entrance examinations be feasible.

In her volume on *The Rise of a New Federalism,* Professor Clark has devoted some attention to the practice of joint Federal-state appointments to office,[9] and she cites the elimination of unnecessary duplications of Federal and state services as the major advantage of the policy. Undoubtedly this simplification is often desirable, and other advantages could certainly be found. In answer to the major objection that administrative responsibilities of the official who holds a joint appointment are divided, Professor Clark admits the necessity of— and defends the sufficiency of—a planned and co-ordinated scheme. The danger that such a scheme might undermine two basic principles of our federalism—(1) a division of political power, and (2) administrative decentralization—she does not discuss. Perhaps this danger is visionary, but it would be well to investigate the possibilities thoroughly before indorsing the new technique.

Topics for Research

In concluding, the author wishes to repeat that this brief article is designed only to raise questions and to suggest methods of approach. The whole field of Federal-state relations offers rich opportunities for discussion and research, and this note will close with a very partial list of possible topics: [10]

1. Are there actual instances in which minimum qualification requirements worked against experimentation in state programs?

2. Have such requirements appreciably limited the possibility of selecting capable persons in given states?

3. Can poor administrative performances be traced to political overturns in an appreciable number of instances?

4. Has the furnishing of examination questions by Federal agencies been conducted in accordance with state policies?

5. What have been the actual results of state use of Federal registers?

6. How much Federal partisan politics has been discernible in Federal approval or disapproval of state employees?

[9] See the interesting Chapter IV on "Co-operative Use of Government Personnel," and also pp. 296–300. (Columbia University Press, 1938.)

[10] It is suggested that persons who are in a position to write up specific cases on these or related questions communicate with Mr. Charles S. Ascher of the Committee on Public Administration of the Social Science Research Council.

George C. S. Benson is associate professor of political science and director of the curriculum in public administration at the University of Michigan, Ann Arbor. He is a member of the Board of Directors of the National Civil Service Reform League, a member of the Michigan State Planning Commission and of the Civil Service Advisory Board of the Michigan Unemployment Compensation Commission, and consultant for the National Resources Planning Board.

Municipalities and the Federal Government

By Raymond S. Short

THE new and more intimate relation of municipalities to the Federal Government has been one of the most significant developments of the present decade. Officials—both local and Federal—are just beginning to realize that this new relationship, born of the depression, is likely to be permanent. The depression, the growing complexity of society, and an expanding concept of civic needs have imposed new demands upon every level of government, the satisfaction of which has forced the adoption of new channels for intergovernmental co-operation.

Viewed in terms of the volume of services today, the principal governmental units are, first, the municipality and, second, the National Government.[1] Yet in spite of this, the first mention of municipalities in a Federal statute came in 1932 when the Reconstruction Finance Corporation was authorized to make loans directly to cities for self-liquidating projects upon approval of the application by the governors of the states affected. The depression created a situation in which cities found themselves in dire need of immediate aid. The states were not in a position to offer the needed assistance, nor had they developed adequate channels through which the Federal Government might extend the aid. On the other hand, Congressional remedies for recovery called for the co-operation of local governments. From this situation developed direct contacts between Washington and the local governments.

During the early years of the depression emphasis was placed upon attaining certain objectives rather than upon the proper allocation of functions or upon the development of permanent principles for intergovernmental co-operation. For the most part, Congress seemed little nearer the consideration of these problems in 1939 than in 1933.

FEDERAL-MUNICIPAL CONTACTS

Growing out of the interrelation of a Federal Government which needed the co-operation of local governments in instituting recovery measures, and local governments which were in dire need of Federal financial aid, came several types of Federal-municipal contacts. By way of contrast it may be well to note the character of the great majority of pre-New Deal Federal-municipal relations. These relations, for the most part, were casual and incidental, developing from the administrative necessity for contact between governmental levels. Aid was in the form of statistical, research, informational, and advisory services.[2]

Of course, this type of relationship is not confined to the predepression period. It characterizes many of the contacts which have developed during the last seven years in the expansion of the work of the regular branches of the National Government.

Then, too, some municipal functions came under the direct control of Federal agencies as incidental regulations under powers conferred upon the National Government but which parallel to a certain extent local functions. There has been an expansion of this type of con-

[1] *Urban Government*, Volume I of the Supplementary Report of the Urbanism Committee to the National Resources Committee, Washington, 1939.

[2] For a detailed account of these developments see *Urban Government*, Vol. I, Part II, Sec. 1; P. V. Betters, *Federal Services to Municipalities*, Municipal Administration Service, 1931; and P. V. Betters, "The Federal Government and the Cities: A Problem in Adjustment," THE ANNALS, Sept. 1938.

tact also in the past few years, as, for example, the licensing and regulation of municipal airports.

With the coming of the depression, unemployment and relief became such acute problems that the National Government set up the now familiar relief and work relief agencies to cope with them. Since unemployment and need for relief were most urgent in urban areas, and state organizations adequate to serve as channels for the distribution of Federal aid were lacking, national agencies dealt directly with municipalities.

As a result, an important class of contractual relations between municipalities and the public works and work relief agencies developed. In this class of relationships the states acted primarily as authorizing or promotional agents through the passage of enabling legislation. The Work Projects Administration and its predecessors illustrate a type of contractual relationship in which the Federal rather than the local agencies took the primary responsibility for making the contracts. This developed, according to the Urbanism Committee, because of the fact that the agreements for selecting, supervising, and sharing the costs of work relief projects approached a uniform nationwide function.[3]

A different type of contractual relation was set up with respect to public works involving such agencies as the Public Works Administration and the Reconstruction Finance Corporation. Although not primarily a public works project, the United States Housing Authority falls in the same class of relationship. In these cases, contracts are made with individually selected agencies. Local agencies initiate the contracts and the primary responsibility is theirs.

Direct contacts have likewise been established in those fields in which the National Government has set up regular services which would benefit local governments but where the states do not perform functions parallel to municipal services. The Federal Bureau of Investigation deals directly with cities in cases of criminal investigation and in conducting a training school for police officers. Federal recreation contacts have been maintained directly with the municipalities. The recently created Civil Aeronautics Authority plans to work with cities in the development of a Federal airport plan. In fact, since the state does not participate in the transportation field, we may expect direct relations between the National Government and municipalities whenever the interests of the two merge.

The grants-in-aid system has been given new significance in the development of Federal-municipal relations. The older types of grants-in-aid, such as those for vocational education and rehabilitation and for highways, had only a limited effect upon urban government. Now, however, Congress is using the grants-in-aid system to extend financial aid to the states and through them to urban communities. The most important new grant-in-aid project is the social security program; but the training program authorized under the George-Deen Act of 1936 and the extension of Federal aid to municipalities for highway construction conducted under the Bureau of Public Roads are not without significance.

The general development of Federal aid aside from emergency aid is well expressed in the report of the Urbanism Committee:

The Federal agencies administering the aid systems informally contact the municipalities, but chief reliance is centered upon the responsibility of the states for the performance of functions. Where the Federal agency was in operation before the institution of Federal aid, as with the Public Health Service, the municipal advisory

[3] *Urban Government*, Vol. I, p. 97.

services are numerous and not lacking in importance. . . . Where the state grants antedated the municipal contacts, as in the case of the Bureau of Public Roads, the Federal view is to continue working through the state as the unit indispensable to the administration of a far-flung activity.[4]

Indirect Financial Aid

Municipal finances have been aided materially in the Federal Government's attempt to buttress the economic system by giving aid and providing safeguards to private business. Activities of the Home Owners' Loan Corporation in saving hundreds of thousands of homes from the sheriff's hammer, and of the Federal Housing Administration in adding in the current taxes as a part of the carrying charges on mortgages insured by it, have greatly improved tax collections in many cities. The Federal Housing Administration, through its favorable mortgage insurance terms, has stimulated building, which in turn has added to the assessment rolls.

Aid may come from unexpected quarters. Recently, at the request of the United States Conference of Mayors, the Federal Trade Commission instituted investigations into identical bidding on building supplies bought by cities. There is the prospect that large sums might be saved by breaking up collusive bidding.

However, the operation of some of these agencies has not been an unmixed blessing. Carl H. Chatters, executive director of the Municipal Finance Officers Association of the United States and Canada, reported at a conference of the American Municipal Association on October 5, 1938, that the amount of Federal property which is exempt from local taxes is increasing as a result of foreclosures by the Home Owners' Loan Corporation. Likewise, legislation governing the Federal Deposit Insurance Corporation and the Federal Reserve Board, which prevented banks from paying interest on public fund deposits in 1937, has resulted in a considerable loss of interest to local governments. An attempt was made to amend this in the recent session of Congress, but without success.

Operation of Grants-in-Aid Not Wholly Satisfactory

Municipal benefits from Federal grants-in-aid have not been all that was hoped for. It is not denied that this form of aid has been a helpful influence in the improvement of local conditions, although some local officials have pointed out that it has encouraged additional spending which cities could ill afford.

Dissatisfaction over the operation of the aid system has sprung from two factors—the difficulty which municipalities have in getting funds to which they are entitled, and the tendency of Congress to attach conditions which would sap them of authority over their own expenditures.

Both the appropriations for highway construction and those for categorical aid under the social security program have become important to municipalities. These illustrate the manner in which the grants may be administered by the states. In the case of highway aid, municipalities had to appeal to Federal agencies to get the states to apportion part of the funds to municipalities for street construction purposes.

Prior to 1934, states were prohibited from spending any portion of the regular Federal-aid highway funds in municipalities of more than 2,500. But Congress made available $125,000,000 in 1932 and $400,000,000 in 1933 as outright grants for highway and grade-crossing-elimination work. Municipal projects were made eligible to participate in these. Nevertheless, municipal officials had to appeal to the Bureau of Public Roads over the heads of several

[4] *Urban Government*, Vol. I, p. 73.

state highway departments to get any benefit from the appropriations. The Bureau directed that 25 per cent of the appropriations should be spent on municipal projects—a provision which was incorporated into both the emergency and the regular Federal-aid highway legislation in 1934.

When the social security program was up for consideration, the United States Conference of Mayors sought to have incorporated in the Social Security Act a provision to insure that the state share of the cost would specifically be paid out of state government revenue, to prevent the states from shifting a large share of the financial burden back to the localities. Paul V. Betters, executive director of the Conference, points out that because the law did not clearly incorporate the amendment proposed by the Conference, in some states the localities have had to share some if not all of the burden. He concludes that those

who believed that the states would come in and do their share now realize that it is highly improbable that the state governments will accept their proper responsibilities unless there are mandatory provisions in the Federal statute.[5]

Both municipal and state officials fear that the grants-in-aid system will be used as a vehicle to force a Federal pattern upon them. The Senate in 1938 attempted to require a uniform licensing law for operators of motor vehicles as a condition for receiving Federal-aid highway funds. In the same bill it incorporated a provision of the Hayden-Cartwright Act of 1934 which would have prevented the states from reducing the percentage of proceeds from highway-use taxes which would be available to the state highway department. This was to be accomplished by withdrawing aid in case of violation. The provision was killed by the Conference Committee after strong protest from municipal officials. The effect, according to Earl D. Mallery, executive director of the American Municipal Association, would have been to make it next to impossible for a state to share highway funds to an effective extent with counties or municipalities, even though the funds were to be expended only for roads and streets.[6]

Allocation of Funds

Federal aid is reaching the stage where a reconsideration of the methods of allocation of funds becomes imperative. But reallocation of funds must be based upon comprehensive studies into the allocation of functions between the different levels of government, and a consideration of the financial ability of the different levels of government to support the functions which they are most competent to administer. Unfortunately, those in positions to determine policies have all too frequently acted without the benefit of thorough study.

Unemployment relief, for instance, a problem which has been in the front rank of public questions for nearly a decade, to use the words of Carl H. Chatters, has been handled as a temporary emergency. Nothing far-reaching, nothing forward-looking or statesmanlike, has been done.[7] However, recent realization that the problem is of more than temporary character has led both houses of Congress to authorize committee investigations. The Senate Committee headed by Senator Byrnes made a report in January 1939. The subcommittee of the House Appropriation Committee investigating the W.P.A. is

---

[5] "The Federal Government and the Cities: A Problem in Adjustment," The Annals, Sept. 1938, p. 195.

[6] "Federal-City Relations in 1938," *Municipal Year Book*, 1939.

[7] "Is Municipal Government Slated for a Headache?" address before the Conference of the American Municipal Association held in Chicago, Oct. 5, 1938.

still at work, although a preliminary report was made before the adjournment of Congress in August. The Byrnes Committee recommended: (1) discontinuance of the W.P.A. type of relief and adoption of a public works program in its place—a part of the slack would be taken up by an expanded social security program; (2) establishment of a department of public works to handle the public works program; (3) adoption of a formula based upon the population of the states and the number of unemployed in the various states, under which aid would be granted to the states; (4) limitation of Federal contributions to not more than two-thirds of the cost except in states whose average per capita income is less than the average per capita income in the United States. The Committee did not think it justifiable to maintain two organizations, each engaged in construction work, the one requiring a local contribution of 55 per cent and the other an average of 22 per cent. Senator Byrnes favors allocation on a state basis with the one-third rule applying to projects in the state as a whole.

The development of a formula for distributing Federal funds for unemployment relief has been very troublesome. The House Committee agrees with the Senate Committee that state and local contributions should not be less than 33⅓ per cent, with a minimum of flexibility permitting lower amounts in some places. On the other hand, the President does not look with favor upon the use of the Byrnes formula. A formula should take into account not only the factor of population but also the constantly changing economic and unemployment conditions in various sections of the country. To be acceptable, a formula should be sufficiently flexible to meet specific situations. The President does not believe that states and local units should be required to contribute so large a percentage of the total cost.

Local officials contend that Federal aid should be accorded in proportion to the number of jobs necessary to relieve unemployment, rather than in fixed sums allotted to states. The issue is an important one, which will in all likelihood come before the next Congress. Consideration of the problem by the recent session of Congress was influenced by such bitter politics that an acceptable solution was out of the question.

The same problem is faced in the distribution of Federal funds for highway purposes. Legislation provides that the funds be granted to the states with the stipulation that 25 per cent be spent on highways within municipalities. However, the Bureau of Public Roads refrains from ordering the proportion or the method of distribution within a state. This has led to the contention that some state highway departments have slighted their cities. In defense of some states it should be noted that they may not legally spend state funds on municipal streets.

The pertinent comment of the Urbanism Committee anent this situation expresses a principle that might well be observed generally in applying Federal funds. Wrote the Committee:

No continuing validity can be attached to the 25 per cent rule; nor can internal distributions within states be left to haphazard decision. Urban needs and capacities do not run uniformly to an arbitrary percentage, like the 25 per cent used as an emergency rule; and road needs, engineering and social requirements, and financial capacity cannot be safely neglected for long in determining the fund distribution.[8]

Facts are needed to determine the proper allocation for road building as well as for any other function. In this connection the recent report of the

[8] *Urban Government*, Vol. I, Part II, Sec. 2, p. 115.

United States Bureau of Public Roads is important. The Bureau in conjunction with state highway departments has been making a survey of highway users. The report shows a much greater urban use of all highways than most municipal officials would have guessed. Most traffic begins and ends in cities, so that the belt line is not so important in an integrated highway program as was once supposed. The report has important possibilities for securing to municipalities a fair and reasonable share of state-collected highway revenues. It likewise provides the basis for a better Federal distribution.

RECENT POLICY CHANGES

A serious problem for municipalities in their contacts with the Federal Government is the change in Federal policies. Often changes in policy adversely affecting the municipal budget are made suddenly, and often these changes come in the middle of the city's fiscal year. As long as some of the most important direct Federal-municipal contacts are due to emergency legislation, this is to be expected. Two factors might help the municipal budgetary problem. First, Congress might adopt a permanent program for the problems growing out of unemployment and relief instead of treating these as emergency problems; and second, Congress and Federal agencies might establish better channels for consultation with municipal officials. It is reasonable to suppose that sudden changes would be less likely to occur if channels existed for more direct and frequent contacts between national and local authorities.

Congressional legislation of 1939 was not without its shock to local government. Congress seemed to be in a mood to return much of the responsibility for public construction and relief to the state and local governments. No new public works appropriations were authorized, although at the close of 1938 a total of 6,246 applications were in the hands of the Public Works Administration for consideration if Congress should authorize another appropriation.[9] The demand for this type of aid is shown by the fact that these requests remained after the allotment of $965,000,000 appropriated in 1938 to the Works Progress Administration and after Congress had made available $400,000,000 for this purpose from the revolving fund of the Reconstruction Finance Corporation. The President's "lending-spending" program which was defeated in the closing days of the session called for $350,000,000 for non-Federal public works of a self-liquidating character, and $750,000,000 for self-liquidating toll roads, bridges, high-speed highways, and city by-passes.

The relief act [10] made some important changes which are of concern to local governments. The salient features of the act which are likely to affect municipal budgets are: (1) reduction in the amount appropriated over 1938 by about one-third, entailing a cut in W.P.A. rolls by approximately one-third; (2) prohibition against varying the rate of pay for workers of the same type in different geographical areas to any greater extent than may be justified by differences in the cost of living; (3) the furloughing for thirty days of all persons except veterans who have been continuously employed on W.P.A. rolls for eighteen months; (4) requirement that local sponsors contribute at least 25 per cent of the total cost of a project; (5) reduction of the ratio of administrative expenditures to total costs; (6) substitution of the security wage for the

[9] E. D. Mallery, "Federal City Relations in 1938," *The Municipal Year Book*, 1939, p. 154. A summary by types of projects approved under the 1938 appropriation is contained in this article, pp. 153–54.

[10] Pub. Res. No. 24, 76th Congress.

prevailing wage; and (7) prohibition of the use of any of the funds after January 1, 1940 for the construction of any non-Federal building the portion of which payable from Federal funds exceeds $52,000.

It is too early to weigh the effects of these changes. Unofficial information from several states showed increases in the state and local relief rolls about in proportion to the number dismissed from W.P.A. rolls. The United States Conference of Mayors warned Congress late in July that the Federal work relief program would collapse unless the present law was amended "to meet the needs of the situation." It contended that it was already unmistakably clear that the whole work program was jeopardized as a result of certain provisions of the law and that the already heavily burdened taxpayers were faced with an additional load. War in Europe may relieve the pressure on local relief rolls, but conditions at the time of the passage of the act scarcely warranted Congress in assuming that industry would take up the slack caused by reduced W.P.A. rolls.

Since 1933 there had developed a plan of intergovernmental co-operation in dealing with the relief problem which fixed within general limits responsibility among the three levels of government for various types of relief. That program has been upset, with the result that a readjustment of responsibility and financial obligations must now be sought between state and local governments if the relief problem continues to be acute.

HOUSING AND TAXATION POLICIES

A third important change in policy has occurred in the field of housing. The National Government did much to stimulate local interest in public housing. Aside from aid for limited-dividend housing projects, the first public projects were built and managed by the Housing Division of the P.W.A. Congress by the passage of the United States Housing Act of 1937 changed its housing policy from one of Federally administered housing to decentralized, locally administered housing. Local authorities were responsible for the initiation and management of projects under nationally prescribed standards.

Congress came to the aid of these local authorities by authorizing the United States Housing Authority to lend them up to $800,000,000. Ninety per cent of the cost of a project might be borrowed from the Housing Authority. In addition, Congress agreed to provide $28,000,000 annually for sixty years to be allocated to local authorities to enable them to bring the rents within the means of the lowest income groups. Local authorities were only required to put up one-fifth of the amount received from the United States Housing Authority.

By April of 1939, thirty-seven states had passed enabling legislation and 230 local authorities had been established. A number of these had not been created in time to participate in the grants of 1937 and 1938. A new housing bill was introduced in 1939 authorizing the Housing Authority to lend an additional $800,000,000 to local authorities and to contribute annually up to $45,000,000 for sixty years.

Local interest in the program is shown by the fact that early in 1939 the United States Housing Authority had earmarking requests for more than the amount sought in the bill before Congress. At this point further Federal aid for housing was stopped by the action of the House in dropping the bill although the Senate had passed it. This probably means the death of further low-cost housing and slum-clearance projects for the time being.

Following the Supreme Court's recent decisions that salaries of officials of one government are not immune from taxation by another, Congress passed the

Public Salary Tax Act, which provided for the taxation of salaries of officers and employees of states or their political subdivisions. More controversial is the question of taxing public securities. An amendment to include public securities in the Public Salary Tax Act was withdrawn. But hearings have been held by a subcommittee of the House Committee on Ways and Means on a measure to accomplish this purpose, and the measure is scheduled to come before Congress in January, 1940. Many feel that if such a measure passes, state and local bonds cannot be floated on such favorable terms, and that the cost to local governments will be greater than the revenue secured by the Federal Government.

New Activities and New Needs

Each year the activities of the National Government which affect municipalities grow more numerous. Bills were under consideration during the session of 1939 which would increase Federal activity in such fields as education, health, stream pollution control, and personnel relations. The services of the regular agencies grow more numerous. Many of the new contacts which grew out of the depression are certain to continue. The last few years mark a period of swiftly changing emphasis in the apportionment of authority among the different levels of government. As yet no clear line of policy has emerged with respect to the distribution of authority.

Two important needs have emerged; first, more thorough studies in intergovernmental relationships, and second, better channels through which Federal-city co-operation may be carried on. Although Federal services have been expanding which are very beneficial to cities, little effort has been made to develop services for cities as such. Legal concepts of the city and its relation to the state have dominated the thinking of Federal and state authorities. The city as an economic and social entity which plays an important role in the national economy has not been given proper consideration. An intelligent policy for Federal-municipal co-operation can only be built upon comprehensive studies into the interrelation of functions at different levels of government, together with a consideration of the financial and administrative resources of each level of government for performing those functions. It is a problem of the proper allocation of powers and functions between the national, state, and local governments.

Until recently, little has been done along this line by those in official capacity. It is for this reason that the comprehensive study and recent reports of the Urbanism Committee [11] appointed by the National Resources Committee stand as a landmark in the development of Federal-municipal relations. They mark the blazing of a trail which Congress, the National Administration, and state and local authorities might explore to their mutual benefit. In this connection a report of the United States Bureau of Public Roads on the allocation of highway funds and highway uses, made public in 1939, is important in the development of better intergovernmental responsibilities with reference to the highway function.

New Channels for Federal-Municipal Co-operation

Not only does the need exist for more thorough knowledge on the allocation of functions, but equally important is the need for better channels of co-operation between the national and local governments. Municipal officials have no spe-

---

[11] *Urban Government,* Volume I of the Supplementary Report of the Urbanism Committee to the National Resources Committee, Washington, 1939; *Our Cities: Their Role in the National Economy,* Washington, 1937.

cific regularized channel for contact with the executive and legislative branches of the National Government. The Urbanism Committee listed seventy-one Federal agencies dealing with urban government. Because the services offered are so widely scattered, municipal officials are often unaware of their existence. Moreover, the same type of services may be rendered by more than one Federal agency, and this causes confusion.

The creation of some agency for centralizing information concerning Federal services to municipalities has been preached for more than a decade. Some would go beyond the mere clearing-house stage by favoring the offering of more concrete aids to local governments, in line with what the Federal Government does for agriculture.

Several recent developments are likely to improve Federal-municipal relations. By the President's Reorganization Plan Number 1,[12] the P.W.A., the W.P.A., the Bureau of Public Roads, the Public Buildings branch of the Treasury's Procurement Division, the Buildings branch of the National Park Service, and the United States Housing Authority were consolidated into a new Federal Works Agency. Also, the United States Employment Service, the Office of Education, the Public Health Service, the National Youth Administration, the Social Security Board, and the Civilian Conservation Corps were consolidated under a new Federal Security Agency. By an Executive Order issued September 9, 1939, providing for White House staff reorganizations, the President directed the National Resources Planning Board to consult with Federal, regional, state, local, and private agencies in developing orderly programs of public works and to act as a clearing house and a means of co-ordination for planning activities—linking together various levels and fields of planning. An Office of Government Reports has been set up under the Executive Office, which among other things will: (1) provide a central clearing house through which citizens, state and local governmental bodies, and, where appropriate, agencies of the Federal Government may transmit inquiries and complaints and receive advice and information; (2) assist the President in dealing with special problems requiring the clearance of information between the Federal Government and state and local governments and private institutions; (3) keep the President currently informed of the opinions, desires, and complaints of citizens and groups of citizens and of state and local governments with respect to the work of Federal agencies.

In addition to these changes, a municipal reference bureau has been established in the Bureau of the Census. The National Resources Committee (now the National Resources Planning Board) recently named a special committee to discover and make available aids to local planning. One of the problems which faces this committee is to decide upon what kind of planning aids to make available. Shall it deal in drafting general plans, or shall it widen the scope of its work to enable it to assist in the implementation of the recommendations of the Urbanism Committee? Many hope that it will undertake this broader task.

Treatment of municipalities by the National Government as wards of the state which should be dealt with through state channels has been a major retarding influence to the development of better official contacts between cities and the Nation. In the absence of official contacts, cities have had to develop and rely upon unofficial representation at Washington to get a proper hearing on Federal-municipal problems. Especially valuable have been the representations

[12] Approved June 7, 1939, Public Resolution No. 2, 76th Congress.

carried on through the American Municipal Association and the United States Conference of Mayors. These organizations are likely to continue to act as important liaison agencies between the two levels of government.

THE PRESENT PERIOD OF TRANSITION

Criticisms as well as praise have been characteristic of this transition period. One local government official has remarked that the Federal Government has alternated between preserving the cities financially, placing new burdens upon them, and sapping their authority and influence.[13] It is to be expected in this period of rapidly changing conditions that maladjustments would be experienced.

The distinctive characteristic of the present period, as the Urbanism Committee has so clearly pointed out, is a groping toward a new synthesis in allocating powers. The task of governing through various levels of government has yet to attain an equilibrium by harmonious intergovernmental relations.

[13] C. E. Armstrong, City Comptroller, Birmingham, Ala., "Troubles and Trends in Municipal Finance," *Texas Municipalities*, Feb. 1939, p. 43.

Raymond S. Short, Ph.D., is assistant professor of political science at Temple University, Philadelphia, Pennsylvania. He has aided in legislative surveys of school costs and state-local relations in Pennsylvania.

Trade Barriers Between States

By F. Eugene Melder

TRADITIONALLY, the United States is an area in which internal free trade exists as long as the trade is not detrimental to the public safety and morals. This tradition is based on the Constitution's limitations on the activities of the states, which forbid a state to ". . . lay any Imposts or Duties on Imports or Exports, except what may be absolutely necessary for executing it's Inspection Laws . . ." or to ". . . lay any Duty of Tonnage . . . ," without the consent of Congress. Furthermore, the Constitution forbids discriminations against commerce, ships, and citizens of other states.

Nevertheless, a considerable variety of state and local statutes and regulations have been enacted or practiced which accomplish results similar to those served by tariffs in the relations between nations. Like international tariffs, these laws have tended to accomplish any of three ends: first, to provide a protected market for home producers and merchants by discouraging the consumption of "imported goods"; second, to retaliate against governments which have protected their own producers; and third, to raise public revenues at the expense of those who produce, market, or consume "imported" products or services.

The principal forms of state and local trade barriers which have received court sanction are classified as "indirect burdens" on interstate commerce. These laws are based on the states' rights or powers to tax and license those enjoying property or other privileges or rights in the state, and the states' police and general regulatory powers, which include sanitary protection of the health and goods of persons resident in the state, including the power to impose quarantine, and which provide for the safety of the persons, the property, and the morals of populations. Other types of laws which tend to clog the arteries of trade and which are sanctioned by the courts are based on the sovereign proprietary powers of states or on specific grants of authority to the states by Congress or constitutional amendment. The proprietary or corporate powers relate to the conservation of natural resources and ownership of public works and property.

Although the Constitution forbids the states, without the consent of Congress, to levy duties on imports and exports, and prohibits discriminations against commerce, ships, and citizens of other states, the revenue powers of the states have often been used so as to discriminate against outside goods, persons, and corporations.[1]

EXERCISE OF TAX AND LICENSE POWERS

The leading types of discriminations based on the tax and license powers of the states, which may be delegated to local governments, are as follows:

1. Special taxes on certain commodities which compete with products made within the state. Thus today we have the spectacle of thirty states attempting to limit the sale of margarine within their borders in order to protect various of their home producers. Of these, nine states apply their "protective tariffs" to all margarine, in order to protect butter producers. Fifteen states protect producers of cottonseed oil or other domestic fats and oils against the competitive menace of coconut and other imported oils in their state markets, by excise taxes on the sale of margarine

---

[1] F. Eugene Melder, "Trade Barriers and States Rights," *American Bar Association Journal*, Vol. XXV, No. 4 (April 1939), pp. 307–9.

containing such foreign ingredients. Six states levy only a license tax, while nine states which levy excise taxes also employ licenses to collect fees from dealers, manufacturers, and other handlers of the product. Used-car import laws and carbonated-beverage license laws at times appear to combine similar features.

2. Special taxes on certain types of merchandising organizations, as for example, state taxes on chain stores and other integrated merchandisers, aimed to protect the merchants in older marketing channels such as the traditionally independent retailer and wholesaler. One-half of the states enforce such a tax.

3. Use taxes levied by sales-tax states and applied to purchases from outside merchants by state residents without "offsets" for sales taxes paid in the state of origin. At least five states have such consumer tax laws.

4. Taxation of nonresident commercial motor vehicles so as to discriminate in favor of resident trucks and busses.

5. Special taxes and license fees levied on "foreign" corporations in return for the privilege of doing business within the states.

6. Vendor licensing by municipalities and states which apply to merchant-truckers and nonresident canvassers.

7. Discriminatory premium taxes applicable to each foreign insurance company doing business within the state. Twenty-nine states appear to fall in this category. Exemptions from a part or the whole of state premium taxes are sometimes granted to those insurance companies which have a certain proportion of their reserves invested within the state. Ten states have such a feature in their laws.

8. Discriminatory liquor tax laws have been enacted by many states since the adoption of the Twenty-first Amendment to the Federal Constitution in 1934. These are used to curb or destroy out-of-state competition with resident liquor producers or dealers, or to protect the resident farmers who produce raw materials usable in the manufacture of alcoholic beverages.[1a] These laws have been based upon a section of the Twenty-first Amendment which was intended to protect "dry" states from illegal liquor imports under the protection of the "Commerce Clause," but which has been so construed as to enable "wet" states to erect protective tariffs and discriminatory police measures against out-of-state alcoholic products. During the past five years an amazing variety of such restrictions on the import of out-of-state liquors have been adopted. While many represent barriers under the police powers, the most effective discriminatory measures undoubtedly are found in the field of taxation.

Protection of a state's manufacturers and wholesalers of alcoholic beverages takes at least five forms: (1) lower excise taxes on alcoholic beverages, especially wines, which are manufactured from domestic rather than out-of-state or partly out-of-state materials; (2) higher license fees on wholesalers who handle imported alcoholic beverages than on those who handle domestic products only; (3) special license fees or "certificates of approval" for nonresident manufacturers who wish to ship into states; (4) requirements that a manufacturer qualify to do business in the state as a foreign corporation before he can secure a license; and (5) explicit or implicit advantages to domestic products given by the liquor stores in those states which themselves monopolize the retailing of liquor.

Preference to farmer producers of raw materials usable in liquor manufacture

[1a] Thomas S. Green, Jr., *State Discriminations Against Out of State Alcoholic Beverages*, Trade Barrier Research Bulletin Series, Council of State Governments, March 17, 1939.

may likewise take several forms: (1) lower tax differentials on wines made from local raw materials than on those made from "foreign" grapes; (2) sale by domestic producers directly to retailers rather than through wholesalers; and (3) requirements that a certain percentage of the alcoholic beverage be made from specified products grown in the state.

Police and Regulatory Powers

Under the police and general regulatory powers, states exercise the functions of protecting the public health, safety, and morals. In performing these functions it is often necessary to interfere with interstate and interregional commerce. When such occasions arise, a trade barrier exists if the measures taken go beyond the necessities of the situation and operate to the economic advantage of local residents and industries at the cost of persons or products of sister states. Often trade barriers and legitimate police measures are so indistinguishable as to cause the experts to disagree. However, the courts, as well as economists and public authorities, have often made such distinctions.[2]

Some of the more or less significant types of barriers based on police or regulatory powers of the states are:

1. Milk-market exclusion by limitation of the area or milkshed from which fluid milk may be supplied to city markets, through refusal to inspect the premises of some dairymen who wish to supply the market, or by arbitrary and questionable changes in the sanitary requirements applicable to milk producers, from time to time.[3]

2. Exclusion of plant or animal products of competing areas by means of quarantines based on economic considerations under the guise of pathological or biological titles. Laws controlling the entry of nursery stock into the state are closely related to quarantine exclusions. Such requirements as the filing of large surety bonds, permit tags to accompany each interstate shipment, and the filing of special invoices with state officials prior to shipment of nursery stock tend seriously to discourage such imports.

3. Restrictions on the movement of laborers across political boundaries by requiring monetary proof of migrants' ability to remain self-supporting or by enforcement of settlement laws.[4]

4. Regulations of dimensions, weights, and equipment of interstate trucks and busses and the use of ports of entry on interstate highways so as to curb the use of the highways by the motor carriers of neighboring states.[5] The lack of uniformity of state motor-vehicle codes is the primary cause of this form of hindrance to interstate shipping. Conflicting requirements are so numerous that several legal volumes would be required to print all the contradictory legislation.

Even though an interstate truck operator receives equal treatment with intrastate truckers, nevertheless he must comply with such a variety of dimension, safety, and liability requirements that at times he finds himself violating one state's laws in order to comply with the laws of an adjacent state. Such legislation can and does constitute a serious hindrance to interstate commerce. For instance, a trucker in one

[2] F. Eugene Melder, *State and Local Barriers to Interstate Commerce in the United States* (University of Maine Studies, Second Series, No. 43, 1937), pp. 125–41; Geo. R. Taylor, Edgar L. Burtiss, and Frederick V. Waugh, *Barriers to Internal Trade in Farm Products* (United States Department of Agriculture, Special Report, Government Printing Office, 1939), pp. 85–97.

[3] Melder, *op. cit.*, pp. 106–24; Taylor, Burtiss, and Waugh, *op. cit.*, pp. 5–16.

[4] Melder, *op. cit.*, pp. 142–53.

[5] Melder, *op. cit.*, pp. 72–85; Taylor, Burtiss, and Waugh, *op. cit.*, pp. 36–57.

eastern state may not drive a vehicle whose loaded weight exceeds forty thousand pounds, while in the next state he may operate a truck of three times that weight. A truck operator in the second state may not be able to drive into the adjoining state because of the relatively low maximum weight limit permitted there, while trucks of the first state move freely into the second state, as far as maximum weights are concerned.

In addition to being restricted by a maze of nonuniform state requirements, the interstate trucker sometimes finds his operations hindered by "ports of entry." About eight western states operate these ports on highway entrances to the respective states, as a means of enforcing their motor-vehicle laws, collecting ton-mile taxes, and regulating the entry of nursery stock and other commodities. Although in theory the port officials do not discriminate against outside trucks, in practice shippers and truckers and even private pleasure car travelers lose time and suffer other annoyances to such a degree that complaints are constantly heard against these stoppages. Ports of entry are of such a spectacular nature that some observers consider them the outstanding example of what they term the "Balkanizing of the United States."

5. Establishment of state grades, standards, and labels which do not conform to Federal or other state specifications, with the result that the free movement of goods between states tends to be interrupted.[6] Some of these laws go so far as to require out-of-state eggs to be branded as "shipped," while eggs from resident poultrymen are branded with the name of the home state.

CORPORATE OR PROPRIETARY STATE POWERS

As the sovereign, a state is proprietor of the public domain, the public works, and such natural resources as have not been reduced to private possession. Furthermore, as a corporate entity a state possesses the power and the duty of spending large amounts of public moneys in carrying out its proprietary, police, and other functions. Under their powers as proprietors in conserving natural resources and owning public property and in performing their spending functions, the various states may exercise several types of preferences which favor residents or discriminations which penalize nonresidents, with very little restraint from the courts.[7] The leading forms are as follows:

1. As employers, states may refuse employment on public pay rolls to any but legal residents. By "legal residents" is meant those persons who have maintained their homes in the state for a minimum period varying from six months to five years depending upon the state, and qualified in other possible ways, such as by the payment of a poll tax.

2. Many states have also followed a policy of favoring residents in the expenditure of public moneys. One way in which this is carried out is to require that public printing contracts shall be awarded only to resident printing firms. Twenty-six states have had such a policy. This means that printers do not have to worry about outside competition in making bids for state printing contracts in these states.

This principle of protecting residents against nonresident competition by means of granting preferences in the expenditure of public moneys has been extended in recent years to other groups. Thus, twenty-eight states exercise some degree of preference for state-produced products when buying supplies for public institutions or building materials for public works. These laws demonstrate

[6] Taylor, Burtiss, and Waugh, *op. cit.*, pp. 68–84.

[7] Melder, *op. cit.*, pp. 12–36, 154–65.

an interesting variety. For instance, six states purchase for public use only coal mined within the state. Seven states require building stone and other materials produced within the state to be used in the construction and repair of public buildings, whenever such are obtainable. Three others have similar restrictions, but limit the preferences application to domestic producers whose prices are not more than 5 per cent above the prices of outsiders for like products. A fourth sets the limit of preference at 3 per cent. Some states provide preferential treatment of resident contractors in awarding contracts for the construction of public buildings and other public works. One state even requires that textbooks for the public schools shall be printed within the state. Another requires that home-produced butter be served in its state hospital and penal institutions.

In all, forty-seven states of the Union exercise at least one type of such citizen-preference laws, intended to restrict the movement into the state of products or residents of other states and to protect some residents or home groups from the competition of outsiders. In so far as higher prices are thus paid for home-produced products, such practices tend to increase the cost of state government at the expense of the taxpayers as a whole. Furthermore, such measures may at times injure the outside market for residents, because, as in international trade, in order to sell abroad, a group must permit outsiders to sell their goods inside.

3. As conservator of public or even privately owned natural resources, a state may place limitations or absolute prohibitions on the export of products of natural resources, such as hydroelectricity, in order to force industry which would obtain such products at advantageous prices to locate within the state.

It would be a mistake to give the reader the impression that the growth of trade barriers between the states necessarily represents deliberate attempts of state legislators to wall off their respective states from the rest of the Union. Many times lawmakers enact such laws in almost complete innocence of their consequences. The trade-barrier effects of many motor-truck specification laws and highway ports-of-entry statutes are usually not foreseen. However, most such legislation is probably motivated by the desire to furnish protected markets to various resident special-interest groups.

Trade Barriers Unsupported by Special Legislation

Such trade barriers as exist without benefit of legal sponsorship are invariably intended to give market protection to special groups. By its very nature, this type of trade barrier between states, cities, or other sections is secretive. Such barriers exist extralegally or illegally—which is sometimes the best reason for their effectiveness. A barrier law may ultimately be recognized as such by those adversely affected, and if sufficient protest results, it is sometimes repealed. A trade barrier which operates without legal basis is seldom recognized in its true colors, so surreptitious is its nature. As a consequence, it may exist successfully for years with few consumers, taxpayers, or other injured parties being the wiser, and to the great benefit of the protected groups.

In fact, so little is known of such interstate trade barriers that they have almost entirely escaped the attention of barrier-law investigators. A few examples will suffice to give a partial idea of their nature. In a western state, nonresident brewers recently found it difficult or impossible to sell their product, without any apparent legal reason. Investigation showed that the reason for the lack of orders for outside beer, despite generous advertising within the state, was to be found in a verbal agreement between resident brewers and several labor union leaders, by which the brewers agreed to foster the labor leaders' interests in return for the promise of union members to handle only beer produced in domestic breweries.

Another barrier of the same general type is that to be found in some cities, in the building industry. Assistant Attorney-General Thurman Arnold recently brought it to public attention as a result of Federal investigations preparatory to enforcing the antitrust laws. According to his statement, whole building industries, including labor unions, are so organized in some cities as virtually to force home builders to pay exceedingly high building costs as compared with the costs of construction in neighboring areas, by the device of excluding outside competition through extralegal means.

Sometimes public construction contracts are awarded to local high bidders in lieu of the legally mandatory "lowest responsible bidder." In such cases it is probable that there is some sort of illegal collusion between the favored bidders and the awarding officials. Yet the fact remains that such discriminations are as effectual barriers to free competition as any tariff laws could be. They may operate for years without discovery, simply because the victims cannot or dare not divulge the practice to the public. Probably no broad study of such state and local barriers will ever be made, because of the difficulty of gathering data on such practices.

Consequences of Trade Barriers between States

It is outside the scope of this article to discuss all the consequences of state trade barriers. Needless to say, their effects have not been uniform. Doubtless, favored groups have often benefited at the expense of consumers, competitors, taxpayers, or the public. On occasion, barrier laws have been boomerangs to the very groups which sought their creation and benefits. Probably in the majority of cases their economic consequences are unmeasurable. From another approach, however, their consequences are more certain and are observable. This approach is their influence on interstate relations. Here their consequences are invariably the same. Trade barriers, if discovered, always increase tensions between the lawmakers and business groups of the states involved. The principal proof of this statement lies in the fact that so many trade barrier laws and practices have come into existence as reprisals for real or fancied injuries by other commonwealths. Innumerable boycotts have also been threatened, and reams of paper have been consumed in exchanges of threats, recriminations, and arguments over trade barriers, between officials of the several commonwealths.

Progress against State Tariffs

The picture of national disunity arising from interstate trade barriers and related activities would be very dark indeed were it not for the recent growth of a strong movement in opposition to provincial economic legislation.

State trade barriers largely escaped public attention until recently, perhaps because of the desire of interested business groups to minimize Federal regulation through the appeal to states' rights, and because of the general acceptance of the traditional existence of free trade among the states. Not until Governor James V. Allred of Texas appointed a Trade Barrier Commission in September 1938 to investigate and recommend policies which would tend to remove the obstructions of other states to the free sale of Texas' products therein, did any state governor express alarm over this abuse of state rights. In rapid succession the Annual Governors' Conference, the Council of State Governments, the United States Department of Agriculture, and various agricultural and business groups began to take cognizance of the situation.

An intensive campaign was begun to check the rising tide of state "autarchy" laws when the Council of State Governments and co-operating state agencies called a National Conference on Interstate Trade Barriers. The conference met in Chicago early in April 1939 to air the whole situation and to work out a program of action to be taken by the groups concerned. This conference was attended by delegates from forty-three states, including six state governors and the representatives of several interested agricultural, business, and consumer organizations. At the end of three days the conferees adopted resolutions condemning the principle of trade barriers, and reports of special committees on various types of such laws. Of more importance, the conference prepared a program which recommended that the states adopt a "good neighbor" policy and work through the machinery of existing state Commissions on Interstate Co-operation and the Council of State Governments, to the end that existing barrier laws be repealed or amended so as to remove discriminatory features. Specifically, it proposed:

Discouraging the adoption of any retaliatory legislation by states which feel themselves aggrieved by the legislation of their neighbors.

Encouraging the repeal of trade barrier legislation which may have already been adopted by the several states.

Encouraging the enactment of uniform laws, and the adoption of reciprocal agreements, which have for their aim the reduction of trade barriers between the states.

Initiating regional hearings throughout the United States, such hearings to be officially called by the Commissions of Interstate Co-operation in conjunction with the Council of State Governments, in order to follow through the recommendations made by this conference.

Undertaking surveys and factual studies as proposed by this Conference or the Commissions on Interstate Co-operation.

Following that conference very little new state trade-barrier legislation was enacted in the sessions of the forty-four legislatures which met in 1939, while dozens of trade-barrier bills were defeated in legislatures or vetoed by state governors. The press and the radio of the country gave a great deal of publicity to the conference and its background in provincial laws. Many Federal and state agencies actively contributed to bringing public attention to the situation which has come to exist as a result of such petty special-interest laws. There seems to be little doubt that the educational and propagandistic influence of this publicity, plus the active interest of state and Federal authorities which grew out of the Chicago conference, is responsible for nipping in the bud the growth of economic national disunity by state political devices.

Attempts to pass repeal measures have achieved some success. For instance Indiana, Missouri, and one or two other states have repealed or amended liquor trade-barrier laws.

STATES' RIGHTS ARGUMENTS WEAKENED

The general tenor of the Chicago conference indicated that in future discussions of relations of government to private enterprise, more emphasis should be placed on state interference with internal free trade than in the past, and the appeal to states' rights as a guardian against Federal control should receive less attention than heretofore. The gist of most of the published material, a well as much of the oral discussion of recent months, is that the states have too often used their "rights" and powers to regulate interstate transactions to the disadvantage of persons, business agencies, or commodities of other states, and to the advantage of local residents and industries.

F. Eugene Melder, Ph.D., is assistant professor of economics at Clark University, Worcester, Massachusetts. He has written the first general treatise on interstate trade barriers, published under the title: "State and Local Barriers to Interstate Commerce in the United States" (1937), as well as numerous articles in the same field. He acted as economic adviser on trade barriers to the Council of State Governments in preparing for the National Conference on Trade Barriers in April 1939.

Tax Competition Between States

By James W. Martin

GENERALLY speaking, three varieties of state tax policy are traceable to interjurisdictional competition. The specific forms are almost as numerous as the multitude of statutes which impose them. Neglecting refinements, the major policies may be stated categorically, then discussed in turn. (1) Many states employ exemptions and other tax favors as a means of fostering "home industry." (2) States frequently impose tax measures designed to discriminate against out-of-state industry or business or against the use of raw materials produced outside the state. (3) Legislators and tax administrators often try to reach beyond the state for tax resources.

Interstate Tax Competition through Tax Favors

One of the most usual—and one of the crudest—forms of interstate tax competition is found in several varieties of tax favors to economic enterprise, prompted in some measure by a desire to lure it away from other places or to promote its development within the taxing state.[2] The tax favor is bestowed in various forms, a few of the most important of which will be outlined.

The most obvious variety of tax favor is the outright exemption of the favored property, income, sale, or other activity. Although exemptions for this purpose occur in all sorts of tax measures, property tax practice will afford sufficient illustration.

Almost invariably, state laws provide for certain agricultural exemptions. The most usual type is exemption of growing crops. This is prompted by other considerations—economic and administrative—so that it may be ignored for present purposes as long as confined to usual practice. However, the situation is different where under such a guise Tennessee exempts all raw tobacco in storage or Maine exempts mature livestock on farms or Mississippi provides a five-year exemption for livestock almost generally.

Another type provides partial or complete exemption for specified kinds of industrial or agricultural property. The Jensen study already cited enumerates a variety of instances, and a more recent announcement by the National Association of Assessing Officers adds numerous others which reflect subsequent legislation. It is in this area that interstate bidding with tax favors for industrial development, especially manufacturing, becomes most extreme and to many minds most offensive.[3]

Among the specific cases of these special exemptions, a few illustrations will suffice. The Kentucky Constitution provides that the General Assembly may authorize granting temporary exemption from municipal taxes to manufacturing plants. Mississippi and Louisiana have become notorious for the character and the extent of such exemptions. However, they are not alone, for nearly all

---

[1] In fairness to Dr. Martin, I should like to record that the manuscript of this article was received and acknowledged by me on August 11, 1939, one month prior to the publication of Professor Mabel Newcomer's somewhat parallel article in the September issue of *Tax Magazine*.—The Editor.

[2] Jens P. Jensen, *Tax Exemption as a Means of Encouragement to Industry* (University of Kansas), especially pp. 42 ff. See also James W. Martin, "General Theory of Tax Exemption," Chap. I in Martin and others, *Tax Exemptions*, pp. 3 ff., as well as sources cited pp. 223 ff.

[3] One of the most interesting current discussions is found in Kenneth McCarren, "Luring Industry through Tax Exemption," Martin and others, *ibid.*, Chap. III.

the southern as well as the New England and other states have some such exemptions—some of them concerning one or more types of industry, some involving manufacturing indiscriminately.

A related practice is the partial exemption of specified types of property. Kentucky affords adequate illustration. The Blue Grass State exempts from all local taxation livestock, farm machinery, manufacturing machinery, and manufacturers' raw materials and goods in process. Thus, the elective tax assessor must place tobacco in the hands of the farmer who produced it (or his agent) in the class of wholly exempt property, which is not assessed; must place similar tobacco held in a manufacturer's warehouse as raw material on hand at a place of manufacture in the class subject to state taxation only; and must put exactly the same product stored by a manufacturer but not at his manufacturing plant in the class which is subject to state taxation and to nominal local rates; however, if the tobacco has been processed, the assessor must treat it as finished product subject to full state and local rates.[4] Over-all tax limitation has become the basis of a whole interstate tax competition movement.[5] These limitation measures have been inserted in the constitutions of at least six states.[6]

A kindred competitive device is found in limitations deliberately placed on the taxing power by the legislature, or even by the constitution, in a form which precludes imposition of certain kinds of tax measures. If this is done by the constitution, it may apply to the state, to subdivisions thereof, or to both of these. In Illinois, for example, graduated income taxes and certain types of excises are unconstitutional. In Florida a constitutional amendment was adopted to make income and death taxes impossible.[7] If the tax applies to localities alone, it may be and usually is imposed by the legislature. Of course some such restrictions are motivated in part by considerations of an entirely different complexion, but there can be little doubt that competition for economic advantage has been *sine qua non* in many instances.

PUNITIVE TAX MEASURES

The several varieties of tax measures designed to discriminate against out-of-state competition are, for the most part, of recent vintage. Some of them have been on the statute books for many years; but the past ten years have witnessed remarkable new legislation, especially that incident to taxation of transactions in certain foods and beverages.

Although a number of minor developments may be ignored by the procedure, it seems best to present the problem through three characteristic examples: retaliatory insurance taxation, alcoholic beverage license and gallonage taxes, and taxes on margarine and related products.

Retaliatory and reciprocal [8] policies in

---

[4] In the *Twentieth Annual Report of the Department of Revenue*, 1937-38, recommendations for simplification are reiterated. They were made by the Kentucky Efficiency Commission. (*Revenue and Taxation*, Advance Pamphlet III, 1923, pp. 97 ff.; *Government of Kentucky*, I, pp. 315 ff.)

[5] For full discussion of the pros and cons, see Glen Leet and Robert M. Paige (Eds.), *Property Tax Limitation Laws*, P. A. S. No. 36. See also *Problems Relating to Taxation and Finance*, Vol. X of New York State Constitutional Committee Report, Chap. XI, and A. Miller Hillhouse and Ronald Welch, *Tax Limits Appraised*, P. A. S. No. 55. In the last is a well-selected bibliography.

[6] Hillhouse and Welch, *op. cit.*, p. 38.

[7] After the decision in Florida v. Mellon, 273 U. S. 12, the restriction as to death taxes was removed by further amendment.

[8] "Retaliatory" and "reciprocal" are words variously defined in this connection. In his exceptionally able address on "Reciprocity and Retaliation in Insurance Taxation" (*Proceedings*, National Tax Conference, 1938, pp. 462 ff.), Professor K. M. Williamson defines the terms in the following language: "Under the

insurance taxation began in 1832.[9] The practices originated in an attempt to protect home companies against tax discrimination by other states in which the companies might do business.[10] The policy seems to rest essentially in the notion that the state which charters an insurance company has a peculiar stake in nurturing that concern, but is totally or largely indifferent to the prosperity of concerns organized under the laws of other states. Occasionally, there is a grain of truth in the assumption.

The principal basis of retaliation is the premium tax. Philip L. Gamble [11] defines half a dozen methods of taxing insurance business, but the area within which retaliation in the ordinary sense is fiscally important does not reach much beyond the premium tax.

One illustration will suggest the reasons for student and insurance-executive objections to these discriminations.[12] An

reciprocal plan, as the term is used here, a state enacts no specified mandatory taxes to be imposed upon foreign insurance companies but provides that such companies should be subject to the same special tax laws and fees as are imposed by the states chartering such companies. Under the retaliatory plan, however, as that term is used here, a given state, A, imposes upon foreign insurance companies doing business within its borders its own primary or mandatory tax at fixed rates on legally defined bases, but provides that if any other state, B, imposes upon A's companies a higher tax, B's companies shall be taxed in A by B's law. The retaliatory system thus assures the taxing state of a mandatory minimum tax and permits an alternative conditional maximum, while the reciprocal plan provides only for such charges as are fixed by the chartering states." The word "retaliatory" is used for both forms of discrimination in the following paragraphs.

[9] *Loc. cit.*
[10] George B. Young, "Discussion on Reciprocity and Retaliation in Insurance Taxation," *ibid.,* p. 480.
[11] *Taxation of Insurance Companies,* New York State Tax Commission, Special Report No. 12, Chap. III.
[12] Williamson, *loc. cit.,* and Young, *ibid.,* p. 484.

insurance company chartered under the law of one state does business in another. To find out its liability, it must ascertain the rates of various taxes in each, apply them, and pay the larger amount. On the state's side, it is necessary, if the task is to be properly performed, that the tax official keep current not only as to the statutes and regulations of his own state but also as to details for every state which has chartered any insurance corporation collecting premiums on business within his own state.

There is also a mercantilist policy of introducing differential premium tax rates if the insurance company invests in specified types of local securities. In South Carolina, for example, there is a reduction of one-fourth of a point for each one-fourth of the fire insurance premium invested in specified South Carolina securities; so that, in the event all the premiums collected on account of South Carolina policies were thus locally invested, the rate would be reduced from 2 per cent to 1 per cent. In Colorado, if the fire company invests 50 per cent or more of its assets in the state's specified securities, the 2 per cent premium tax is entirely waived.[13]

REACHING BEYOND THE STATE FOR TAX SOURCES

The practice has been common for states to reach beyond their own boundaries for taxable resources. In many instances the practice is deliberate on the part of the legislature or the tax administration. In other cases it arises from technical difficulties which the state intentionally or inadvertently resolves in its own favor. Several illustrations will make clear the characteristics of this most direct and obvious

[13] Data as to both states from P. L. Gamble, "Special Taxes Applicable to Fire Insurance Companies as of October 1, 1935," *Tax Systems of the World,* 1937, pp. 205–6.

form of tax competition between the states.

Death taxes

Possibly the form of overreaching jurisdictional bounds which has been most widespread, and about which most has been written, is found in multiple bases of death-tax jurisdiction. At one time or another, individual state legislatures have asserted authority to tax the transfer of estates or bequests on the basis of the decedent's domicile [14] and, in the case of corporate securities, on the basis of corporate domicile,[15] the location of the property of the corporation,[16] and the place of the physical depository of corporate securities.[17] In addition, of course, tangible property having a fixed situs in another state is subject to transfer tax wherever the property is located.[18] In a series of decisions by the Supreme Court of the United States, some of these jurisdictional grounds have been declared unconstitutional; though some now outlawed, as for example corporate domicile, were perhaps as logical as decedent's domicile as the determinant of taxable situs of stocks and bonds. At the present time, therefore, in respect of most intangible property, jurisdiction rests on the domicile of the decedent alone, and in the case of real estate and tangible personal property having a fixed situs, on the location of the property alone.

It is not to be inferred, however, that all of the problems in connection with situs for death taxation have been solved. Transfer of trust property under certain circumstances, for example, can be taxed in two states.[19]

The principal competitive point in connection with death taxation results from the fact that states have chosen those bases of jurisdiction which would result in the largest tax revenue. For example, if an eastern state enjoyed jurisdiction on the basis of decedent's domicile and a western state had jurisdiction on the basis of the location of corporate property, then the estate of a decedent resident of the eastern state who owned securities in the western state corporation would be called on to pay two taxes. If another eastern state successfully asserted jurisdiction on the ground that it was the domicile of the corporation owning the property, then a third tax would be imposed. Moreover, some states have claimed jurisdiction, speaking logically, on two or more mutually exclusive bases. It has been shown that theoretically claims amounting to substantially more than the entire estate could arise from the statutes in force in 1924.[20]

Corporation taxes

Another area illustrating the same principle but involving an entirely different technique of reaching out for tax sources, is found in connection with excise and income taxes on corporations. One of the most obvious forms of discrimination, formerly practiced even more widely than at the present time, arose from discriminatory excises on foreign as compared with domestic corporations. The Supreme Court approved this type of discrimination on the ground that the equal-protection clause of the

---

[14] This is generally the law now. Curry v. McCanless, decided May 29, 1939 (No. 339), 83 L. Ed. 865 (Adv. Sheets).

[15] First National Bank of Boston v. Maine, 284 U. S. 312.

[16] Rhode Island Hospital Trust Co. v. Daughton, 270 U. S. 69.

[17] Baldwin v. Missouri, 281 U. S. 586.

[18] Frick v. Pennsylvania, 266 U. S. 497.

[19] Curry v. McCanless, *supra.*; Graves v. Elliott, decided May 29, 1939 (No. 372), 83 L. Ed. 880 (Adv. Sheets). See also First Bank Stock Corporation v. Minnesota, 301 U. S. 234.

[20] W. B. Belknap, *Proceedings* of Preliminary Conference, Inheritance and Estate Taxes, 1924, p. 5.

Constitution does not apply to corporations.

A second form of corporation excise, income, and property tax discrimination is found in defective allocation formulas. In a number of states the statutes prescribe allocation formulas which are particularly adapted to securing a large proportion of the corporation within its bounds. For example, a railroad company subject to an income, excise, or property tax may find that a western state having a large amount of single-track mileage will employ line mileage as a basis of apportionment; whereas an eastern or midwestern state in which the same railroad has much double track and extensive yards will employ all-track mileage, the consequence being that the railroad is allocated to an aggregate extent of more than 100 per cent.[21] Exactly the same result may follow from administrative action. If the assessing officers are inconsistent in the utilization of formulas, the discrimination may be multiplied. Industrial corporations having property and business in two or more states give rise to kindred effects.

Use taxes

Much has been written recently about the employment of use taxes as a means of tapping revenue sources without the state's boundaries. Most of the discussion has no factual basis other than irritation caused by the administrative machinery necessary to handle these measures. The enforcement structures are admittedly more complicated and irritating than are those employed in connection with other taxes. They are essentially no different in principle, however, from methods invoked in the administration of other commodity taxes.

Notwithstanding the fact that the taxation of outsiders by means of use taxes has been grossly overstated, there is a limited area within which the tax discriminates against interstate commerce. It appears that such discrimination is accidental and exists, aside from inadvertences, in only five of the numerous states which levy use taxes. Generally speaking, use-tax laws elsewhere provide that articles purchased from without the state and subject to a sales tax may have the amount paid offset against the use tax which would ordinarily be payable. For example, if a resident of the state buys personal property from without and pays no sales tax at the place of purchase, he must pay a 3 per cent use tax in his own state; if, however, he pays a 2 per cent sales tax, he will be relieved of the use tax to the extent of the amount paid to the other state. Failure to incorporate some such provision in five states discriminates to a minor extent against the commerce of other states, and under certain circumstances may be contrary to the Fourteenth Amendment to the United States Constitution.

Margarine taxes

A movement to tax certain food products made from raw materials competitive with others produced in the taxing state is of more recent vintage and of more deleterious character. The outstanding example is found in margarine taxes imposed in about half the states.[22]

[21] The literature suggests that the error is well-nigh chronic. Cf., e.g., E. A. McCrary, "Terminal vs. Bridge States in the Allocation of Unit Values," *Proceedings,* National Tax Conference, 1938, p. 300; and Robert S. Ford, *The Allocation of Corporate Income for the Purpose of State Taxation,* New York State Tax Commission Special Report No. 6.

[22] Oppenheim, "Nature and Extent of Trade Barrier Legislation," *Proceedings,* National Conference of Interstate Trade Barriers, Council of State Governments, April 1939, pp. 23 ff. Other surveys of margarine taxes include Rodman Sullivan, *The New Margarine Taxes,* Bureau of Business Research, University of Kentucky, 1934; *Barriers to Internal Trade in*

The state taxes include both heavy licenses on individual manufacturers and dealers and excises of five to fifteen cents a pound. In some states the tax depends on whether or not the product is colored.

The purpose of such legislation, in early days ostensibly designed to prevent fraud, is now generally "protective." This motive was obvious in the record which went to the Supreme Court in the Washington case; the court nevertheless sustained the act.[23] In consequence of the purpose to "protect"—that is, discriminate against products competitive with local raw materials—in some states no revenue is collected, and in others practically none. Iowa, a state having an excise of 5 cents a pound, derives more revenue from the margarine sales tax than does any other state—roughly a quarter of a million dollars annually.[24] Analysis by the Bureau of Agricultural Economics leaves no doubt as to the effectiveness of the tax at ten- and fifteen-cent rates in preventing sale of margarine.

Margarine taxes as interstate tax competitive devices resulting in trade barriers have been deplored by the United States Secretary of Agriculture,[25] by state officials in a general representative conference,[26] and by students generally.[27] The measures are doubly subject to condemnation when, as in Minnesota, Nebraska, and Wyoming, they are made well-nigh administratively impossible by providing exemption if containing specified percentages of animal fats.

The results of margarine tax legislation have included widespread retaliation, threats of retaliation, and general ill feeling.[28] In the case of Wisconsin, for instance, an extensive boycott of Wisconsin products is said to have ensued. The cancellations of orders alone may have amounted to more dollars (estimated at several millions) than the total amount of margarine sold in the state for several years prior to passage of the act. It is not yet clear how widely retaliatory legislation will be adopted and the extent to which it will be confined to related products.

Alcoholic-beverage taxes

Discriminatory tax legislation has appeared in connection with alcoholic beverages in about half of the states.[29] For the most part these measures impose licenses, though in a number of cases discriminatory excises on volume have been enacted. Fortunately for freedom of trade between the states, a counter movement appears to have set in during 1939 legislative sessions.

Speaking generally, tax competition of this variety is in part based on situs of production of the beverage and in part on origin of the raw material used. In several states licenses for beer importers are higher than for other beer distributors. Some states have placed higher excises on out-of-state beer. Export taxes on distilled spirits are imposed in two states. At least four states have imposed higher excises on imported than on domestic wine. As illustrative of the mercantilist discrimination based on character of raw material employed, a few examples may be cited. If raw materials for wine production are grown locally, Maine imposes a preferential rate. A similar provision applies to

---

Farm Products, a special report to the Secretary of Agriculture by the Bureau of Agricultural Economics, pp. 17 ff. (cited *Barriers*); and the factual table published in *Tax Systems of the World.*

[23] A. Magnano Co. v. Hamilton, 292 U. S. 42. Cf. *Barriers,* pp. 19–28.
[24] *Barriers,* p. 20.
[25] *Barriers,* Foreword, p. iii.
[26] *Proceedings,* National Conference on Interstate Trade Barriers, pp. 95 ff., 100 ff., and 15.
[27] See footnote 22.

[28] *Barriers,* pp. 28 ff.
[29] Oppenheim, *ibid.,* p. 24.

beer. The alcoholic beverage license in that state is dependent on the origin of the raw materials.[30]

Legislation of this sort affecting alcoholic beverages has been condemned, as has margarine tax legislation. Retaliations have been even more vigorous, so that today numerous states have general retaliatory statutes. In Michigan the retaliation was in the form of an outright embargo on products from a state which discriminates against Michigan beer.

CRITICAL ESTIMATE OF TAX COMPETITION POLICY

Politically, the tax competition devices which have been outlined are persuasive. Mercantilism generally attracts those who, like the average citizen, have had little opportunity to study economic theory and political history. It is perhaps apparent to social scientists that tax plans like those outlined above are unsound from the point of view of the whole country. Can it be said also that they are unwise from the viewpoint of all the people of the state which is directly concerned?

It appears certain that general prosperity—that is, economic well-being—is fostered by a nondiscriminatory state tax policy. The burden of proof, then, must be assumed by one who seeks legislation which will restrict the sovereignty of the state or favor one enterprise or economic class at the expense of another. Tax exemption or partial exemption for one group which does not perform public service at the expense of other citizens, it is believed, cannot be defended on grounds of public policy.

[30] Data have been assembled from *Barriers*, pp. 31 ff.; Thomas S. Green, Jr., *State Discriminations against Out-of-State Distilled Spirits* and *State Discriminations against Out-of-State Beers*, Council of State Governments, 1939; see also release by Council published July 10, 1939, in the *Louisville Courier-Journal*.

What a farmer receives from a livestock subsidy—tax exemption—or what a manufacturer gets from a subsidy for his manufacturing machinery must be paid by other members of the community or by the same ones through other taxes. Taxes designed to burden commodities produced elsewhere bring in little revenue and invite economic and political reverberations wholly deleterious. The administrative difficulties and wastes introduced by discriminatory policies are prodigious incidental objections.

These economic wastes, without considering the larger ones due to retaliation, cannot but adversely affect the general economic welfare and hence the prosperity of the individual state. The situation is analogous to that of national economic policy in peacetime. In that area it is well recognized that artificial restrictions on the free flow of commerce are injurious to the national economy. Internationally, however, not more than perhaps 5 per cent of our trade is involved. Probably 95 per cent of it moves interstate. Thus, the effect of relatively insignificant restrictions which may be introduced by tax competition between states is very much greater quantitatively than that of a similar international restriction. The force of this observation will be more apparent if it is remembered that the national economy is much more truly a unit than is the world at large.

Retaliation

Possibly the most objectionable feature of "unfair" tax competition between the states is found in the retaliations involved. In 1787, it will be recalled, import duties imposed by one colony were met by the producer colony with economic weapons which sometimes took the same form but which often took an entirely different form. Today, if Mississippi introduces half a dozen kinds of tax favors to manufacturing, Louisiana introduces a dozen. If Ohio sets a bogus fifteen-mill limit on tax rates, West Virginia virtually abolishes local government (pending uneconomical readjustments) by setting a limitation which actually works—to some extent. If Wisconsin enacts a fifteen-cents-a-pound tax on margarine, not only do the cotton-oil states object with kindred weapons, but Illinois (which manufactures large quantities of margarine) cancels orders for paper products and bathroom equipment theretofore sought from Wisconsin manufacturers. If western states usually allocate interstate railroads to themselves by a formula which overemphasizes miles of line, the east retaliates with one which unduly stresses yard property. Thus, discriminatory, competitive tax legislation or administration is characteristically met with similar or dissimilar reciprocal weapons by the people or states which are injured.

Ineffectiveness

The inequalities introduced by competitive tax legislation are not only objectionable positively, as has been suggested, but they are also for the most part open to the charge that they do not effectively serve their immediate purpose. It has been abundantly demonstrated that tax favors to industry fail materially to affect industrial location.[31] There is good reason to believe that margarine taxes and alcoholic-beverage tax discriminations fail to promote significantly the local consumption of butter or to stimulate home manufacture of alcoholic beverages respectively.[32]

In view of the sense of unfairness engendered by a policy of discrimination, the injurious economic, political, and administrative effects invited by aggressive tax competition, and the inefficiency of such a policy in achieving its purpose, there can be no doubt that the wisest general revenue plan is one of religious zeal to treat every taxpayer alike. Whether the taxpayer is a local citizen or a nonresident should have no bearing —except of course in the case of taxes which are peculiarly the obligation of residents. Experience indicates that the soundest tax competition in the long run is undeviating, nondiscriminatory fairness.

[31] McCarren, *loc. cit.*
[32] See especially discussion in *Barriers* and *Proceedings,* National Conference on Interstate Trade Barriers, 1939.

James W. Martin is professor of economics and director of the Bureau of Business Research at the University of Kentucky, Lexington. He has served as president of the Kentucky Academy of Social Science, the Southern Economics Association, and the Tax Research Foundation. He is active as a consultant in public finance. For the past few years, until his recent resignation, he has headed the state tax administration of Kentucky, and incidentally served as a member of the State Legislative Council and as chairman of the Kentucky Planning Commission.

The Supreme Court and Interstate Barriers

By Robert H. Jackson

The oppressed and degraded state of commerce, previous to the adoption of the constitution, can scarcely be forgotten. . . . Those who felt the injury arising from this state of things, and those who were capable of estimating the influence of commerce on the prosperity of nations, perceived the necessity of giving control over this important subject to a single government. It may be doubted, whether any of the evils proceeding from the feebleness of the federal government, contributed more to that great revolution which introduced the present system, than the deep and general conviction, that commerce ought to be regulated by congress.[1]

THE history of the times which immediately preceded the Constitutional Convention abundantly justifies the opinion thus expressed by Chief Justice Marshall. The Revolutionary War was followed by an economic breakdown and an accompanying commercial war between the states. Beginning in 1784 protective tariffs were erected by New England and most of the Middle states. Connecticut levied discriminatory duties on goods from Massachusetts, and Pennsylvania discriminated against Delaware. Tribute was exacted from the coasting trade, notably by New York, through the imposition of clearance fees. Even market boats from New Jersey, carrying butter and cheese and garden vegetables, were subject to entrance fees when rowed across from Paulus Hook to Cortlandt Street. Madison drew a classic picture of "New Jersey, placed between Philadelphia and New York, . . . likened to a cask tapped at both ends; and North Carolina, between Virginia and South Carolina, to a patient bleeding at both arms." Discrimination was followed by retaliation, and the meetings and resolves of embittered merchants bore an ominous resemblance to those which in 1775 had prepared the way for revolution.[2]

On the anvil of this experience the Constitutional Convention of 1787 hammered out one of the great implements of federal power.[3] Article I, Section 8, paragraph 3 of the Constitution provides: "The Congress shall have Power . . . to regulate Commerce with foreign Nations, and among the several States, and with the Indian Tribes."

Difficulty in Application

These concise words have been a source of almost continuous litigation and vexation for the Supreme Court. The clause has been the focus of many of the most important conflicts between federal power and states' rights. It forms the warp into which theoreticians have woven strange designs of laissez faire and patterns to separate acts of commerce from antecedents such as production or mining and from subsequent acts such as distribution. Its application has always been difficult and its breadth not always consistently understood. Marshall described it as a "sovereign" power, "complete in itself." This majestic concept was narrowed until in 1918 in the Child Labor case [4] the majority found it a puny power indeed. Now we are returning to its authentic

---

[1] Brown v. Maryland, 12 Wheat. 419, 445–446.

[2] See Fiske, *The Critical Period in American History*, Chap. IV; Story, *On the Constitution*, Secs. 259–61.

[3] See *The Federalist*, No. XLII; 5 Elliot, *Debates*, Introduction by Madison, pp. 109–22.

[4] Hammer v. Dagenhart, 247 U. S. 251.

rigor and simplicity. The Supreme Court again holds that Congress may regulate commerce among the several states.[5]

No more difficult problem has arisen under the commerce clause than its application to break down barriers to interstate trade erected by a state to obtain some provincial advantage. Some of these barriers are obvious and easy to strike down. Others are disguised in inspection laws which actually serve or at least simulate a public good. Others are subtle discriminations in administration which usually elude the judicial power. But the decisions of the Supreme Court show how frequently commerce has invoked the clause to save it from local pride, jealousy, or selfishness.

CHIEF JUSTICE MARSHALL'S OPINION

The problem was first presented to the Supreme Court in *Gibbons* v. *Ogden*, in 1824.[6] Chief Justice Marshall, speaking for the Court, held invalid a New York statute granting to Livingston and Fulton the exclusive privilege of navigating the waters of the state by steamboat, and refused to enjoin Gibbons from navigating between New York and New Jersey. Gibbons had invoked the protection of both the commerce clause and a coasting license under an Act of Congress of 1793. Marshall's opinion is far from lucid, but part of his discussion emerges as the broad doctrine that power over interstate commerce is confided "exclusively" to Congress. This interpretation ignores the reliance of counsel and Court on a conflict between state and Federal laws covering the same subject, but it has, with modifications, become central to our whole constitutional scheme: the commerce clause, by its own force, without national legislation, puts limits upon the power of the states which the Supreme Court may delineate.

A few years later, in 1827, *Brown* v. *Maryland*[7] provided the occasion for a practical application of the intimations in *Gibbons* v. *Ogden*. A Maryland statute had levied a discriminatory tax on an importer selling articles of foreign origin in their original packages. The opinion of Marshall ignores the feature of discrimination and discusses the case as though the Maryland tax were on the selling of goods of whatever origin. With considerable ingenuity, Marshall found a license in the Federal Tariff Act giving an importer the right to sell "in the original package." He then dispensed with the relevance of the argument by declaring that the majority "suppose the principles laid down in this case, to apply equally to importations from a sister state." The "principles" were limitations which Marshall derived from the existence of the commerce clause, upon the power of the states to impose general taxes upon dealings with goods yet in the original packages in which they arrived from other states. This particular application was formally rejected in *Woodruff* v. *Parham*, in 1869,[8] sustaining a nondiscriminatory tax on goods in the original package,[9] but the doctrine survived to restrict state regulation.[10] Considerable time elapsed before discrimination against interstate and foreign commerce, as to which Marshall remained ambiguously silent, was decisively prohibited in *Welton* v. *Missouri*, in 1876.[11]

CHIEF JUSTICE TANEY'S OPINION

The opinion of Taney in The License

---

[5] Currin v. Wallace, 306 U. S. 1; Mulford v. Smith, 307 U. S. 38.
[6] Gibbons v. Ogden, 9 Wheat. 1.
[7] See *supra* note 1.
[8] Woodruff v. Parham, 8 Wall. 123.
[9] See Brown v. Houston, 114 U. S. 622; Sonneborn Bros. v. Keeling, 262 U. S. 506.
[10] Leisy v. Hardin, 135 U. S. 100; cf. Baldwin v. Seelig, 294 U. S. 511, 526–528.
[11] Welton v. Missouri, 91 U. S. 275.

Cases [12] illustrates an approach quite different from that of Marshall. It appeared to Taney to be

very clear that the mere grant of power to the general government cannot, upon any just principles of construction, be construed to be an absolute prohibition to the exercise of any power over the same subject by the States. The controlling and supreme power over commerce with foreign nations and the several States is undoubtedly conferred upon Congress. Yet, in my judgment, the State may nevertheless, for the safety or convenience of trade, or for the protection of the health of its citizens, make regulations of commerce for its own ports and harbours, and for its own territory; and such regulations are valid unless they come in conflict with a law of Congress.

Even the protection afforded by the original-package doctrine, Taney insisted, is derived from an act of Congress and does not emanate from the commerce clause.[13]

The reasons which induced Taney to refuse to place limitations upon the power of the states because of assumed conflict with the "dormant" commerce clause also led him to restrict the interpretation of Federal laws when used to show a conflict with state enactments. The considerations are brought into focus in the suit by Pennsylvania to enjoin as an obstruction to navigation the maintenance of a bridge across the Ohio River authorized by Virginia. The suit was part of a struggle between steamboat and railroad interests for dominance in transportation. The variety of interests at stake led Taney to urge against the assumption of jurisdiction that Congress "has better means of obtaining information than the narrow scope of judicial proceedings can afford." [14]

Present Status

Neither Marshall nor Taney was to have his approach fully established. Various attempts at social legislation during the period under consideration [15] at length led to a reformulation of theory in *Cooley* v. *Board of Wardens,* in 1851.[16] The doctrine now classic is that over subjects of commerce which are "in their nature national, or admit of only one uniform system, or plan of regulation," Congress alone may legislate, while over subjects concerning which there exists "no doubt of the superior fitness and propriety, not to say the absolute necessity, of different systems of regulation," the state may legislate until supplanted by Congress. Thus emerges a basis for supporting state regulations of interstate commerce. The local benefits to be secured are balanced by the Supreme Court against the inconvenience to interstate commerce. Regulations of local matters may be invalid if unduly burdensome to interstate commerce,[17] while a stream of commerce national in character may be subjected to local regulation if the effect is "indirect." [18]

A variety of state regulations intimately affecting interstate carriers themselves has been upheld in the absence of conflicting Congressional legislation. The state may construct dams and bridges over navigable streams,[19] require

---

[12] The License Cases, 5 How. 504, 572.
[13] 5 How. at 574, 577. But see Leisy v. Hardin, *supra* note 10.
[14] Pennsylvania v. Wheeling Bridge Co., 13 How. 518, 592 (1852) (dissenting opinion). See Illinois Central R. Co. v. Public Utilities Comm'n, 245 U. S. 493, 510.
[15] The License Cases, *supra* note 12; The Passenger Cases, 7 How. 283.
[16] Cooley v. Board of Wardens, 12 How. 299.
[17] E.g., Brimmer v. Rebman, 138 U. S. 78 (inspection law).
[18] E.g., Munn v. Illinois, 94 U. S. 113 (grain elevator regulation).
[19] Wilson v. Black-Bird Creek Marsh Co., 2 Pet. 245; Gilman v. Philadelphia, 3 Wall. 713; Lake Shore & M. S. R. Co. v. Ohio, 165 U. S. 365.

fees for policing and regulating the harbor,[20] insure the seaworthiness of tugs,[21] and control the location of docks and impose wharfage and other charges for special services.[22] The safety of its citizens may be thought to require special controls on motor carriers. Accordingly, it may restrict operation to uncongested highways,[23] limit the hours of continuous service of drivers,[24] and regulate the size and weight of the equipment on its highways.[25] Local safety may be the basis for imposing burdens even on interstate railroads.[26] The importance of *The Granger Cases*[27] in the development of the due process clause should not obscure the material effect such permitted regulation has had upon interstate commerce in grain.

THE ORIGINAL-PACKAGE DOCTRINE

The state may also enforce policies directed not at the carriers but at articles of commerce which it considers socially injurious. Subject to conflicting legislation of Congress, the state may regulate the importation of unhealthy swine or cattle,[28] and may protect its citizens against noxious articles or foods[29] and against fraudulent and deceptive substitutions of one article for another.[30] The enforcement of these state policies, however, encounters the original-package doctrine. Rejected as a limitation on the taxing power, the doctrine forms the basis for curtailing state regulation of articles transported from another state as long as they remain in the original packages.

Adequate control of the social problems arising from the use of intoxicating liquors was materially hindered by the application given this doctrine in *Leisy v. Hardin*. Potentially it offered broad means of evasion of state restrictions through shipment of proscribed articles from extrastate sellers direct to the consumer.[31] But the doctrine was confined to "legitimate" articles of commerce; thus noxious articles and articles unfit for consumption or misbranded were not within its scope. Liquor remained a legitimate subject of commercial intercourse, however, and some other expedient had to be found. The restrictions imposed by the Court on local control were effectively overcome by Congressional action complementing the state laws. The Webb-Kenyon Act of 1913, sustained in *Clark Distilling Co. v. Western Maryland Ry.*,[32] prohibited the transportation of intoxicating liquors into any state when it was intended they should be received or used in violation of its laws. The same device for effectuating state policies was recently applied to convict-made goods.[33] It has also been used with reference to explosives, diseased plants, and game killed in violation of state law.[34]

---

[20] Cooley v. Board of Wardens, *supra* note 16; Clyde Mallory Lines v. Alabama, 296 U. S. 261.

[21] Kelly v. Washington, 302 U. S. 1.

[22] Packet Co. v. Keokuk, 95 U. S. 80; Cummings v. Chicago, 188 U. S. 410; Ingels v. Morf, 300 U. S. 290.

[23] Bradley v. Public Utilities Comm'n, 289 U. S. 92; cf. Buck v. Kuykendall, 267 U. S. 37.

[24] Welch v. New Hampshire, 306 U. S. 79.

[25] South Carolina Highway Department v. Barnwell Bros., 303 U. S. 177.

[26] St. Louis & Iron Mountain Ry. Co. v. Arkansas, 240 U. S. 518; cf. Seaboard Air Line Ry. v. Blackwell, 244 U. S. 310.

[27] Munn v. Illinois, *supra* note 18; also 94 U. S. 155, 164, 179, 180, 181.

[28] Mentz v. Baldwin, 289 U. S. 346.

[29] Crossman v. Lurman, 192 U. S. 189; Price v. Illinois, 238 U. S. 446; Bourjois Inc. v. Chapman, 301 U. S. 183.

[30] Plumley v. Massachusetts, 155 U. S. 461; Hygrade Provision Co. v. Sherman, 266 U. S. 497.

[31] Cf. Austin v. Tennessee, 179 U. S. 343.

[32] Clark Distilling Co. v. Western Maryland Ry., 242 U. S. 311.

[33] Kentucky Whip & Collar Co. v. Illinois Central Ry. Co., 299 U. S. 335.

[34] Cf. 1 Stat. 474; 14 Stat. 81; 35 Stat. 1137; 45 Stat. 69, 1084.

CURTAILMENT OF STATE REGULATION

The formula expressed in *Cooley* v. *Board of Wardens* also operates to curtail vast fields of state regulation. Thus the commerce clause itself sets limitations on state control of interstate rail carriers so as to prevent local service requirements from unduly burdening the efficiency and convenience of interstate traffic.[35] Matters once thought to be within state competence have been withdrawn: in 1886 the power of a state to forbid discriminatory interstate rates was denied [36]—a decision which gave material impetus to the passage of the Interstate Commerce Act of 1887. Any form of discrimination against interstate commerce and any attempt to gain a local advantage by throwing the attendant burdens of legislation on those without the state are likewise declared to be prohibited by thte commerce clause.[37] It may be observed, however, that this formula is much more difficult of application than of statement. The complicated growth of commerce-clause limitations on the taxing power of the states is a complete story in itself.[38] A brief review of only a few decisions raises considerable doubt as to the feasibility of leveling the barriers to interstate trade by the tedious process of case-by-case adjudication.

Statutes which in terms discriminate against interstate commerce are easily weeded out. Thus in *Cook* v. *Pennsylvania* [39] the Court invalidated a tax on the sale at auction of imported goods which exempted similar sales of domestic goods. Similarly, an ordinance imposing a wharfage fee on vessels landing products other than of domestic origin was stricken in *Guy* v. *Baltimore*.[40] Discriminations in favor of local wines and beers and other local products were of early origin and met with a like disposition.[41]

INSPECTION LAWS

Not all attempts at gaining a local advantage are so obvious. Many are clothed in the plausible garb of inspection laws. In *Minnesota* v. *Barber* [42] the Court invalidated a statute forbidding the sale of fresh meat unless it was inspected in the state within twenty-four hours prior to slaughter. The argument that proper inspection can be made only prior to slaughter was met with considerable skepticism, together with the suggestion that outside inspection could be relied upon. A similar attitude was expressed in *Brimmer* v. *Rebman*,[43] invalidating a statute requiring the inspection of all meat slaughtered over one hundred miles from the place of sale. The law did not discriminate against meat because of its extrastate origin, but merely differentiated between meat slaughtered close to market and that slaughtered at a distance. Nevertheless, the Court held that its necessary tendency was to stop interstate commerce in meat, and accordingly it went beyond the limits of inspection. Only last term, the Court condemned a Florida statute which, in the guise of an inspection law, imposed an onerous and discriminatory exaction on imported cement. Mr. Justice Frankfurter, speaking for the Court

[35] E.g., Herndon v. Chicago, R. I. & P. R. Co., 218 U. S. 135; Chicago B. & Q. R. Co. v. Railroad Commission, 237 U. S. 220.

[36] Wabash St. L. & Pac. Ry. v. Illinois, 118 U. S. 557.

[37] E.g., Steamship Co. v. Port Wardens, 6 Wall. 31; Robbins v. Shelby County, 120 U. S. 489; Baldwin v. Seelig, 294 U. S. 511.

[38] Powell, "Indirect Encroachment on Federal Authority" (1919), 31 Harv. L. Rev. 572, 721, 932; 32 *Ibid.*, 234, 374, 634, 902.

[39] Cook v. Pennsylvania, 97 U. S. 566.

[40] Guy v. Baltimore, 100 U. S. 434.

[41] Welton v. Missouri, 91 U. S. 275; Ward v. Maryland, 12 Wall. 418; Guy v. Baltimore, 100 U. S. 434; Tiernan v. Rinker, 102 U. S. 123; Walling v. Michigan, 116 U. S. 446; Voight v. Wright, 141 U. S. 62.

[42] Minnesota v. Barber, 136 U. S. 313.

[43] See *supra* note 17.

for the first time, referred to Marshall's great decision in *Brown* v. *Maryland* and declared that "such assumption of national powers by a state has, ever since March 12, 1827 . . . been found to be in collision with the Constitution." [44]

Other attempts to protect a particular industry have met with more success. A statute forbidding the sale of oleomargarine colored to resemble butter was upheld as applied to sales in the original package, on the ground that it prevented deception.[45] Recently an excise tax of fifteen cents per pound on all butter substitutes sold within the state of Washington was found to be proper.[46] The limits appear to be delineated by two decisions striking down one statute forbidding the sale of oleomargarine sold in the original package and another prohibiting sales of oleomargarine when not colored pink.[47]

State regulation of interstate motor traffic and the requirement of reasonable fees for special services and the cost of inspection serves an important need in the absence of Federal legislation. Yet the tests of validity often appear merely formal. A fee declared invalid because found to be excessive in one case may be upheld in another after the statute has been rephrased and the accounting method changed.[48] A Tennessee tax on the privilege of using the highways was declared invalid because the measure employed bore no sufficient relation to the extent or manner of use,[49] while a South Carolina regulation of size and weights, which seriously impeded motor truck transportation through the state, was upheld as a reasonable exercise of legislative discretion.[50] Relief from the "border wars" and ports-of-entry restrictions reported in current literature [51] appears to be dependent on the promulgation of uniform regulations under the Motor Vehicle Act of 1935.[52]

The use of inspection laws and of quarantines to protect local industries from injury through the introduction of diseased plants or animals has long been recognized as valid and necessary.[53] A discriminatory statute, such as one forbidding the importation of cattle during a long season of the year, is repugnant to the commerce clause.[54] Yet the Secretary of Agriculture reports current use of inspection laws and quarantines as a means of achieving market restriction.[55]

PRESUMPTIVE VALIDITY

The statement of the cases in many instances demonstrates the presumptive validity of state legislation. There are pressing social and economic needs that call for relief through local regulation. The menace consists in its perversion. The purpose to discriminate may not appear on the face of the most burdensome measure. It often appears only in its administration and application, and this is usually not susceptible of proof. The question before the Court in most instances is not whether state

[44] Hale v. Bimco Trading Co., 306 U. S. 375, 380.

[45] Plumley v. Massachusetts, 155 U. S. 461. See Capitol City Dairy Co. v. Ohio, 183 U. S. 238.

[46] Magnano Co. v. Hamilton, 292 U. S. 40.

[47] Schollenberger v. Pennsylvania, 171 U. S. 1; Collins v. New Hampshire, 171 U. S. 30.

[48] Compare Ingels v. Morf, 300 U. S. 290, with Clark v. Paul Gray, Inc., 306 U. S. 583. See Dixie Ohio Co. v. Comm'n, 306 U. S. 72.

[49] Interstate Transit Co. v. Lindsey, 283 U. S. 183, 190.

[50] South Carolina Highway Department v. Barnwell Bros., *supra* note 25.

[51] See Report to the Secretary of Agriculture, *Barriers to Internal Trade in Farm Products* (1939), pp. 38–54.

[52] See Welch v. New Hampshire, 306 U. S. 79.

[53] See inspection laws listed in Gibbons v. Ogden, 9 Wheat. 1, 119–123, and in Turner v. Maryland, 107 U. S. 38, 51–54. Also 1 Stat. 474.

[54] Railroad Co. v. Husen, 95 U. S. 465.

[55] Report, *supra* note 51, pp. 68–97.

regulation is preferable to Federal regulation, but whether state control is better than no control at all. Unable to solve the problems in any practicable manner, the Supreme Court must be slow to condemn laws which do not clearly discriminate against interstate commerce. As the Court recently observed: "Its function is only to determine whether it is possible to say that the legislative decision is without rational basis." [56]

The difficulties implicit in attempts to invalidate state legislation on grounds other than discrimination are recorded in the decisions. The original-package doctrine as a limitation on nondiscriminatory regulation of intoxicating liquors was overcome by Congressional enactment.[57] The confusion in the tax field is illustrated by two recent decisions of the New York Court of Appeals. In *Sears, Roebuck & Co.* v. *McGoldrick*,[58] the Court sustained a tax upon sales of bulky merchandise contracted for in New York. The goods, so the parties understood, were to be delivered direct to the buyer from factories and warehouses located in other states. On the same day the Court held invalid a tax upon quantities of oil for steamships contracted for in New York and to be delivered in New York by barge from tanks located in New Jersey.[59] The first case was distinguished on the ground that the delivery from extrastate warehouses was a matter of indifference to the buyer, while the oil in New Jersey was specifically contracted for.

These confusions arise from attempts to apply some of the nice distinctions that have grown about the doctrine that a tax "on" interstate commerce is invalid.[60] A nondiscriminatory tax by the state of destination on a sale negotiated *prior* to interstate transportation is a tax on an "interstate sale" and hence invalid;[61] but a nondiscriminatory tax by the state of destination on a sale negotiated *subsequent* to interstate transportation is not repugnant to the commerce clause.[62] The doctrine is further refined by distinguishing between vendors and agents of extrastate sellers.[63] Finally, the equivalent of a tax on an interstate sale may be imposed by means of a tax on the "use" within the state.[64] The latest decisions of the Court have shown a tendency to explain earlier decisions in terms of the risk of multiple taxation.[65] Even here, dissenting opinions suggest that actual multiple taxation may be a more practical test of discrimination than the mere possibility of it.[66]

Entirely apart from the inability of the Court to eliminate barriers to trade through adjudication of the issue of discrimination, many types of discrimination exist completely free of commerce-clause restrictions. Thus, the state may use its purchasing power substantially as it pleases. Employment policies on

[56] Stone, J., in Clark v. Paul Gray, Inc., 306 U. S. 583, at 594.

[57] See *supra* note 32.

[58] Sears, Roebuck & Co. v. McGoldrick, 279 N. Y. 184.

[59] Compagnie Generale Transatlantique v. McGoldrick, 279 N. Y. 192.

[60] See Robbins v. Shelby County, 120 U. S. 489, 492; Helson v. Kentucky, 279 U. S. 245; cf. Wiloil Corp. v. Pennsylvania, 294 U. S. 169, 175.

[61] The Court has so assumed: Robbins v. Shelby County, 120 U. S. 489, 492; Sonneborn Bros. v. Cureton, 262 U. S. 506, 515; Henneford v. Silas Mason Co., 300 U. S. 577, 583.

[62] Woodruff v. Parham, *supra* note 8; Sonneborn Bros. v. Cureton, 262 U. S. 506.

[63] Compare Robbins v. Shelby County, 120 U. S. 489, with Banker Bros. Co. v. Pennsylvania, 222 U. S. 210.

[64] Hannaford v. Silas Mason Co., 300 U. S. 577; Southern Pacific Ry. Co. v. Gallagher, 306 U. S. 167.

[65] Western Live Stock v. Bureau of Revenue, 303 U. S. 250; Adams Manufacturing Co. v. Storen, 304 U. S. 307; Gwin, White & Prince Inc. v. Henneford, 305 U. S. 434.

[66] See dissenting opinions of Black, J.: 304 U. S. at 316; 305 U. S. at 442.

state public works favoring local residents and business firms have been sustained.[67] The ensuing discrimination and retaliation may impose difficult barriers to trade between the states, all secure from constitutional attack.

The Twenty-first Amendment reserved certain powers to the states to insure adequate control of the social and moral problems incident to the liquor traffic. The power thus given to protect social policies many states have turned, under pressure from local liquor interests, to protection of home industry. Discriminatory sales taxes and special restrictions are placed on those who sell out-of-state wines and beers. The Court is powerless to prevent economic provincialism from perverting such state power to purposes not intended by the amendment but not precluded by its provisions.[68]

Means of Protecting Interstate Trade

We must not forget that while the commerce clause of itself will not keep open the channels of interstate trade, the Congress has a wide choice of means to use the grant of power effectively to achieve that end.

Litigation to enjoin or to resist the enforcement of interstate barriers is successful against most of the obvious or declared discriminations against interstate commerce by states and municipalities. The Government has not hesitated to intervene to assist private litigants in that endeavor,[69] but litigation has definite limitations. Federal executive power, like the judicial power, is properly reluctant to attribute any undeclared and improper purpose to a sovereign state where its acts are asserted to be innocent of the purpose to discriminate, and where they serve a useful local end. If local regulations are within the state's power—and that power is considerable—the Federal Government cannot assume or ask the courts to assume to explore the motives.

The Supreme Court has held, however, that where an application of state power, such as the regulation of local rail rates, is in practice to discriminate against or to burden interstate commerce, then regardless of motive, the Federal power is adequate to prevent that result.[70] This power can be made effective through a Federal administrative agency, such as the Interstate Commerce Commission,[71] with authority to invalidate local regulations found to burden the national commerce unduly.[72] Local inspection and quarantine laws which prove burdensome because of their very diversity might be superseded by uniform regulations.[73] It has been suggested that even state taxation powers may also be restricted so as not to burden interstate trade unduly.[74] To shield the national commerce from regulations which, however well intended, have the effect of an undue burden on the national commerce, Congress may make its own choice of means and procedures.

Whether the protection of interstate trade shall be accomplished by existing controls or by a further extension of Federal controls, the most important thing is the existence of an informed public opinion which will identify and condemn efforts to fasten parochialism upon the national commerce from any

---

[67] Heim v. McCall, 239 U. S. 175; Atkin v. Kansas, 191 U. S. 207.
[68] Mahoney v. Triner Corp., 304 U. S. 401; State Board v. Young's Market, 299 U. S. 59.
[69] Hale v. Bimco Trading Co., *supra* note 44.
[70] The Shreveport Case, 234 U. S. 342; McDermott v. Wisconsin, 228 U. S. 115.
[71] See 223 I. C. C. 109.
[72] The Shreveport Case, *supra* note 70.
[73] See Oregon-Washington R. R. & Nav. Co. v. Washington, 270 U. S. 87.
[74] See Black, J., dissenting in Gwin, White & Prince Inc. v. Henneford, 305 U. S. 434, at 451–52, 455. But cf. The Federalist (Lodge ed.), No. XXXII, pp. 185, 187.

source. Balkanism is as much a state of mind as a condition of geography. We cannot afford to let trade selfishness set up legal frontiers in America where trade must halt. Such petty barriers have long since proved to be not only economically futile but also disastrous to peace and good will. A realization of these facts by the residents of each locality would make the choice of means to level trade barriers relatively unimportant.

Robert H. Jackson, Washington, D. C., is Solicitor-General of the United States. From 1913 to 1934 he was engaged in general law practice. Since that time he has served as General Counsel of the United States Bureau of Internal Revenue, Assistant General Counsel for the Treasury Department, Special Counsel for the Securities and Exchange Commission, Assistant Attorney-General in charge of the Tax Division, and Assistant Attorney-General in charge of the Antitrust Division.

Uniform Legislation in the United States

By Rodney L. Mott

THE United States would appear to be a fertile soil for the growth of uniformity in legislation. The forty-eight states present no wide differences in political ideals or governmental machinery; there are no deeply diversified legal habits, economic interests, or social classes; our people have a common cultural heritage and a common language; the Nation possesses a form of business organization and a system of communications which has steadily centralized commercial life; and the constitutional framework promotes, rather than impedes, common action by the states.

If uniform laws thrive where there is social homogeneity, American conditions should furnish not only an ideal setting for them but also the generative forces necessary for their development.

Federal Powers and State Legislation

A long tradition of increasing legal uniformity, moreover, has resulted from the gradual extension of national powers. The Federal Constitution was established to eliminate commercial discriminations between the states, and as the need for unvaried regulation has grown, the powers of the central government have grown to meet that need. This has been accomplished in part by amendments to the Constitution and in part by the decisions of the United States Supreme Court giving an increasingly broad interpretation to the power of the Federal Government to regulate "commerce among the several states." With the approval of the Court, uniformity has been established in such a variety of matters as railroad fares, labels on canned foods, regulation of monopolies, licensing of radio broadcasting, and control of securities exchanges.

There are, however, very definite limits to the use of Federal powers to reduce variation in the legal systems of these United States. Even a nationally minded Supreme Court could not bring itself to decree that the regulation of local as well as interstate business, which was attempted under the National Industrial Recovery Act, was within the powers granted to Congress by the Constitution.

If there were no constitutional doors to unlock, high barriers would still need to be hurdled before uniformity could be secured by Federal fiat. The experience with national control of the liquor traffic under prohibition, and with price regulation under the short-lived National Recovery Administration, was not entirely happy. It was evident in both cases that legislative uniformity which was not accompanied by intelligent and skillful administration of the law would be a mirage.

Every field which the Federal Government enters produces conflicts between the national statute and state laws at innumerable points. One of the principal objections to the proposed amendment giving the Federal Government control over child labor is that under it the National Government might attempt to centralize education as well. A national marriage and divorce law has often been proposed to replace the present situation under which the states compete for marriage and divorce business by being more lenient than their neighbors. A single code in this field would certainly be desirable, but only a legal neophyte would fancy the task of adjusting a national law on this subject to the diverse state rules on such correlative subjects as property rights, inheritance, legitimacy, guardianship, public health, and the criminal code.

Legislative Copying

The constitutional, administrative, and legal difficulties which the National Government meets in prescribing uniform laws are trivial compared with the practical political obstacles to harmonious action by the forty-eight states. A certain amount of unplanned, fortuitous uniformity has been achieved by sheer luck. Framers of state constitutions and drafters of state statutes have often taken similar documents from convenient sister states or from the Federal Government as models for their efforts. Legislative copying has thus cast many pieces of legislation in similar molds, although sometimes the results of this process have not been too fortunate. The inland prairie state of South Dakota, with scarcely a navigable river or lake in its boundaries, solemnly stipulates in its constitution that its governor shall be the commander-in-chief of the "military and *naval* forces of the state" —a phrase from the early constitutions of seaboard states. The tenement-house law passed some years ago by a well-meaning but unimaginative western legislature was copied from the statute enacted for New York City. As a result, every farmer was required to provide his hired hands with rooms having running water and sanitary toilet facilities, although such features were almost unknown in the rural areas at that time.

Fortunately, many states have taken steps to prevent the more serious evils of indiscriminate copying of statutory provisions from other states. Many legislatures provide for a careful survey of any important problem by a small investigating commission before a new statute is passed to solve it. More than two hundred of these commissions are appointed in each biennial period. In many cases the commission is given funds to employ an expert staff to study the problem, go over the legislation in other states, and draw up a proposed law. The use of investigating commissions not only tends to make the state statutes on a given problem more uniform by enabling each state to profit from the experience of the others, but a really thorough piece of investigation will often result in an act which is so well constructed that other states soon find it desirable to incorporate its provisions in their own laws. The splendid report of the New York Commission on Old Age Pensions under the leadership of Senator Seabury C. Mastick was widely used as a basis for legislation in other states as well as in New York.

Legislative Reference Services

The legislatures of more than three-fourths of the states have established permanent legislative reference agencies to guide their members through the mazes of legislation. Many of these agencies are well organized with a trained staff, adequate library facilities, and convenient offices. They compile digests of the laws of other states on subjects of current interest; prepare summaries of technical information for busy legislators; and sometimes more detailed investigations of the social and economic effects of various types of laws. In some states they draft a large proportion of the bills which are introduced in the legislative bodies, and a few legislatures submit all bills to them for revision as to form before they are finally enacted. Through the constant study of legislation, these agencies are in a position to suggest the statute in another state which is most likely to produce the results the lawmakers desire. This practice tends to promote a practical kind of similarity in the state statutes, if not precise uniformity.

To assist these legislative reference

services in securing data on the legislation of other states, the Interstate Reference Service has performed a useful service. This organization acts as a clearing house of information on legislative problems, answers inquiries from the legislative reference services, prepares bulletins on legislative topics, and issues a monthly magazine, *State Government*, in which legislative matters are discussed. It is now possible for improvements in legislation to become known to legislative draftsmen throughout the United States in a very short time. During the banking crisis in 1933, copies of emergency statutes were sent by air mail and were on the desks of the directors of the legislative reference bureaus within two days. This service has already proved its value in harmonizing the laws of the various states, and as it becomes more firmly established, its influence in this direction should increase.

LOBBYING ORGANIZATIONS

Lobbying organizations also have had a considerable share in the work of promoting uniformity of legislation in a number of fields. A directory published by the Public Administration Clearing House lists a hundred and fifty agencies which seek common legislative action in the various states on some subject. A few of them are very strong, and have qualified research staffs which do some excellent work. Thus, the National Safety Council with a staff of ninety-five has exerted considerable influence in the direction of more uniform laws to promote safety in factories, on highways, and in the home. Even more influential is the American Automobile Association, with its staff of two hundred and its representatives in every state capital. Through a very extensive propaganda campaign it is able to exert a considerable influence toward greater uniformity in motor-vehicle legislation. Many of these organizations are supported by public-spirited citizens, and while they are interested only in promoting uniformity in a limited field, they do not have any selfish interest to protect. Thus, the American Association for Labor Legislation has been influential in spreading information on labor laws and has helped to prevent needless variation in them. Most of these organizations engage in a wide variety of other activities as well as the promotion of uniformity in legislation. The American Uniform Boiler Law Society, however, is interested solely in securing the adoption of the uniform boiler code formulated by a committee of the American Society of Mechanical Engineers.

In general, these organizations represent individuals, societies, or business firms outside the government. There are, however, a number of organizations of public officials which are national in scope and which further legislation in their respective fields. Thus, the American Public Welfare Association provides, among other things, a technical staff to advise state legislative committees concerning changes in their poor laws or statutes affecting their public welfare institutions. With a membership composed of state and municipal officials, it has great technical resources for its work, and is able to do much for the unification of welfare legislation. The National Tax Association, composed of tax officials, citizens interested in taxation, and professors of public finance, has been particularly active in studying the problems of double and conflicting taxation and in promoting a more harmonious tax structure for the states and the Nation.

It is only natural that the members of the state legislatures should look with more or less suspicion on the representatives of all these organizations. Their propaganda tactics, their limited interest in special fields of legislation, and in some cases the sources of their finances have been such as to prejudice their work. In spite of their handicaps, these organizations have been of real assistance in promoting more harmonious legislation. Their enthusiasm, the vigor of their educational campaign, the continuity of their work year after year, and the intelligent and informed character of their leadership have been a tremendous source of strength. While they have not promoted uniformity of text so much as uniformity of ideas, their work has laid the basis for a more consistent legal structure in the United States.

National Conference on Uniform State Laws

The National Conference of Commissioners on Uniform State Laws is by far the most important organization striving for uniformity of legislation in the United States. It is an official body, created by state statutes. The three commissioners appointed by the governor of each state or territory are invariably leading members of the bar or teachers in law schools. The Conference is now forty-seven years old, and has counted among its members many of the most prominent American scholars in the field of comparative law and legislation. The public spirit of the commissioners is such that although they are all unpaid, and many do not even receive travel expenses for their journeys to the annual meetings of the Conference, the attendance at these meetings is usually very good.

TABLE 1—Attendance at Annual Meetings by Commissioners on Uniform State Laws

Year	Attendance	Jurisdictions Represented
1935	74	38
1936	85	40
1937	71	37
1938	88*	44

* There were five Associate Members in addition.

The procedure of the Conference is such as to inspire confidence in its work. A uniform act is considered over a period of years and usually passes through several editions for discussion, correction, and amendment before it is released to the public. If the Conference decides that a uniform act on a given subject is desirable, a subcommittee is appointed to draft it. These subcommittees have often engaged legal experts, men of outstanding reputation in their fields, to draft acts on the more intricate subjects. Thus, several of the statutes in the Uniform Commercial Code were drawn by Professor Samuel Williston of Harvard University, the most widely recognized expert in that field. The text as prepared by the draftsman is then considered by the subcommittee, which may modify it, refer it back for redrafting, or approve it for submission to the Conference at its next annual meeting. Here it is discussed section by section, objections are considered, and modifications proposed. The act is then referred back to the subcommittee for reconsideration. This process may be repeated several times before a draft is presented which secures the approval of the Conference. The Uniform Bills of Lading Act was approved by the Conference only after five separate drafts had been prepared, printed, and revised.

Uniform acts which are approved by the Conference are submitted to the Section on Uniform State Laws of the American Bar Association for its approval, and then are promulgated for consideration by the state bar associations. Only those acts which can secure this widespread support are submitted to the state legislatures for their action. This painstaking procedure has made the uniform laws models of draftsmanship, and the standards which the Conference has set exert an important influence toward the technical improvement of American statutes. The meticulous care which is taken in preparing the uniform laws is an indication of their importance, and in itself should make it difficult for the state legislatures to ignore them.

This meticulous procedure, however, is better adapted to some types of legislation than to others. Although it is admirably suited to the drafting of laws governing commercial transactions, it has not operated so well in the field of social legislation. The prosperous lawyer is continually meeting commercial problems in his practice, and the attorneys who compose the Conference are likely to be well informed on those branches of the law. On the other hand, they are frequently out of touch with some of the more fundamental social needs which would be well known to economists, political scientists, or sociologists. Furthermore, since the Conference does not hold hearings, it is deprived of the wisdom of those who do have the specialized knowledge of these problems. As a result, the legislation which has been drafted in the social field has sometimes failed to take account of important aspects of the problem. Because of this, the legislatures have been inclined to favor social legislation which has the support of those interest groups which are affected by it, even though their objects may be selfish ones.

Activities of the Conference

During the first forty-six years of its existence (up to 1938), the Conference had drafted and approved ninety acts, and in addition had approved seven acts which had been drafted by other organizations.[1] Some of its earlier acts had been declared obsolete or had been withdrawn by the Conference, leaving seventy-six acts which were being pressed on the state legislatures.

The constitution of the Conference states that its object is "to promote uniformity in state laws on all subjects where uniformity is deemed desirable and practicable." In general, a rather strict view has been taken of this object. The Conference has tended to confine its recommendations to subjects of interest to the country at large in those fields where the principles of law are fairly well settled, and has shunned the domain of public policy. Although it has rapidly expanded the number of acts which it has approved, the Conference has generally refrained from promoting new laws or legal reforms. As one of its members declared, "You cannot make uniform that which has not yet been formed."

The Conference operates on a relatively small budget of about $10,000 a year.[2] About two-thirds of its funds come from an annual contribution by the American Bar Association. The rest of the budget is raised by contributions from state or municipal bar associations and by appropriations from state legislatures. During the past thirty years legislatures in thirty-two jurisdictions have made one or more contributions to the work of the Conference. While the amount of public money spent for this work has been small, it indicates an interest in the work.[3] The only other siz-

---

[1] Since 1914 the Conference has discontinued the practice of approving acts drawn by other organizations. In 1928 it withdrew its indorsement from one of the seven it had formerly approved.

[2] The largest item of expenditure is for the secretary's office, with printing and the expense of the annual meeting making the bulk of the other disbursements.

[3] The states most frequently contributing to the work of the Conference are: Ohio (26 years), Pennsylvania (24 years), Connecticut (23 years), Massachusetts (23 years), Maryland (20 years), Rhode Island (18 years), South Dakota (18 years), Wisconsin (17 years), Delaware (16 years), Maine (15 years), New York (15 years), District of Columbia (15 years). Few states have voted more than $500 a year, the typical appropria-

able financial support the Conference has ever received was a contribution in 1905 from the American Warehousemen's Association to pay part of the costs of drafting the Uniform Warehouse Receipts Act. There is no evidence that the Conference has allowed any of the contributions which have been made to it to influence its judgment on proposed uniform acts.

POOR RESPONSE

The response to the efforts of the National Conference of Commissioners on Uniform State Laws has been, on the whole, rather disappointing. After an expenditure of some $200,000 and the time and effort of several hundred of the most capable and public-spirited lawyers of the country during nearly half a century, it is a little discouraging to find that the typical uniform law has been adopted by only one-quarter of the states. Only one act has been adopted by all the states and territories (the Uniform Negotiable Instruments Act); only eight others have been adopted by half the states and territories;[4] and only twenty-three have been adopted by one-fourth of the legislatures. On the other hand, there are eighteen acts which have not been adopted by more than a single legislature. Stated another way, about one-fifth of the work of the Conference has not resulted in any uniformity at all, while only one-tenth has had any substantial effect.

Time, of course, is required to familiarize the legislators in forty-eight states with the provisions of these acts and to break down their natural hesitancy to accept laws drawn by other agencies. Nearly all the eighteen acts which have failed of adoption by more than one legislature were less than ten years old. Nevertheless, this by no means tells the whole story. The first act to be approved by the Conference (the Uniform Acknowledgments Act) has been adopted by only nine states in the forty-five years it has been before the legislatures, and the Uniform Public Utilities Act, which was approved by the Conference ten years ago, has not been approved by any legislature. It is evident that the Conference has failed to acquire the prestige necessary to enable its acts to be adopted by the legislatures without opposition.

The difficulty is in part legal and in part political. In spite of the fact that many of the uniform acts contain sections and clauses which are found in the statutes of many different states, it may be hazardous to adopt them entire in any one jurisdiction. Very often the terms used must be changed to conform to the legal phraseology in other statutes of the particular state. Thus, the term "felony" has a wide variety of meanings in American criminal law, and civil and criminal procedures vary from state to state. Since the acts must be enforced in the state courts, it is often necessary to change a statute in order to have it operate with a minimum of difficulty in a given jurisdiction.

These legal difficulties are by no means trivial, but where they are honestly met and a sincere effort is made to produce a statute which will harmonize with the laws of other states, they can generally be overcome. They account for certain of the changes which have been made in the uniform acts as they have been adopted in the various states, but by no means for all.

---

tion being about $200. Thirteen states have never contributed (either through their legislatures or through their bar associations) anything to the work of the Conference.

[4] Uniform Sales Act, Uniform Warehouse Receipts Act, Uniform Bills of Lading Act, Uniform Veterans' Guardianship Act, Uniform Declaratory Judgments Act, Uniform Narcotic Drug Act, Uniform Proof of Statutes Act, and Uniform Stock Transfer Act.

The Political Obstacle

An even more serious obstacle to uniformity is the political one. Those who organized the National Conference of Commissioners on Uniform State Laws failed to take into account the short tenure of American legislative bodies and the rapid turnover in their membership. Nearly half the members of the forty-eight legislatures serve but two years, during which period there is only a single legislative session. In any legislature, a count of the members will show that only a small fraction have seen legislative service for four or more sessions. There is thus little continuity of personnel, and consequently little continuity of policy from one session to another. Even if one session determines to support the work of the Conference, both by giving it financial aid and by approving its proposed laws, there is no assurance that such support will be continued in the next session. Everything depends upon the interest of individuals in the legislature, and the task of interesting anew a majority of the 7,500 members of the American state lawmaking bodies every two or four years is one which the Conference has never been able to meet.

A newly elected legislator is deluged with proposals for laws. Many of these come from organizations whose names and letterheads indicate as great a degree of interest in the public weal as has the National Conference on Uniform State Laws. Some indeed insist that they are dedicated to the promotion of uniformity in legislation. There is little wonder that the novice in lawmaking is confused. Even after he arrives at the state house, he finds no fellow legislator who has been a member of the National Conference of Commissioners on Uniform State Laws, for legislators are never appointed during their term of office. If he is a member of the American Bar Association, he may support the proposals of the Conference; but only one-quarter of the lawyers in the United States are members of this organization, and those who are not members often join the non-lawyers in the legislature in their natural suspicions of the motives of the Conference. Accordingly, even when a legislature is favorably disposed toward the principle of uniformity, it scrutinizes the proposals of the Conference very closely.

Modification of Uniform Laws

The result has been twofold. The acts proposed by the Conference have not been widely adopted, or else they have been modified by the legislatures in such a manner as to impair their uniformity. The reports of the Conference show that the proposed uniform laws have been modified by every eighth legislature, and, what is even more ominous, this tendency has been much more marked during the past decade. This is clearly shown by Table 2.

TABLE 2—Modification of Uniform Laws by Legislatures

Year	Acts Approved by Conference	Total Number of Adoptions	Number of Adoptions with Modifications	Per Cent Modified
1920	22	274	11	4.0
1925	34	375	18	4.8
1930	48	540	67	12.4
1935	58	695	88	12.7
1938	76*	783	95	12.1

* Including amendatory acts.

If these modifications were merely changes in detail, the situation would not be so serious. It has been estimated[5] that in at least two-thirds of the cases, the modifications were serious enough to impair the uniformity of the act. A comparative study of the text of some of the uniform laws as they have been adopted by the various states indicates that this is a very conservative estimate. If every change which was made in the text of the uniform law were counted, the number of identical adoptions would be very few. The Uniform Negotiable Instruments Act has been altered in some particular in forty-seven of the fifty-three states and territories in which it is the law. Changes have been made in 117 of the 197 sections of this act. Many of these changes are, of course, of minor significance, and some of them were obviously errors. Nevertheless, a surprising number of states have rewritten sections, added clauses not in the uniform act, omitted clauses, or even omitted entire sections. Table 3 indicates the extent to which this one act has been mutilated by some of the legislatures. These changes do not include obvious errors in the enacted statute, or even intentional alterations which change only a single word or two, although such changes may alter the meaning of the act more than the omission of an entire section.[6] The difficulties which the Conference has had to face in the state legislatures are obviously very great.

The adoptions of the Negotiable Instruments Act have been chosen for detailed analysis because that act has been the only one to be adopted by every state and territory, and because it is generally considered to be the most striking success which the Conference has had in promoting uniformity. A study of the other acts, however, tells much the same story.[7] In general,

TABLE 3—LEGISLATIVE CHANGES IN THE NEGOTIABLE INSTRUMENTS ACT IN SELECTED STATES—1936

State	Sections with Clauses Added	Sections with Clauses Omitted	Sections Rewritten	Sections Omitted
Arizona		3	2	2
Georgia	1	1	2	1
Illinois	2	2	14	2
Kentucky	1	4	1	2
Massachusetts		1	3	1
North Carolina	3	2		1
South Dakota	3	2	8	5
West Virginia	3	2	3	1
Wisconsin	10	2		1
Total for all others	34	35	46	33

[5] W. Brooke Graves, *Uniform State Action*, p. 52.

[6] See for example the substitution of "endorsers" for "indorsees" in the Negotiable Instruments Law, Sec. 68, as adopted in Nebraska, North Carolina, and West Virginia, or the omission of the word "not" in Sec. 141 of that act in Arkansas. At least six states have corrected errors in the Negotiable Instruments Act by subsequently passing amendatory acts.

[7] Section 4 of the Uniform Sales Act requires written contracts, acceptance of goods, or payment of earnest money for sales in excess of a stipulated amount. This amount varies from $2,500 in Ohio to $50 in eight states. Iowa even fails to specify any amount. The Conference recommended $500 as the stipulated amount, but fewer than two-thirds of the states adopting this act by 1936 had accepted its recommendations.

it has been found that the acts which have been adopted quickly by a large number of states have suffered less mutilation than those which have raised controversial issues. Likewise, it may be said that the efforts to bring uniformity in the various fields of social legislation have met with more legislative resistance than have efforts in the field of commercial law. The only piece of uniform social legislation to be adopted by one-quarter of the states by 1936 was the Uniform Desertion and Non-support Act, which had been adopted in nineteen jurisdictions. This act was altered by every legislature which placed it on the statute books, and there is not one of its eight sections that is identical in all the nineteen states. The same forces which cause some legislatures to reject uniform social legislation have forced modifications and alterations of it in others. The latter result is, of course, less unsatisfactory than the former, because a uniform act, however modified, will produce a considerable body of rules which are common to the states adopting it. But it is deplorable that the legislatures should feel it necessary to alter statutes which have been so carefully drawn.

A similar situation exists with respect to the amendments which may be made to an act once it is adopted. The Conference has never taken the position that the acts which it draws are infallible and should never be changed. Indeed, it has itself drafted and approved amendments to four acts [8] and now has under consideration a long series of amendments to the Uniform Negotiable Instruments Act. But the unauthorized amendments which have been adopted by the legislatures have far exceeded, both in number and in importance, the approved amendments which have been enacted. By 1936 the Uniform Negotiable Instruments Act alone had been amended in twenty-nine of the fifty-three states which had enacted it. Changes were made in thirty-two of its 197 sections. About a third of these amendments brought the law more into harmony with the uniform act, but the great majority were in the direction of less uniformity rather than more. The amendments to uniform social legislation have been even more drastic. By 1936 three states had repealed the Uniform Desertion and Non-support Act and had substituted for it a statute drawn along other lines. Thirteen other states had passed substantial amendments to it, and in only two cases were the amendments designed to bring the law of the state into harmony with the uniform act.

Adverse Interpretation

Adverse legislative action, however, is not the only peril which a uniform statute must face. Even more dangerous may be an adverse interpretation of its provisions by the courts. The doctrine of *stare decisis* is so strongly entrenched in American legal thinking that it is sometimes difficult for the courts to realize that the legislature, in enacting a uniform act, really intended to change the ancient rules which had been enforced in that state. The cases where the courts have ignored the statute have fortunately been few, but the danger of diverse interpretation in different states is a much more serious one. Under the American legal system there is no judicial body which can harmonize the decisions of the different state courts on the construction of state statutes and enforce a common interpretation on them all. The United States Supreme Court is supreme only as far as Federal law

---

[8] One of these (the Criminal Extradition Act, approved in 1926) has been both amended by the Conference in 1932 and revised by it in 1936. Fifteen jurisdictions adopted the original act, two adopted the 1932 amendments, and ten adopted the 1936 revision.

and the Federal courts are concerned; on all matters in the domain of state law, each state is a law unto itself.[9]

The danger from diverse interpretations of the law became so great that the Conference since 1906 has included a clause in each of its approved acts to the effect that the courts should interpret the act to produce uniformity with the laws of other states. This has not entirely solved the problem, for it still happens that courts decide cases to which the uniform acts may apply without citing them,[10] or without referring to the interpretation which may have been given the same statute in a sister state. In a few cases, adverse interpretations of the acts have led the legislatures to enact clarifying amendments. The fault is only partially with the judges on the bench, however. The lawyers who plead before them are so steeped in the principles of the common law that it is difficult for them to see the implications of legislative amendments, especially when these are, as are some of the uniform acts, based on European statutes.

The national character of legal instruction has served to reduce this situation to some extent. The stronger and more progressive law schools give training in the principles of the law rather than in the rules of any single jurisdiction.

This practice has both its light and its dark sides, however. It has undoubtedly tended to keep the general development of judicial decisions more uniform throughout the country, and if the tendency continues another generation, an American common law may develop. Indeed, this is being hastened by the American Law Institute in its Restatements of the Common Law, a work which is for judicial decisions somewhat similar to the work that the National Conference of Commissioners on Uniform State Laws is doing for statutes. It should be observed, on the other hand, that since there is so little statutory material which is common to all the states, the national law schools tend to ignore the study of the statutes. The student is much more likely to know the rules of the common law with respect to fiduciaries than he is to know the meaning of the provisions of the uniform act on that subject. But this situation is by no means hopeless, for as the uniform acts grow in number and in popularity, they will undoubtedly be more frequently studied. When this day comes, America will have progressed a long way toward real uniformity in its legal structure.

The Commissioners on Uniform State Laws are fully aware of the difficulties which they have encountered. The proceedings of their annual conferences often contain discussions of these problems, and numerous suggestions have been put forth to remedy the situation. These suggestions range all the way from the proposal to confine the work of the Conference to statutes which are non-controversial or are exclusively in the commercial field, to proposals to tie the hands of the state legislatures by means of interstate treaties and thus to prevent amendments which will destroy the uniformity of the law. None of these

---

[9] The difficulties arising from diverse interpretation of identical statutes has led Grant to urge the state adoption of national laws as a road to uniformity. "State adoption of national laws unifies the laws of all co-operating states. It does this to a greater extent than can be accomplished through the National Conference of Commissioners; for the National Government, unlike the Conference, has a supreme court to give definitive meaning to its laws. . . . Indeed, in adopting the law of the Nation the state would be adopting, not a particular statute, but a complete product: statute, administrative rulings, and judicial decisions." J. A. C. Grant, "The Search for Uniformity of Law," 32 *American Political Science Review* (Dec. 1938), 1097.

[10] See for example the amazing situation described in 25 *Illinois Law Review* (April 1931), 964–65.

proposals, however, has taken hold.[11] The Conference has steadfastly refused to confine its efforts to a single group of laws or to recommend that the legislatures abdicate their power to bring the statutes into harmony with changing conditions.

PRESSURE FROM FEDERAL GOVERNMENT

There is real danger that the Conference may find its usefulness declining unless it develops methods of overcoming the difficulties which confront it. A competing method of securing uniformity has been gaining in popularity during the past decade, and may push the Conference on Uniform State Laws to the side lines. The Federal Government has belatedly discovered that it has within its own powers the strength to induce the states to act in the common interest. These powers have been used in various ways. Herbert Hoover as Secretary of Commerce called several National Conferences on Street and Highway Safety which were attended by representatives of the automotive interests, motor-vehicle owners, state and municipal officials charged with the enforcement of traffic laws, and Federal officials from the Bureau of Public Roads. These conferences drafted a Uniform Vehicle Code and after careful deliberation approved it for presentation to the state legislatures and municipal councils. This code was thereupon considered by the National Conference of Commissioners on Uniform State Laws, approved by it, and made a part of its program. The code has been rather widely adopted, although the legislatures have so altered parts of it that it is difficult to measure its influence in quantitative terms.

TABLE 4—ADOPTIONS OF THE UNIFORM VEHICLE CODE

Act	Jurisdictions Adopting Act	Jurisdictions Adopting Act with Modifications
Motor Vehicle Registration Act	11	3
Motor Vehicle Antitheft Act	10	2
Motor Vehicle Operators' and Chauffeurs' License Act	14	1
Act regulating traffic on the Highways	19	18

Various other Federal bureaus have been active in promoting uniform legislation. The Narcotic Drug Act, which was approved by the Conference on Uniform State Laws, was drafted by the Federal Bureau of Narcotics, which has also pressed for its adoption in the states. The Department of Labor has taken a keen interest in state labor legislation, and through the collection and dissemination of information has exerted a steady influence toward uniformity in that field. A similar line of activity is undertaken by the Federal Office of Education with respect to educational legislation. More recently the Federal Department of Justice has entered the field of state legislation. The development of criminal activities on an interstate basis has virtually forced the Federal Government to give assistance to the states in the enforcement of the criminal laws. Obviously, this assistance would be more effective if the divergencies in the state laws were reduced. To this end, the

---

[11] In the century and a half—from 1789 to 1939—only 45 interstate compacts have been approved by Congress and ratified by two or more states. Only 9 of these have been ratified by more than 2 states. These 9 all date from 1922. Most of the compacts involve only administrative problems and do not bind the states to uniform statutes. The Colorado River Compact (1922) ratified by 6 states, the Oil Conservation Compact (1935) ratified by 6 states, and the Interstate Crime Compact (1937) ratified by 32 states, are, however, close to uniform acts in their effect. None of these three has been sponsored by the National Conference. *Book of the States*, 1939–40, pp. 124–27.

Attorney-General called the National Crime Conference in 1934, appointed a special officer to develop contacts with the states, and fostered state crime conferences.

This was followed by the establishment, through the leadership of the Council of State Governments, of the Interstate Commission on Crime, in October 1935. This agency took several of the uniform acts drafted by the Conference on Uniform State Laws, made such changes in them as experience had shown to be necessary,[12] and, with the help of experts from twenty-six of the leading law schools, drafted two other model acts. These acts were very widely adopted during the next three years. Thus twenty-nine states have adopted the Act for the Fresh Pursuit of Criminals across state lines; nineteen states have adopted the Extradition Act; twenty-seven states have adopted the Act for the Rendition of Witnesses Across State Lines in criminal proceedings; and thirty-two have adopted the Act for the Supervision of Out of State Parolees and Probationers. The last-named of these acts is especially significant, because it contains an interstate compact binding any state approving it to continue its provisions until the compact is formally renounced by that state. Six months' notice must be given of such renunciation. Within a year after it had been drafted, nineteen states had adopted it, and under its terms 1,691 parolees were being supervised by a sister state of the one granting the parole.

The success of the co-ordinated effort of the Conference on Uniform State Laws, the Department of Justice, and the Interstate Commission on Crime was clearly phenomenal. With the exception of the Narcotic Drug Act and the Veterans' Guardianship Act, no other of the uniform acts had ever been adopted nearly so rapidly. Each of these exceptions had received Federal support, and in addition, the first had been promoted by the Interstate Commission on Crime and the second by powerful lobbying agencies. Indeed, the only other uniform act to be adopted by the states with anything approaching the rapidity of the Crime Commission Acts was the Warehouse Receipts Act. With the help of a powerful lobbying organization, this great initial success of the Conference was approved by seventeen states during the first four years after it was drafted. It became evident that real uniformity in legislation could be secured only by the joint work of several agencies.

In 1938 it seemed as if the National Conference on Uniform State Laws recognized this necessity, for it joined hands with the Council of State Governments. The co-operating arrangement provided that the Conference was to draft the proposed uniform laws, while the Council, with its superior legislative contacts, was to promote their adoption. With insufficient time to test the value of this arrangement, the Conference on Uniform State Laws terminated its agreement the following year, preferring to rely solely on such legislative support as the American Bar Association could give. It remains to be seen whether the states will be able by themselves to achieve real uniformity in their statutes, or whether pressure from the Federal Government will be necessary to attain the desired goal.

The National Government has demonstrated its ability to induce the states to take common action in many fields in addition to those of traffic regulation, narcotic control, and law enforcement. The Federal Deposit Insurance Corporation has promoted a substantial degree of uniformity of state legislation, particularly with reference to bank supervision. Under pressure from the

---

[12] These changes were subsequently approved by the National Conference on Uniform State Laws.

Soil Conservation Service, twenty-two states passed acts providing for the creation of soil conservation districts. In the field of planning, however, an even more spectacular success was scored by the Federal Government. The National Resources Committee, in a short period of two years, was able to induce forty-six states to establish state planning boards—most of them being set up by statutory authority. This unprecedented example of uniform state action was accomplished by the simple expedient of offering to the state the assistance of a technical expert in the field of planning if it would set up a board patterned on the Federal model. The uniformity thus secured is one in fact rather than in form, for the provisions of the state planning acts vary considerably from state to state. The fear that Federal aid might be withdrawn, however, has been sufficient to prevent any important deviations in essential points.[13]

Social Security Board

Perhaps the outstanding example of Federal leadership in promoting uniform state legislation was the work of the Social Security Board. This agency, which was established by the Social Security Act in 1934, had charge of the general administration of the Federal program for unemployment insurance. This program required the co-operation of the states, and thus the enactment of state laws in conformity with the Federal statute. The Board carefully refrained from dictating a uniform act which every state must enact to receive the benefits of the Federal law. Two different model acts were prepared, either of which fulfilled the requirements of the Federal law. Furthermore, the Board was willing to accept modifications in even these laws as long as uniformity with respect to certain essential features was retained. An act as passed by the state legislature was reviewed by the Board, and if it were found to conform to the Federal requirements, employees in that state received the benefits of substantial taxes levied under Federal law.

The Social Security Act carries one step farther the method applied several years ago in connection with inheritance taxation. By giving the taxpayer credit on his Federal estate tax for 80 per cent of his state inheritance tax, the Federal Government induced every state but one to adopt this form of taxation. Thus one of the very few features of uniformity which we find in the American taxation system was achieved. The Social Security Act provides that state taxes may be credited on the Federal tax return only if the state enacts an unemployment compensation which is approved by the Social Security Board. This establishes an administrative control over state legislation through which essential uniformity can be demanded without sacrificing experimentation in certain states or the adjustment of laws to local conditions.

By July 1937, state unemployment compensation laws which met the approval of the Board had been passed in all the states. It had not been found necessary, indeed, to reject any act passed by a state legislature, since the bills were for the most part framed on the Federal models, and changes in the models were made with the help of the representatives of the Board itself. The rapidity with which the Federal Government was able to secure uniformity in essential points of a highly controversial statute like that dealing with unemployment compensation is in itself no small tribute to the success of this method.[14]

---

[13] Numerous other illustrations will be found in W. Brooke Graves, "Influence of Congressional Legislation on Legislation in the States," 23 *Iowa Law Review* (May 1938), 519–38.

[14] Without the impetus of Federal action, it is doubtful if the states could have enacted un-

Similar success has crowned the work of the Social Security Board in the field of public-assistance legislation. The Social Security Act authorizes Federal aid for three types of public assistance: (1) aid to needy persons of sixty-five years or over; (2) aid to needy blind persons; and (3) aid to dependent children under sixteen who have no parental support. By July 1938 three-fourths of the states had enacted approved plans for all three of these forms of public assistance. All but one had passed an approved old-age pension act, and acts for the second and third types were lacking in only ten states.

INCREASED FEDERAL CONTROL

It may be that this new method of securing similarity in state laws is merely a prelude to greater centralization in the Federal Government. Indeed, with the states drawing one-fifth of their revenues from Uncle Sam, it is difficult to see how increased Federal control can be avoided. Many have suggested that the price of a Federal bureaucracy is too dear for the uniformity which is secured. This is, however, in the final analysis a counsel of inaction. It is not standardization of legislation that is destroying states' rights, but rather the development of American industry and society on a national basis. If uniformity is desirable in legislation on controversial subjects, experience has shown that some inducement is necessary to impel the states to act. The motivating force may be pressure from selfish private interests organized into lobbying groups, or it may be benefits which the National Government may confer on the states. Between the two, there is an obvious advantage in Federal leadership. It is infinitely preferable that the uniformity be flexible enough to meet the special needs of the different states than that a dead level of legal mediocrity settle down on all of them. The use of a Federal administrative agency to furnish this flexibility seems admirably suited to the twin purposes of securing essential similarity in legislation and preserving the states as experimental laboratories in government.

---

employment insurance laws for many years, because they would have thereby burdened their own industries in competition with those of other states. V. O. Key, Jr., *Administration of Federal Grants to States* (Chicago, 1937), p. 20.

Rodney L. Mott, Ph.D., is professor of political science and director of the School of Social Sciences at Colgate University, Hamilton, New York. From 1930 to 1934 he was research consultant of the American Legislators' Association and managing editor of its monthly publication, State Government. He is the author of a treatise on "Due Process of Law" (1926) and of numerous articles. In 1925 he edited a collection of "Materials Illustrative of American Government," and in 1938 he compiled (with W. L. Hindman) "The Constitutions of the States and the United States" for the New York State Constitutional Convention.

Interstate Compacts and Administrative Co-operation

By Garland C. Routt

THIS paper is concerned with the operation and effect of some of the formal and informal governmental devices which tend to blur the historical pattern of federalism in the United States. These devices may be described as "short circuits" which have developed between the various parts of the Nation's federal system. They violate the "pure" theory of federalism in that they provide contacts between governmental units which are theoretically insulated from each other. The Constitution itself, while it apparently did not contemplate the development of administrative relationships between the states and the central government, departed from federal theory in giving recognition, under certain conditions, to agreements and joint action by the states.

The Federal-State Issue

Conflict and controversy over the "proper" scope for the application of state and national powers have played a dramatic part in the political history of the United States. The unending tug of war between the governmental center and circumference has been one of the principal topics of political discussion and debate since the Constitutional Convention and the *Federalist Papers*. Even the superior strength which forced national unity after the war between the states failed to give a final answer to the question. Nor does any final solution seem likely to be found. While the Nation and its parts continue to develop in a changing world, there is little reason to suppose that the balancing process between state and Federal authority will reach a permanent equilibrium.

It is likely, however, that solutions to certain pressing problems of government will continue to be sought, in increasing numbers, by formal and informal collaboration between Federal and state governments on the one hand, and among the states on the other.

The American system of federalized government, at the time it was embodied in the Constitution, was a practical and necessary compromise between jealous and suspicious states which were just emerging from colonial vassalage to a distant and arbitrary government. No political theory dictated that the central government be one to which limited powers be delegated by the states which were members of the federation. Experience with the Confederation had demonstrated that the central government must be more powerful than any of its members, and that, within its authorized sphere of action, it must be independent of state interference. The Constitutional Convention faced the task of framing a system of government which would have as few as possible of the undesirable features both of the autocratic British tyranny and of the chaotic and powerless Confederation. The Constitutional framers retained much of the general pattern of the Confederation, but greatly strengthened the authority of the central government by assigning to it certain of the sovereign powers of the states. While this brought greater unity among the states, it offered no final solution to the Federal-state issue. However, by making the central government at least equal to any of its parts, it established an equilibrium on the basis of which compromise was possible. Dr. Jane Perry Clark describes the nature of our federal system as follows:

In any federal system, government may be said to consist essentially of the art of compromise between the interests of the component parts. Two governments are always in the picture, and no matter how limited their spheres of authority, they cannot be combined or prevented from occasional collisions and duplications. But there are advantages in the division of authority in the federal system in the United States. In the expansion of governmental services, there is a line beyond which centralized administration cannot go without falling because of its own weight. A federal division of powers, in accordance with American tradition, may aid in the avoidance of a too-highly centralized administration and offer an opportunity for political and economic experimentation without the necessity for waiting to convert an entire nation to the hopes and beliefs of a particular program.[1]

Closer Relationships

Dr. Clark's study discusses the social, economic, and political forces which have brought about closer administrative relationships between Federal and state agencies. The operation of the same forces has brought about an expansion of the responsibilities of state governments and has increased the necessity for co-operation among them for the better performance of old and new services.

"All over the world," says George Fort Milton, "government is on the march from dedication to narrow ministerial duties to the performance of an economic function; and no nation, whether dictatorship or democracy, is exempt ... the whole pattern of government, in a practical if not a constitutional sense, has been recut."[2]

The effects of the increased use and new applications of governmental devices for communication and joint action between Federal and state governments have been extensively discussed during recent years.[3] Less attention, however, has been given to the role of interstate co-operation and the effect which it may be expected to have on the Federal-state equilibrium.

This discussion is directed at two general problems involved in the development of interstate relationships: first, the operation of state administrative co-operation and of interstate compacts in the developing trend toward general governmental collaboration and co-ordination; and, second, the effects of interstate communication and joint action on the future patterns of federal relationships in this country. Underlying the discussion is the assumption that at the present time these devices are necessary instruments of governmental action for supplementing a relatively inflexible federal division of powers which was based on the expectations of the eighteenth century. A further assumption is that a sound evaluation of these instruments of government will be based on their contributions toward accomplishing the purposes of government in general, rather than on any effect they may have upon expanding or contracting the scope of state, as contrasted with Federal, authority.

State governments are intrusted with the performance of a multitude of odd jobs for their populations. Some of these tasks are of the utmost importance, others are trivial by comparison; but very few are without some bearing on the activities of the governments of other states. Interstate governmental relationships have developed because of this, and they have been extended and have become increasingly important as industrial and economic changes have made the Nation an economic unit. Because this process has involved a high degree of skill-specialization and divi-

[1] Jane Perry Clark, *The Rise of a New Federalism* (New York: Columbia University Press, 1938), p. 7.
[2] George Fort Milton, "New Services to Perform: An Opportunity," *State Government*, Sept. 1939, p. 156.

[3] Jane Perry Clark, *op. cit.*; V. O. Key, *The Administration of Federal Grants to States*.

sion of labor, and because modern invention has whittled away the barriers of time and space which once separated states, decisions made in one state are important to the citizens of other states. These realities have given rise to problems which have broken down the isolation of state governments, and forced communication, co-operation, and compromise among them.

The states have developed a number of methods for solving interstate problems and for organizing harmonious interstate action. These have been utilized in dealing with many different interstate situations, with varying degrees of success. A careful evaluation of the effectiveness of the various interstate devices when applied to different types of interstate problems would be particularly helpful to state officials whose duties involve interstate negotiations. However, this problem lies outside the scope of the present discussion. Among the more important methods for dealing with matters which concern two or more states are the following: (1) uniform state laws; (2) reciprocal or contingent state legislation; (3) interstate administrative co-operation; and (4) interstate compacts and agreements.

Administrative Co-operation

This discussion is primarily concerned with the last two of the above methods. Administrative co-operation is the most informal of the four, and is the only one which can be initiated and carried on without legislative authorization. Interstate compacts and agreements, on the other hand, are the most formal of the types of collaboration mentioned above, and they require the approval not only of the legislatures of the states involved, but also of the Federal Congress. Some compacts provide by law for subsequent administrative co-operation between the signatory states in working out the details of the agreement.

Administrative co-operation is one of the important lubricants which make possible the simultaneous operation of forty-nine semi-independent governmental authorities inside the boundaries of one nation. Without it, the resulting friction would create a great deal of heat, and perhaps would damage sensitive parts of this complex mechanism, if not stall it altogether.

Administrative co-operation between officials of two or more states may take a variety of forms ranging from informal understandings concerning minor problems to continuing collaboration in regard to major social and economic questions. Between these extremes the form of such agreements varies from informal verbal understandings to formal contracts. The types of interstate administrative co-operation may be roughly classified under the following headings: (1) adoption of uniform rules and regulations for the interpretation of identical or similar legislation; (2) adoption of uniform or contingent rules, regulations, and procedures to govern interstate dealings; (3) negotiation or arbitration, rather than litigation, of interstate difficulties; (4) mutual recognition and acceptance of findings of fact by state agencies in regard to interstate problems; (5) exchange of reports, rules, regulations, and so forth; and (6) participation in interstate conferences, and active membership in associations of public officials.

Uniform state laws can be of little value if those charged with their administration promulgate rules and regulations which are radically different or are in actual conflict. Such differing interpretations of identical laws may pose academic questions for the philosopher, but to those who have spent half a lifetime in securing the adoption of uniform legislation, it is a practical problem which demands a practical solution.

In recognition of this difficulty the

National Conference of Commissioners on Uniform State Laws has recently devoted considerable effort to drafting uniform administrative rules and regulations on which to base enforcement of certain of the uniform laws which the Conference has sponsored. As a general rule, decisions of state and Federal courts have also helped to maintain the uniformity intended by legislatures in the enactment of such laws.

Uniform or contingent rules, regulations, and procedures may contribute to the systematic handling of interstate difficulties. Once properly established and recognized, they may become an effective part of the machinery for interstate negotiation. When, in this connection, custom and tradition have made them a part of the regular institutional routine, many interstate problems can be solved automatically without unusual or extraordinary negotiation.

Direct negotiation by state administrators for the settlement or arbitration of interstate difficulties is usually less expensive and more satisfactory than litigation. Solutions reached by this method may not be permanent, but in a rapidly changing world they are likely to be more durable than those resulting from litigation. If the negotiators reach an agreement, a pattern of mutual confidence has been set for dealing with related problems in the future. Legal action, on the other hand, usually results in an even wider separation of the contesting parties. The latitude of administrative discretion which is given officials by state laws is an important factor limiting their authority to arbitrate certain problems.

Political considerations may also exercise a very real restraint, as the following example illustrates: A few years ago an official of Wisconsin arrived at an understanding with officials of a neighboring state regarding the registration of motor trucks which operated in both states. The arrangement apparently worked satisfactorily until the next Wisconsin legislative session, when a resolution censuring the action of the official was introduced. The agreement was terminated soon afterward.

The mutual recognition and acceptance by state agencies of findings of fact in matters related to interstate problems and the exchange of agency reports, rules, and regulations may help to provide a sound basis for intelligent interstate dealings. Familiarity with the methods and the problems of agencies in other states, in even the most general terms, may be expected to promote "full faith and credit" among state administrators. This attitude is basic to the successful settlement of common problems by negotiation.

In the past and at the present time, associations of state officials have made and are making important contributions to the development of "full faith and credit" among state officials who administer similar functions of government. The friendships and the appreciation of common problems which are fostered by the annual conferences of such associations have provided the basis for many of the present co-operative relationships between states. At the present time almost every division and function of state government is represented by an association of administrative officers drawn from all states. The organization and the programs of many of these groups have been analyzed and discussed by Professor W. Brooke Graves in his volume, *Uniform State Action*.[4]

Administrative co-operation, as a device for preventing confusion and conflict and for improving the operation of certain governmental services, has demonstrated its value. However, its chief

[4] W. Brooke Graves, *Uniform State Action: A Possible Substitute for Centralization*, Chapel Hill: University of North Carolina Press, 1934.

virtue—informality—may in some situations become a vital defect. Most interstate administrative agreements and understandings have only the moral obligation of a "gentlemen's agreement." Unless authorized by legislative enactment in the states involved, such agreements have no legal basis. Without the mutual good will among administrators which has been emphasized throughout this paper, the necessary process of concession and adjustment between states, even in minor details, may become the subject of litigation or a political question for legislative decision.

INTERSTATE COMPACTS

The Constitution made no provision for continuous contact between the governments of the several states. However, it did include a provision prohibiting the states from entering into any "Agreement or Compact" "without the Consent of Congress." The essence of this negatively worded compact clause was borrowed from the Articles of Confederation, which in turn had derived it from the practice of American colonies in negotiating boundary disputes through joint commissions whose settlement required the approval of the Crown.[5] Frankfurter and Landis describe the requirement of Congressional consent for compacts as the "republican transformation of the needed approval of the Crown."[6]

Interstate compacts are more formal and permanent in nature than the types of co-operative activity which have been discussed in preceding paragraphs. They have been applied to the more important interstate and regional problems which lie outside the traditional realms of Federal or state powers. History shows that the first and most frequent use of compacts has been in the settlement of disputes concerning the location of interstate boundaries. Since the beginning of the present century, however, the compact method has been used in attempts to solve an increasing variety of interstate and regional difficulties.

Compacts have been utilized in seeking interstate solutions to problems in the following fields of governmental interest and action: (1) boundary and jurisdictional adjustments; (2) regulation of interstate streams, harbors, and water resources; (3) construction and maintenance of interstate public works; (4) conservation of natural resources; (5) interstate tax adjustments; and (6) regulation of certain types of activities for social or economic reasons.

As the Nation has become a more closely knit economic unit and the states have become more interdependent, interstate agreements dealing with problems in any of these fields have had increasingly important social and economic repercussions. For example, an agreement for the abatement of pollution in an interstate stream and its tributaries may affect the economic interests of many individuals and public and private organizations. It is likely to interfere with the customary disposal of industrial wastes in such streams, and to require the construction of municipal sewerage-treatment plants at public expense. The disposal of waste and garbage from boats would probably also be regulated. On the other hand, the value of the stream as a source of water supply and for recreational purposes would be greatly increased by such an agreement.

No procedure for the negotiation of interstate compacts is set out in the Constitution or by Federal law. Consequently, there has been no established pattern of action for initiating and carrying on the discussions necessary for

---

[5] Frankfurter and Landis, "The Compact Clause of the Constitution—A Study in Interstate Adjustments," *Yale Law Journal*, Vol. XXXIV, No. 7 (May 1925), pp. 692–93.

[6] *Ibid.*, p. 694.

arriving at such agreements. Ordinarily, however, the terms of a compact are drawn up by representatives of the compacting states who have been designated to act for their states by legislative or executive authority. The compact must then receive the approval of the legislatures of the states involved and of Congress before it becomes effective.

In the past the negotiation and ratification of compacts have been slow and cumbersome, but there is already evidence that the activities of such interstate organizations as the Council of State Governments are resulting in the development of recognized procedures and more adequate machinery for the initiation and negotiation of interstate compacts and other less formal agreements. The Interstate Commissions on the Delaware, Potomac, and Ohio River Basins which were developed under the sponsorship of the Council have already agreed on the terms of interstate antipollution programs which are now awaiting the legislative approval of the states involved. The membership of the commissions which drafted these plans was drawn largely from the Interstate Cooperation Commissions of the states represented. These latter commissions are the component parts of the Council of State Governments and are discussed elsewhere in this volume.

Classes of Compacts

On the basis of the *permanence of solutions reached*, three general classes of compacts may be pointed out. The first of these classes includes compacts which provide a definition and permanent settlement of the rights of the compacting states with respect to the interstate problem under consideration. However, not all interstate problems can be solved so simply. In the past, compacts of this class have been concerned largely with boundary disputes, although many of those dealing with the extension of concurrent jurisdiction also belong with this group.

Compacts of the second class also attempt to set forth the rights and duties of the compacting states in connection with the difficulty in question, but the type of problem involved precludes the possibility of a permanent settlement. Often such solutions are thought to be final, until changed conditions demand that the terms of the compact be changed accordingly. Agreements concerning problems of this kind offer at most a solution which can only be temporarily satisfactory to the parties concerned.

For example, interstate compacts providing for the allocation of the waters of interstate streams for irrigation and domestic and industrial uses may prove too rigid for easy adaptation to the social and economic development of compacting states. Changes in populations and increases in the industrialization of certain areas within the watershed of an interstate stream may create new demands which were not foreseen by the negotiators of the original agreement. This criticism may likewise apply to compacts dealing with certain interstate problems of a social nature. In some instances provision has been made for periodic revision of the terms of the compact with a view to keeping it abreast of changing conditions. Such amendments as are made to the original agreement, however, must again run the gauntlet of legislative approval in the states, and secure Congressional consent in Washington. This process may be as slow and difficult as the negotiation and ratification of the original compact.

Interstate compacts of the third class have been used to create continuing interstate jurisdictions or authorities and to provide for the establishment of permanent administrative agencies with sufficient discretionary power to decide problems incidental to main objectives. This type of agreement eliminates the necessity for periodic revision by delegating authority to administrators to adapt rules and methods to changing conditions. Successful examples of interstate authorities set up by compact are the Port of New York Authority, the Palisades Interstate Park Commission, and the Interstate Sanitation Commission dealing with the waters of New York Harbor, the lower Hudson River, and the western end of Long Island Sound. Now in process of formation are several similar interstate agencies dealing with other problems.

DIFFICULTY OF RATIFICATION

In some instances the compacts creating such interstate administrative units have narrowly limited the scope of administrative discretion. In such situations, major questions of policy must be referred back to the legislatures. The process of securing the ratification of such proposed policies is often not much less difficult or tedious than that of securing the ratification of the original compact.

A case in point demonstrating the precarious position of major decisions which interstate commissions must refer back to the states for legislative approval is that of the sanitation agreement which was developed by the Ohio River Valley Sanitation Compact Commission and the Interstate Commission on the Ohio River Basin. This agreement was presented to the legislatures of Illinois, Indiana, New York, Ohio, Pennsylvania, Tennessee, and West Virginia during 1939.[7] It was approved in all states except Pennsylvania. The Pennsylvania Senate also failed to approve legislation designed to control pollution in the Delaware River by joint state action. It is alleged that the opposition of certain large industrial interests was responsible for the defeat of these proposals.[8]

These examples illustrate one of the more important arguments which have been advanced against the effectiveness of forms of interstate co-operation which require legislative approval. The possibility of securing agreements among states on matters of major importance is said to be remote, and at best it is a method not suited for problems which require immediate action by government. The problems which have been attacked by the compact method up to the present time have not had this critical urgency. In most cases compacts have been used to correct undesirable situations which have been tolerated in the past. Neglect of such problems may often give them an urgency which is not generally recognized. In a crisis situation, however, where the emergency is apparent, it is likely that the compact process would be speeded up in much the same manner as the general legislative process.

The negotiation of compacts bears more than a superficial resemblance to the negotiation of international treaties. Although state sovereignty is hedged about with restrictions which do not limit the actions of independent nations, the compact method, like the treaty method of solving difficulties, is one of voluntary participation and agreement. Under normal conditions, the terms of a treaty may be worked out over a period of months or years. In critical situations, treaties may be negotiated and ratified almost overnight. The analogy may be pursued further. Effective co-

[7] The legislatures of Kentucky and Virginia did not meet in regular session in 1939.

[8] Statement by the Speaker of the Pennsylvania House, quoted in the *Philadelphia Inquirer*, May 21, 1939. However, the existing powers of the Pennsylvania Health Department are so broad that it is expected that the state, falling back on its adherence to the "gentlemen's agreement," may still be able to do her part in these co-operative ventures.

operation under both compacts and treaties is based on ethical or moral sanctions rather than on those of law or force.

It is now well recognized that interstate compacts are not likely to be successful in operation unless they include all states which affect, or are affected by, the problem under consideration. Any such problem which has economic ramifications—as indeed most interstate problems have—requires for its solution the sincere participation of all interested parties. Almost every interstate problem which is likely to be the subject of future compacts will probably touch the economic interest of some minority group. It remains to be seen whether such groups will continue to oppose the social legislation on an interstate or regional basis which they were able to defeat in individual states a few years ago.

Congressional Consent

Only a few discussions of interstate compacts have referred more than casually to the Federal-state aspects of such agreements. Current controversy concerning the Interstate Oil Compact and the New England Flood Control compacts, however, has centered attention on the effect of Federal policies on such interstate action. The so-called Connally "Hot Oil" Act which was passed in 1935 has a bearing on the Oil Compact. This Federal law prohibits the movement in interstate commerce of oil produced in violation of state laws or regulations. Although it applies to all states, its most important effect is to provide penalties which support the effectiveness of the Oil Compact.

The refusal of Congressional consent, on the other hand, has prevented the Connecticut and Merrimac flood-control compacts from becoming effective. There was acrimonious public discussion involving "states' rights" and "national interests" while Congress deliberated on this question. Since there can be no question concerning the power of Congress to withhold approval, the only question that can be involved is the wisdom of the public policy followed by Congress. Consideration of this question is not relevant here, but it brings up the proposal advanced by Mr. Ernest C. Carman that Congressional authority to approve or reject compacts be removed by Constitutional amendment.[9] He insists that the reasons for requiring Congressional consent have now disappeared.

While it may be agreed that the original reasons for requiring Congressional approval are apparently no longer important, it seems to the writer that there are even more important reasons which may be found in the present situation. There is some evidence that Congressional approval was originally intended to protect the supremacy of the central government from the threat of political alliances among the states. This danger seems remote today. However, only a static and very narrow conception of what constitutes the "national interest" would hold that interstate and regional problems have no bearing on the welfare of the Nation as a whole. Without the necessity for Congressional consent, there would be no opportunity for considering such agreements in the light of broad public policy.

Mr. Carman would also place in the Constitution an amendment giving the Supreme Court original and exclusive jurisdiction in controversies arising from compacts between the states. In other words, he proposes to substitute judicial review of compacts for Congressional preview. Under such an arrangement compacts would be judged on a purely

[9] Ernest C. Carman, "Should the States Be Permitted to Make Compacts Without the Consent of Congress?" *Cornell Law Quarterly*, Feb. 1938, pp. 280 ff.

legalistic basis, and, once agreed to by the states involved, would be valid until found to be contrary to the Constitution or to Federal law by the Supreme Court. There would be no consideration of compacts in terms of national policy or future national welfare. Conflict and confusion between various sections of the Nation would be the inevitable result, and the defeat of any co-ordinated program of state conservation on a nationwide basis would be assured.

The possibility of the adoption of such an amendment is too remote for serious consideration. The matter is discussed here only as an example of an extreme position taken by one of those who would use the compact as a device for interstate action without regard to its effects on the citizens of more remote areas.

A Sectional Basis

Within recent years there has been an increasing growth of various forms of interstate co-operation on a "sectional" rather than a "regional" basis. In this case the word "sectional" is used to describe the political and economic unity of a geographic region which is based on a "united front" of the dominant economic interests of that area against a similar "united front" in another area which is in competition either economically or politically. *Regional* collaboration, on the other hand, has meant interstate agreement and action to solve problems *within the region,* and not the development of plans of aggression or defense against other regions.

Growing intersectional rivalry and competition is evident today. In many instances it has been well organized and well financed by state governments through the very co-operative devices that have been the subject of this paper. The recent multiplication of interstate trade barriers was one evidence of this competition and rivalry between individual states. Fortunately the states themselves, through their Council of State Governments, have taken effective steps to correct this situation. But now the spirit of rivalry, retaliation, and reprisal has infected whole regional areas. The migration of industries in search of lower labor costs, bitter debate over intersectional freight rate differentials and their adjustment, and competition for tourist patronage are merely the more obvious aspects of the struggle. These and many other issues are being fought out between rival regional organizations of states. Commercial advertising campaigns, tempting offers to migrating industry, and well-managed propaganda and political pressure are the weapons of the battle.

To point out these aberrations of the use of co-operative methods in dealing with interstate problems is but to emphasize that these methods, like other instruments of government, are neither good nor evil in themselves. They are but means to ends, and their use will not guarantee a "good" result.

Appraisal of the Compact Method

As a tool of government, the interstate compact has been criticized as slow, uncertain, and cumbersome both in negotiation and in operation. This may be admitted without denying its value as an instrument of government in certain situations. The compact device has been used in solving problems which lie outside the realm of individual state control and beyond the scope of Federal authority. It has been utilized where economic competition between states made individual state action impractical or politically impossible. The alternatives would seem to be: no action, or Federal action which would require Constitutional amendment. The process of amending the Constitution has usually been even slower and more uncertain than the negotiation of compacts.

As the limits of the effective application of the compact method are more clearly marked out, and as a body of custom and precedent for the use of compacts in dealing with the more modern problems of government is accumulated, the negotiation of such agreements may be expected to proceed with fewer unnecessary delays. There can be little doubt that the inherent complexity and technical difficulties of some of the problems which have been attacked by the compact method have been responsible for many delays in negotiation. Present and future research such as that being carried on by the National Resources Planning Board may be expected to provide more readily available answers to some of the problems which have held up negotiations in the past.

The interstate compact offers no short cut around the delays which are accepted as a necessary part of democratic government. Decisions and solutions reached by such agreements can have no greater claim to validity than the products of other democratic deliberations. The difficulties of this, as of other forms of interstate co-operation, are the difficulties inherent in democratic government. The forms of co-operation which have been discussed are important aids to the effectiveness of democratic government. They offer ways and means of getting the tasks of government done when other channels are blocked or not appropriate.

The peaceful compromise of conflicting or divergent state interests by co-operative action is rarely spectacular. Usually it is far from satisfactory to the parties involved. But the mutual give-and-take of democratic compromise is the way of civilization.

Garland C. Routt is editor of State Government magazine and director of publications at the Council of State Governments, Chicago, Illinois. At present he is on leave of absence, serving as consultant on a research project for the United States Department of Agriculture. He has previously served as research assistant in the Department of Political Science of the University of Chicago, and in a field study sponsored by that University's Social Science Research Committee.

Work of the Commissions on Interstate Co-operation

By Hubert R. Gallagher [1]

PUBLICISTS and government officials, including President Roosevelt, have recently expressed their concern over the upsurge of sectionalism in the country, as manifest in the erection of interstate trade barriers and the intensification of the propaganda war between the South and New England over freight rate differentials. There is some hope, however, that these threats to our national unity, as well as other interstate conflicts, can be averted through the work of the Council of State Governments and its Commissions on Interstate Co-operation.

As a result of the effort of these agencies, the drive to erect additional trade barriers in the forty-four legislatures meeting in 1939 was stopped in its tracks. In addition, the Commissions on Interstate Co-operation continued to accomplish much by unifying state laws and ironing out conflicts among the states in other fields, including water resources, conservation of fisheries, liquor control, conflicting taxation, interstate parks, motor vehicle regulation, and crime control.

Growth and Structure of Commissions

Since the co-operation commission is a relatively new device in the field of government, it would not be surprising if the public generally were aware neither of its existence nor of the effective work of the commissions and the Council in bringing about "a more perfect Union." The first commission was established in New Jersey in April 1935. Since then forty-one states have become members of the Council of State Governments by establishing commissions patterned after the model bill drafted by the Council. The attention which the work has attracted in newspapers, in magazines of national circulation, and over the radio networks attests to the broad public interest in the problems attacked by these agencies.

The commissions, with few exceptions, consist of fifteen members, including ten legislators and five administrative officials. Five of the legislative members constitute the senate standing committee on interstate co-operation, and five make up the house standing committee on interstate co-operation. These committees are appointed as are other standing committees of the legislatures. In most cases the speaker appoints the house members, the president of the senate appoints the senate members, and the governor names the administrative committee, usually from the members of his cabinet.

Notable exceptions to this general pattern are Kentucky and Kansas, which have designated the Legislative Council to act as the co-operation commission; New York, which provides for a seventeen-member committee by a joint legislative resolution every year; and Wisconsin, Delaware, and Maine, which have commissions of nine members instead of fifteen. A Joint Committee, composed of appointees of the Governor and the Attorney-General, serves in Texas—the forty-second state to establish an agency to co-operate with other states.

The achievements of the commissions have generally been in direct proportion to the amount of appropriation received from their legislatures. Those commissions which have made a successful record have had sufficient funds to employ an executive secretary and, in some

[1] With the editorial assistance of Virginia Savage Lanahan

cases, a research staff. Outstanding among the commissions have been those of Illinois, Indiana, Massachusetts, New Jersey, New York, Ohio, Pennsylvania, and Wisconsin. The chairmen of these commissions have been usually able, and sincerely interested in solving the difficult problems facing their commissions. Legislative appropriations to the commissions vary from a high of $30,000 per year in New York State to $200 in Vermont.

Efforts of the Council of State Governments were first directed to bringing about the establishment of commissions throughout the country; more recently the Council has been interested in seeing that every commission has funds for its work. At the end of the legislative sessions of 1935 only eight commissions existed and but two were supported by state appropriations. At the end of the regular sessions in 1937 eight states were financing these agencies, and in 1939 fifteen states had appropriated a total of $96,600 to their commissions.

The fact that some of the states failed to appropriate to their commissions does not mean that they failed to function, because in many cases the expenses of delegates participating in conferences were paid out of legislative travel or special contingent funds. The commissions also indorsed the legislative programs of other commissions and were successful in passing legislative proposals drafted as a result of the research studies made available by the better-financed commissions. Interstate agreements were also successfully promulgated by members of commissions whose work was not formally financed by their legislatures. As other states observe the efficiency of those commissions which have a permanent organization, undoubtedly more states will make available funds for the maintenance of an administrative secretary, research assistance, and office space.

WORK OF THE COMMISSIONS

Turning now to the work of these ambassadorial agencies of the states, it is not surprising to find that the organized commissions have been leaders in these states in initiating investigations toward solving interstate problems. Frequently the commissions call regional conferences themselves, with the assistance of the Council's staff; and often they request the Council to call a conference on a specific problem. Massachusetts has taken the lead in conferences among the New England states, and its co-operation commission has been influential in activating other commissions in that region. The New York Joint Legislative Committee on Interstate Co-operation, with the assistance of the Council's New York district office, has called a great many conferences on subjects ranging from conservation of fisheries to banking practices and highway safety. The New Jersey Commission has initiated conferences on labor problems, transiency, and crime control. The Wisconsin Commission requested the Council to arrange a conference of certain midwestern states on conflicting taxation among those states. The Indiana Commission has been particularly active in the Midwest, and at its suggestion regional assemblies have been held on interstate trade barriers and on dairy problems. More significant, the points agreed upon by these groups have been adopted by the states in a gratifying number of instances.

Trade barriers

The National Conference on Interstate Trade Barriers held in Chicago in April 1939 by the Council and Commissions on Interstate Co-operation attracted national attention and inaugurated a successful campaign to eliminate state trade barriers. This meeting was held while most of the legislatures were in session and while there was still time to take legislative action. As a result of this conference, trade barriers were repealed or vetoed in more than twenty states and were defeated in committee or on the legislative floor in other states. In this campaign the co-operation commissions played a key part.

The New Jersey Commission's opposition to a discriminatory liquor-licensing measure and a provision for rebating 50 per cent of the gallonage tax on home-distilled applejack resulted in the defeat of these measures in the legislature. The Indiana Commission succeeded in bringing about the repeal of the port-of-entry and beer-importation provisions of the Indiana Alcoholic Beverage Control Act.

California Commissioners defeated a bill which would have placed a discriminatory tax on beer brewed in certain states. As a direct result of the conference, the California Legislature refused to adopt a number of retaliatory measures proposed against products manufactured in a number of Eastern states. The Missouri Anti-discriminatory Liquor Act of 1937 was repealed; and Connecticut and Oregon, at opposite ends of the land, united in defeating discriminatory liquor legislation.

The strong opposition of the New York Joint Legislative Committee on Interstate Co-operation killed a bill requiring that materials to be used in the construction of public buildings, which were not mined or quarried in New York State, must be fabricated and finished within the state. In Ohio, a proposal to limit the purchase of coal for state institutions to that mined in Ohio was defeated as a result of the work of the co-operation commission.

Vigorous opposition by the co-operation commission of Connecticut defeated a bill which provided that all state contracts for supplies and public works be awarded to resident bidders if their bids were not more than 3 per cent higher than those of out-of-state bidders. Kansas likewise defeated three bills which would have given preference in public purchases of materials, equipment, and supplies to resident dealers. Texas followed suit by defeating a bill to grant a 10 per cent preference to state bidders on public works.

Oregon and Vermont lawmakers refused to adopt bills imposing an oleomargarine tax, and Iowa defeated a proposed increase of taxes on this product. Duties or inspection fees levied on farm products of other states were defeated in Arkansas, California, Florida, and Rhode Island. Connecticut and New Hampshire defeated measures which would have discriminated against out-of-state salesmen.

These are but examples of the type of interstate trade barriers which were defeated as a result of the campaign inaugurated by the Council of State Governments and Commissions on Interstate Co-operation at the National Conference in April. These agencies have been equally successful in solving the more routine conflicts and administrative disagreements among the states.

Palisades Park

Through the efforts of the New York and New Jersey co-operation commissions, an interstate compact was entered into by these two states which ended the impasse which for thirty years had existed with respect to the Palisades Interstate Park. This compact, as finally ratified by Congress, co-ordinates the activities of two separate state boards into a single permanent governmental instrumentality similar to the New York Port Authority, and overcomes certain major and minor difficulties which have hindered effective supervision in the past.

A major problem of the Northeastern states in their relationship with each other is the conservation of wild life, the policing of boundary lines, and particularly of boundary waters. The co-operation commissions of these states are making an effort to secure uniform regulations for the taking of wild life, issuing of reciprocal licenses, and joint stocking and policing of these areas. These statutes provide for the reciprocal enforcement of penalties for violations of fishing laws in boundary waters between New York and New Jersey, and New York and Pennsylvania, and the control of the taking of fish, especially from the Hudson River.

Crime

Commissions on Interstate Co-operation have continued to support the uniform laws drafted by the Interstate Commission on Crime. In addition to the original four bills, the crime commission has revised the Uniform Firearms Act and prepared amendments to the Uniform Narcotic Drug Act. The former, product of intensive study by the Firearms Section of the Commission, represents an improvement and clarification of the Uniform Firearms Act drafted by the National Conference of Commissioners on Uniform State Laws, inasmuch as it removes the points objected to on the scores of national defense and sportsmanship. The latter act, also drafted by the Commissioners on Uniform State Laws, was revised in order to curtail the use of marihuana. Passage of these bills will be urged during forthcoming legislative sessions. At the present time the four original bills have been enacted throughout the country as follows: fresh pursuit of criminals, 29 states; extradition, 19 states; out-of-state witnesses, 27 states; parolee supervision, 32 states.

Fisheries

As a result of commission activity, definite progress has been made toward conserving both marine and Great Lakes fisheries. Along the eastern seaboard, New York and New Jersey by joint action have made provisions looking toward the restoration of shad and sturgeon fisheries in the Delaware and Hudson rivers.

Marine fisheries offer a more difficult problem, since the states themselves have jurisdiction out three miles into the ocean, where the Federal Government takes over. Since the fish can not be expected to observe either state lines or the three-mile limit, both interstate and Federal-state co-operation are required for a solution. A suggested answer is that Congress be requested to give consent in advance to compacts providing for the necessary protection. The compact would establish the Interstate Marine Fisheries Commission charged with the duty of recommending and securing the enactment of essential state legislation, and providing as well for the reciprocal enforcement of legislation by all game wardens of the states concerned. The consent-in-advance measure, S.J.R. No. 139, was approved by Congress but was vetoed by President Roosevelt.

After years of fruitless effort to conserve Great Lakes fisheries, the states through their co-operation commissions requested the President and Congress to establish an International Board of Inquiry for the purpose of considering an international treaty as a means of conserving Great Lakes fisheries. The states' interests in carrying on negotiations would be safeguarded by an advisory committee composed of representatives of the Commissions on Interstate Co-operation and the leaders in the industry. This board is in the process of being established through an exchange of diplomatic notes between the United States and Canada. The Canadian Government has notified our State Department that it would join the United

States in appointing members of the International Board of Inquiry.

Oil

Another conservation problem of interest to the commissions is that of oil. Efforts have been made on the part of some of the commissions to aid the Interstate Oil Compact in furthering its work in the field of oil proration and conservation. Recent discoveries in Illinois have elevated that state to the rank of one of the principal oil-producers. At the request of representatives of the Oklahoma Commission on Interstate Co-operation, the Illinois Commission has taken under consideration the possibility of urging Illinois to become a party to the Interstate Oil Compact. This general subject was also considered by the Western Conference on Governmental Problems which met in San Francisco, October 26–28, 1939.

Highway safety

The Middle Atlantic and New England states have been particularly active in the field of highway safety. Annual conferences on the subject have been held for the last four years, and in the course of these discussions recommendations have been agreed upon in respect to compulsory periodic inspection of motor vehicles, regulation of the interstate transportation and sale of used cars, safety education in public schools, "hours of service" laws for drivers of commercial vehicles, uniform safety equipment, enforcement of pedestrian regulations, and determination of maximum speed limit. The decision of the conferees that a reasonably high enforced speed limit is preferable to a more conservative but unobserved limitation is reflected in changes during the past legislative sessions in Georgia, Nebraska, Maine, Minnesota, Arkansas, and Montana. Further, a number of states changed their laws to provide a higher speed limit during daylight than at night. A draft of an act requiring the reciprocal reporting of motor vehicle accident convictions among states has also been adopted by many of the states.

Banking and securities

In co-operation with the American Bankers Association and a Committee on Uniform Laws appointed by the National Association of Supervisors of State Banks, the Eastern and New England states have held three regional conferences on uniform banking and securities practices. These conferences have resulted in a clarification of the problems connected with these subjects, especially in regard to the regulation of branch banking, the adoption of uniform report forms, and the establishment of minimum standards for chartering requirements, investment policies, loans, and bank operations.

Migration of industry

The Massachusetts Commission on Interstate Co-operation, at the request of the General Court, conducted an extensive inquiry into the industrial losses of that state, the reasons for those losses, and the possible remedies. The survey indicated that at the present time the New England states are more than holding their place in industry; and while it is to be hoped that cotton textile mills will return to the section, tangible recommendations were made for keeping the industries now in New England and encouraging those trades peculiarly adapted to the region.

Transients

Considerable study has indicated that the transient, crossing and recrossing state lines as he does, creates a problem which can be solved only by the help of the Federal Government. A grant-in-aid program, supplemented by uniform settlement laws by the states and administered by the states within a Federal framework, would offer the best solution. In the meantime, states should make reciprocal arrangements in respect to transients and settlement—as, in February 1939, New York and Vermont, as a result of the work of their co-operation commissions, each agreed to care for the transients of the other if those persons had been in residence one year. Transients in residence less than one year were to be transported back to the city of the state from which they came.

Marriage regulation

Co-operation commissions have continued to take an active interest in marriage regulation, provisions for premarital examination, and marriage evasion laws. An act approved by the New York co-operation committee providing for premarital examination for venereal disease has been accepted by the state of New York and has served as a model for legislation in several other states.

Pollution and flood control

The states in the Delaware River Basin together set up the Interstate Commission on the Delaware River Basin, which now has a permanent office and executive secretary, and is entirely financed by the states concerned. The states in the Ohio and Potomac Basins have likewise set up interstate commissions which have initiated activities toward control of pollution and floods in those areas.

The most pressing problem is probably that of the Delaware; more persons depend upon the Delaware for water, and the water is more polluted. The fact that the river is used as a means of disposal of industrial wastes makes it more difficult, since in recent years the industries have been unwilling to go to the expense of providing proper treatment for their wastes. The Commission has been encouraged by revival of business to believe that the objections of those companies may soon be overcome. In the meantime, subcommittees on quantity and quality of water are preparing the way for rapid action at the earliest possible moment.

A compact drawn by the Ohio River Valley Water Sanitation Compact Commission, working as a subcommittee of the Interstate Commission on the Ohio Basin, was adopted by five states in the Ohio Valley during the recent legislative sessions. Since this is a majority of the basin states, the ultimate adoption of the compact seems assured. West Virginia's ratification is contingent upon acceptance by Pennsylvania, however, so that the compact cannot go into actual operation until that state has acted.

In co-operation with the National Resources Committee and the United States Public Health Service, arrangements have recently been completed for a study of the problems in connection with the Potomac Basin. Plans are in operation for a field and research staff centered in Washington.

EFFECTIVENESS OF COMMISSIONS

About two years ago, in an article on the development of interstate co-operation,[2] the writer asserted that the test of the Commissions on Interstate Co-operation would come when they took the offensive in those economic fields which have too frequently been the strongholds of selfish business and industrial interests. Recent communiqués from this front would indicate that a major offensive in behalf of the public interest is now under way. So far, the co-operation commissions have been tested by the campaign to abolish trade barriers. Self-interested business lobbies have frequently met defeat as a result of the follow-up work of Commis-

[2] "The Development of Interstate Government," *National Municipal Review*, July 1937, pp. 345–51.

sions on Interstate Co-operation since the National Conference on Interstate Trade Barriers held in Chicago in April 1939. It appears that there is strength in numbers, and where a co-operation commission has taken a strong stand against trade barriers in our various legislative halls, this has led to the repeal of existing and the defeat of threatened trade-barrier legislation.

It is true that the co-operation commissions suffer from the inefficiency inherent in the democratic process. Their recommendations must stand the test of legislative consideration, and there undergo the attacks of those whose interests they would contravene. Few partisans would contradict the statement that American business is a victim of that common human failing—a disinclination to face a problem which will not become critical during our own lifetimes. It is understandable that a man whose livelihood depends on fishing is more interested in the maintenance of his own income than he is in the number of fish left in Lake Erie after his fishing is done. Corporation executives whose personal lives are more affected by the cost of installing filtration plants for their waste products than they are by the pollution of the Delaware or the Ohio, can be expected to exert their best efforts to maintain the status quo. It is the part of the co-operation commissions to help to determine the long-term best interests of the country, and to endeavor to bring about the changes necessary for those interests.

It is to be anticipated that the commissions will not be successful in every attempt every time. Indeed, their experience has demonstrated that one well-financed lobby can exert a pressure more potent than a combination of the altruistic best interests of all future generations. In the case of trade barriers, due credit should be given, of course, to the fact that frequently strong lobbies have given support to the efforts of the co-operation commissions to defeat this type of mercantilism.

In the case of fishery conservation legislation, the added weight of strong legislative commissions has proved effective in overcoming the objections of elements in the fishing industry which in the past have bitterly opposed legislation to conserve our fisheries. This is worth public commendation because the fishermen's lobbies have been unusually effective, considering their number, in blocking regulatory measures.

Setbacks have been experienced such as the blocking of enabling legislation providing for three interstate pollution-abatement compacts, by a committee of the Pennsylvania Senate in the closing hours of the session. These compacts applied to three interstate rivers—Ohio, Delaware, and Potomac. The legislatures of Illinois, Indiana, New York, Ohio, and West Virginia approved the Ohio River Compact. Tennessee's legislature met and adjourned before the drive for ratification began; Kentucky's legislature did not meet in 1939. The Delaware River Compact, after receiving the approval of New York and New Jersey, met the same fate, and a Pennsylvania Senate Committee also stopped the Potomac Compact a-borning.

It is regrettable that Pennsylvania's failure to accept the compacts prevents their immediate operation. Representatives of the co-operation commissions are now urging Governor James to add pollution-compact enabling legislation to his call for a special session if one should be called within the next few months.

In handling trucking problems in the Midwest, the commissions have been successful in bringing about agreement among certain states in that section regarding their motor-vehicle regulatory problems. These problems were considered by executive session of officials and co-operation commissioners under the auspices of the Council of State Governments. By past experience the Council learned that any public sessions on this subject degenerated into a furious attack and counterattack by the railroad and trucking interests, with the public official caught between and wildly searching for the nearest bomb-proof shelter.

Conclusion

The Commissions on Interstate Cooperation are daily demonstrating that they can deal with these complicated problems of interstate and Federal-state relationships in a constructive manner. This is shown by the fact that governors and legislatures are constantly handing these problems to them for solution. Previously, expensive interim commissions were set up to deal with these interstate affairs in too often a temporary way which frequently ended in costly litigation, border warfare between states, or continued impasse.

The advantage of having statesmen who are acquainted with the personnel of legislatures and officialdom of other states and who have mastered the techniques of interstate diplomacy—be it compact, reciprocity, uniform legislation, or a gentlemen's agreement—is too apparent for further comment. The cooperation commissions of the Council of State Governments have an additional major advantage: their unbiased interest in the country's welfare has never been questioned. The fact that they are not suspected of partisanship has been an inestimable help to them; public officials approach a discussion of the most controversial issues with a confidence in the Council's fairmindedness which can lead only to a successful solution of the problems involved. The commissions stand on their record, ready to serve the United States, convinced that the future is greater than the past, and that the Nation's interests are those of the most of its citizens.

Hubert R. Gallagher has been assistant director of the Council of State Governments, Chicago, Illinois, since 1938, having served for five years as a staff member of the Council, and for three years as district representative in its New York office. He taught in the School of Citizenship of Syracuse University for two years and at Stanford University, and served as a member of the survey staff on the National Commission on Law Enforcement.

Federal Use of Administrative Areas

By James W. Fesler

REGIONALISM is a term whose very vagueness makes its definition largely a personal matter. Those who are regionalists, it seems to me, progressively embrace the following propositions:

1. Social phenomena, in almost a literal sense, grow out of geographic conditions—climate, soil, topography, subsoil resources.
2. Many social phenomena coincide as to area, thereby creating the homogeneous region.
3. Regional institutions, mores, crafts, art, and literature should be protected against the threats of a monotonous national uniformity.[1]
4. Governmental handling of regional phenomena should be at the regional level, rather than at a national, state, or local level.

The four propositions as stated, are, to my way of thinking, incontrovertible. But each, if pushed too far, can become an absurd assertion. There is no valid geographic version of Calvinistic predestination. Many social phenomena do not coincide as to area. Some regional customs do violence to national standards of justice and should give way to the higher national standards. Establishment of regional governments would so complicate the governmental structure that we should soon tire of being governed by such a logical unit.

[1] This third proposition may mean a nostalgic yearning for return of a region's golden age (as the Southern Agrarians yearn for the antebellum South), or it may mean a strong belief in a future in which each region will contribute something distinctive and worth while to the national life. See Howard W. Odum, *Southern Regions* (1936), and Howard W. Odum and Harry E. Moore, *American Regionalism* (1938).

Analysis of Administrative Areas

Analysis of the administrative areas used by the Federal Government can contribute to an evaluation of the regionalists' position. Some instrumentalities of the Federal Government have divided the country into hundreds of administrative districts. The National Recovery Administration's Retail Code Authority had over 700 local agencies, while its Food and Groceries Code Authority used 110 district agencies and over 600 local agencies.[2] The United States Employment Service has 750 districts.[3] However, such small and numerous districts are, in the case of most agencies, merely subordinate areas of administration. The administrative areas next below Washington are characteristically formed by the grouping of several states in such a manner that the resultant scheme provides for not more than seventeen of these major areas.

The fact that an agency has established a scheme of major administrative areas may have little to do with regionalism. The agency may simply be applying public administration's span-of-control principle. The principle was well phrased by the Brownlow Committee: "The number of immediate subordinates with whom an executive can deal effectively is limited. Just as the hand can cover but a few keys on the piano, so there is for management a limited span of control."[4] Applied to the problem of organizing a bureau's field service, this means that the Washington

[2] Leverett S. Lyon, *et al., The National Recovery Administration* (1935), p. 174.

[3] W. Brooke Graves, "The Future of the American States," *American Political Science Review* 30 (Feb. 1936), p. 37.

[4] President's Committee on Administrative Management, *Report* (1937), p. 34.

official responsible for field operations cannot readily supervise more than a few areal chiefs. Administrative convenience, therefore, has often been the primary motive in establishing a few large areas for field administration.

Although recognition of the regionality of problems has not been the first consideration in creating major administrative areas, it has not been completely absent. Almost willy-nilly, the selection of a city in one state as an areal headquarters makes it inevitable that its region be made up of adjoining states, and this generally means states of similar agricultural and industrial interests, political views, historical traditions, and accents of speech. Where one region stops and another begins is not at all clear;[5] therefore, almost any grouping of adjacent states is per se a recognition in some degree of common regional interests.

Some Federal agencies have been genuinely conscious of regional aspects of administration. The National Resources Committee evidenced such consciousness in the report, *Regional Factors in National Planning and Development* (1935), as did the Agricultural Adjustment Administration in *Regional Problems in Agricultural Adjustment* (1935). The Wage and Hour Division has recently adopted a sixteen-region plan on the basis of a report which said:

The use of regions in administration can be most effective if the areas employed in the operation of the program are carefully determined with the primary objective of combining those groups of people and states with similar conditions and needs.[6]

[5] New England is our best-recognized region. But even there, Connecticut is a part of New York City's commuting area, and Maine, New Hampshire, and Vermont are in many ways distinct from industrial southern New England.

[6] Bernard L. Gladieux, "Determination of Regional Administrative Areas" (June 9, 1939), Part IV of *Field Organization of the Wage*

The committee appointed to prepare a system of administrative areas for the Social Security Board based its recommendations on, *inter alia,* geographical grouping, natural trading areas, industrial and commercial density, and homogeneity of population.[7]

BOUNDARIES OF REGIONS

Although some Federal agencies have been concerned over regionality, they are not agreed on the boundaries to be used for "natural" regions. Of the 106 regional schemes that were in use by the Federal Government in 1935, no two were alike. In a way, this is to be expected; for, in spite of the regionalists' belief in the coincidence of areas of social phenomena, the Cotton Belt, the southern coal area, Atlanta's natural trading area, the Tennessee Valley, and the area of Charleston's social mores are not the same. This being the case, there is no valid reason for expecting a greater uniformity among field organization schemes for dealing with these and other phenomena.[8]

Standardization of administrative regional schemes is occasionally advocated by regionalists as a first step toward recognizing that the homogeneous region's problems should be handled on an integrated regional basis by the Federal, state, and local governments. The Tennessee Valley Authority is one experiment in this direction, and bills have been before Congress for a network of such regional authorities.[9] But even

and Hour Division (typewritten ms., 1939), p. 2.

[7] Cited in Albert H. Rosenthal, *The Use of Administrative Areas and Regional Offices by the Social Security Board and Other Federal Agencies* (typewritten ms., June 1938), pp. 76–81.

[8] This position is elaborated in James W. Fesler, "Standardization of Federal Administrative Regions," *Social Forces* 15 (Oct. 1936), pp. 12–21.

[9] E.g., H.R. 7365 and H.R. 7863 in 75th Cong., 1 Sess. (1937).

the Tennessee Valley Authority goes outside the Valley to distribute its electricity, and thus breaks down the doctrine of regional homogeneity.

Almost twenty years ago, Paul-Émile Cadilhac put vigorously and well the case against standardization of administrative regions:

> ... The regionalists ... have not seen, in fact, that there does not exist one homogeneous region but regions—regions which do not agree among themselves, which overlap and get entangled, which, in a word, are complex and multiple, as life itself. There are in our country [France], for instance, some rudiments and traces of industrial regions, of agricultural, tourist, geographic, and intellectual regions; but these regions do not coincide, they cannot be mingled in a single one, and the immense error of [this] administrative regionalism, which is extolled, exalted, and proposed as the ideal solution, is exactly to misjudge that which exists, to be contrary to life, to wish to discipline that which cannot be disciplined.[10]

Although the boundaries chosen for Federal administrative areas give little aid and comfort to the regionalists, the cities chosen as areal headquarters do provide a fairly definite pattern. New York, Chicago, and San Francisco are most frequently chosen by Federal agencies, and there is considerable agreement also, though in diminishing degree, on Boston, Atlanta, New Orleans, the Twin Cities, Denver, and other cities.

SCOPE OF FEDERAL POWERS

Intergovernmental relations are often thought of in the simple terms of nation-state-local government, with very little attention to the internal features of each government which should affect the vesting of powers. One stereotype, for instance, assumes that the Federal Government operates entirely at Washington, or at least that its field officials are mere myrmidons carrying out the detailed orders of Washington bureaucrats. If this stereotype be in the mind, no intelligent decision can be made as to the powers which properly may lodge with the Federal Government.

The vesting of powers in the Federal Government is attractive where a nationally uniform policy or standard is desirable. This is debatable ground, of course, including as it does such standards as those governing child labor, maximum hours, and minimum wages. Beyond the need for a nationally uniform policy or standard as an argument for increasing the Federal jurisdiction are such factors as the Federal Government's excellent administrative personnel, advanced administrative techniques, and superior financial resources. If to these advantages the Federal Government can add a willingness to deconcentrate its administration wherever possible—that is, to give field officials large discretion to adapt administration to local conditions—the stereotype of a Federal centralized bureaucracy may be supplanted by a more realistic picture.

Deconcentration of national administration has its disadvantages. The multifarious Federal administrative activities cannot be very satisfactorily tied together at field centers. The Federal Co-ordinating Service failed to accomplish this in the 1920's, and more recently the National Emergency Council has failed save with the Works Program agencies.[11] The result is, however, probably less chaotic than would be the case if the states were administering similar functions. In many states the governor lacks control over the numerous agencies headed by constitu-

---

[10] Paul-Émile Cadilhac, *Les Projets de Régionalisme Administratif* (1921), p. 124. Translation mine.

[11] James W. Fesler, "Executive Management and the Federal Field Service," in President's Committee on Administrative Management, *Report with Special Studies* (1937), pp. 279-87.

tional officers or by commissions protected against removal. Federal field administration, on the other hand, profits from the fact that at Washington the President effectively controls the agencies with the largest field activities, and this central co-ordination of programs is reflected in the work of the field officials.

There is as yet no objective method of measuring degrees of deconcentration. Among the agencies that reserve to Washington detailed control of field operations can generally be included the Public Works Administration, the Bureau of Internal Revenue, the Bureau of Narcotics, the Children's Bureau, and the United States Public Health Service. But the Bureau of Customs, the Bureau of Public Roads, the Forest Service, and the Secret Service tend to vest discretionary powers in their field agents.[12] The Wage and Hour Division has instituted a regional scheme characterized, according to Administrator Andrews, by "limited decentralization," [13] and the Social Security Board has frequently expressed an intention to delegate extensive authority to its regional directors and regional representatives.

FACTORS AFFECTING DECONCENTRATION

Varying considerations determine the degree to which a bureau should deconcentrate. If the central officials are under civil service and the field officials are patronage appointees, a concentration of power at Washington is desirable.[14] If the activity is one that is unusually open to the danger of corruption and graft, concentration is again the answer.[15] Extreme deconcentration is inadvisable, furthermore, if policies and standards must be uniform to the last detail throughout the country.[16] On the other hand, if the function is one that is affected by local and regional variations, a deconcentration of authority is desirable.[17] If the agency's function is principally that of promotion and personal contact, deconcentration is essential.[18]

There is a vital connection between deconcentration and the use of administrative areas. Deconcentration of a bureau's work can be successful only if the field agents have a clear conception of their respective duties. In other words, a bureau's field officials must not be allowed to tread on one another's toes. The best way to prevent this digital disaster is to mark out the areas within which each official may move. The need for clear demarcation of such administrative areas increases in direct ratio to the increase of deconcentration.

[12] This rough classification is based in part on information in Carroll B. Shaw, *Administrative Control of Field Services in the United States Treasury Department* (abstract of thesis, 1933), and in Albert H. Rosenthal, *op. cit.*

[13] U. S. Department of Labor, Wage and Hour Division, Press Release, July 1, 1939.

[14] Shaw observed that this principle was followed in the Bureau of Customs and the Bureau of Internal Revenue. Carroll B. Shaw, *op. cit.*, p. 10.

[15] Since public construction is traditionally a happy hunting ground for corruptionists, the Public Works Administration is highly concentrated.

[16] E.g., the General Counsel for the Wage and Hour Division cannot very readily delegate to the Regional Attorneys the function of interpreting the Fair Labor Standards Act and regulations issued thereunder.

[17] During the World War the Remount Branch of the War Department drew up a blueprint for construction of stables, and ordered stables constructed in accordance therewith in Oklahoma, Montana, and Virginia. Because of the different climatic and topographic conditions of these sites, the requirement of uniformity had some unfortunate results on the life span of horses and mules stabled in the structures.

[18] The Regional Advisors of the War Industries Board, engaged in promoting coöperation of manufacturers and business men with the military supply agencies of the Government, could not be directed from Washington in any detailed fashion.

Summary

The Federal Government has tended to use regions (usually groups of states) as its major administrative areas. This tendency has resulted in part from application of the span-of-control principle, and in part from recognition of the regionality of social phenomena. These administrative areas, regional or not, offer the framework for increased deconcentration of administrative authority in the Federal Government. Such deconcentration constitutes a significant alternative to bureaucratic, centralized administration at Washington, and as well to chaotic, decentralized administration by the forty-eight states.

James W. Fesler, Ph.D., is associate professor of political science at the University of North Carolina, Chapel Hill, and consultant to the National Resources Planning Board. He has served on the staffs of the National Resources Committee and the President's Committee on Administrative Management, and is the author of monographs and articles in the fields of administrative organization and public personnel.

Voluntary Regionalism in the Control of Water Resources

By David W. Robinson

IF A region may be loosely defined as any area selected for a purpose, a river basin is a natural delimitation for use as a conservation area. Such an area, one in which the resource problem is similar, is for our purposes, the *region*.

The drainage basin is a natural and compact unit; it is a problem area bounding a set of physical conditions which have always affected social and economic possibilities. That it is not an optimum region to the geographer, the planner, the economist, the sociologist, or the political scientist, is true but for the present purpose unimportant, since we are more interested in the matter of *organization* for regionalism—in the types of structural machinery which have been developed to evolve a co-ordination and co-operation of governmental and administrative units.

In this somewhat specialized field of conservation, with particular emphasis on unified water-resources control, there has developed a popular approach to the problem of regionalism.[1] It may be that from the organizations and techniques which are now being demonstrated in scattered sections of the Nation, among different sets of governmental units, in widely varying forms and methods of application, there may be derived generalizations which may be removed from their regional settings and recast to fit other regions, for other purposes. The structure and the method in this field should not be restricted, as, indeed, they are not restricted but related to the much larger field of general regional planning.[2]

Functions

To evaluate the kinds of organization which have been developed to effect unified control of interstate rivers, it is important to realize that such projects have grown steadily in size, in importance, and in complexity over the years. Control of floods has become more and more imperative; domestic water supplies continue to demand greater and more dependable water resources; industries are constantly using larger amounts of water in manufacturing processes; water pollution and sanitation problems insistently press for solution; water power is being sought for and developed more and more; navigation demands greater depth and more uniform conditions; fish and other aquatic life are increasingly valued commercially and by the sportsman; recreational areas are needed and must be developed with the increase of leisure time and improvements in transportation.

How to meet these many and divergent demands upon an interstate stream is, in brief, the problem of unified water-resources control, the function of regionalism in this field. One thing is certain: the protection and enjoyment of the natural resources of our major drainage basins cannot be left to the individual states and their local communities. What were once independent problems

---

[1] *The Regional Approach to the Conservation of Natural Resources,* Bulletin of the University of Wisconsin, Serial No. 2341, General Series 2125, Sept. 1938.

[2] The notable pioneer study, *Regional Factors in National Planning and Development,* prepared and published through the National Resources Committee, includes a series of investigations and analyses particularly pertinent to this discussion of voluntary regionalism.

now affect such a wide variety of interests and communities that complete freedom of action must now give way to some type of co-operation. The present problem must be weighed against the future; specific need against general advantage; the single end against multi-purpose development; local benefit against regional good.

TYPES OF ORGANIZATION

The gradual, halting, varied evolution of water-resources control clearly indicates that some kind of interstate or superstate control is essential. Three plans have been developed, each of which has advantages and disadvantages, special promises, and special dangers. The first two of these, which will be briefly indicated, involve a diminution of state sovereignty as we have it today; the third involves a sharing of such sovereignty among the states, and, to a very limited extent, between those states and the Federal Government.

The first and simplest of these plans, from the administrative standpoint, involves turning over the administration of interstate streams to the Federal Government. In 1933 the Federal Government first took steps to assume control of interstate river systems. In the Tennessee Valley and in the Pacific Northwest, at Bonneville and Grand Coulee, ample evidence exists that the present National Administration views the control of interstate streams as a Federal function, to be directed by Federal appointees, to be paid for by Federal funds.

Obviously, the stages of development through which these experiments have passed up to this time typify a new sort of planning, a new approach to regionalism. Just as obviously, and unfortunately, the regionalism concept which lies behind these demonstrations has been horizoned by the power aspect, and there are many who believe that these extensions of Federal control have brought us no closer to the development of administrative and financial procedures applicable to regional development in general.

This method of river control, imposed on the states from above, has some benefits and some serious limitations. It is not within the range of this paper to discuss either.[3]

A second plan would place the administration of interstate streams under the authority of autonomous agencies created by interstate compacts. This approach to regionalism would project certain state powers upward, or vertically, to a new governmental level intrusting the administration and control of the resources of an interstate drainage basin to a superstate authority. Such autonomous administration is not historically characteristic of the compact device, which has not proved to be an effective instrument when the subject matter involves social and economic, as well as physical, planning. The Port of New York Authority and the Colorado River Compact, as popular examples, have been restricted by a lack of adequate authority and opportunity for initiative, flexibility, and experimentation.

Such criticism clearly implies, however, that when, under the terms of an interstate compact, two or more states project certain of their powers upward so that they focus at some point above the state level but below the Federal level, the regional organization thus created would not differ essentially from the Federal corporation-authority de-

[3] For a discussion of the advantages and disadvantages of Federal control and administration of interstate river systems, see *Toward Unity*, a series of addresses presented at the Second Regional Conference of the Interstate Commission on the Delaware River Basin, Broad Street Station Building, Philadelphia, December 1937, with particular reference to the remarks of Dr. Arthur E. Morgan, pp. 18–28.

vice. Such a superstructure, through which any set of states, with the approval of Congress, would agree to transfer powers of control and administration to a joint agency, would become in fact a legal and administrative unit possessed of corporate powers sufficient to place it beyond the bounds of either state or Federal domination.

A third plan of regional organization suggests a pooling of the governmental and administrative resources of individual states, complemented by the advice and counsel of Federal agencies, under an informal, purely voluntary, functional arrangement. As distinguished from the two types mentioned previously, it attempts to project certain sovereign state powers laterally at the same governmental level, and vertically to the Federal level.

Other articles in this volume have reviewed recent developments in the field of interstate relations. The pattern which now affords the states a means for co-operating with one another, through Commissions on Interstate Co-operation, tied together nationally by the Council of State Governments, has been described. Using this co-operative machinery as a nucleus, interstate commissions—on the Delaware, Ohio, and Potomac River Basins—have been established during the past few years to test the plan of voluntary regionalism.

INCODEL: MACHINERY

In February 1936 the Pennsylvania Commission on Interstate Co-operation called a regional conference, to meet in Philadelphia, on the water-resources problems of the Delaware River Basin. As a result of that conference it was decided that from the membership of the Commissions on Interstate Co-operation in this region, there should be drawn, in each state, one Senator, one Representative, one administrative official, and one member of each state's Planning Board, who should center their combined energies on the problem of conservation, development, and control of the natural resources of the Delaware River Basin.[4]

Under the name of the Interstate Commission on the Delaware River Basin, shortened and popularized as Incodel, governmental machinery was thereby created within the region:

A. To serve as a fact-co-ordinating body and to develop the means and procedure by which the general plans and policies proposed for the development of the region may be carried out;
B. To sponsor the carrying out of properly developed plans which result from surveys and research concerning population, land and water resources and uses, and other related subjects;
C. To co-ordinate the activities of the Commissions on Interstate Co-operation and their joint agency, the Council of State Governments, with the work of appropriate state and Federal agencies for the prevention and abatement of pollution, for flood control, and for the proper general use and control of the waters of the Dalaware River.
D. To encourage interstate compacts and the enactment of uniform state laws for the abatement of water pollution, for flood control and for the proper general use and control of the waters of the Delaware River.
E. To advance, perpetuate, and outline the work recommended by its conferences, and to develop and propose new objectives.

Another section of the Articles of Organization reads: "The Commission requests the co-operation of the Federal Government, through its appropriate agencies, to the fullest possible extent."

The major problems which have been

---

[4] Citations to acts creating Commissions on Interstate Co-operation: Delaware, *Laws*, 1938, No. 69; New Jersey, *Laws*, 1936, Chap. 21; New York, *Laws*, 1937, Chap. 900; and Pennsylvania, *Public Laws*, 1937, No. 35.

dealt with by Incodel up to this time, water pollution and water supply, have been subjected to study by a host of official and private agencies over the past fifty years. Countless costly surveys and studies of these difficulties have been made. Numerous plans have been drawn up and discarded or ignored.[5] Practically without exception, the conclusions and recommendations of this research activity have pointed to the interstate character of the problems involved and the need for concurrent or reciprocal legislation in each of the four states. Because of this constant tendency of plans to require legislative and administrative action, the planners, legislators, and administrators who compose the Interstate Commission on the Delaware River Basin are in an admirable position to make effective a practical program.

All the activities of the Commission are carried on in co-operation with agencies of the four state governments, with Federal bureaus, and with local governments within the Basin. Through its organization on the subcommittee pattern, the Commission is continuously making use of more than a score of Federal and state agencies engaged in some phase of activity related to water-resources use and control in this drainage basin. Through the appointment of advisory members to the Commission, every effort is being made to enlist the services of all those within the four-state region who are qualified to participate in the molding of a joint program for the betterment of existing conditions.

While it is, in fact, a joint governmental agency of the states of Delaware, New Jersey, New York, and Pennsylvania, financed entirely through appropriations from these states, the Commission neither holds nor seeks administrative powers; it attempts to supplement, rather than to supplant in any way, the work of existing water-resources agencies.

The sections which follow illustrate some of the planning activities and a few of the accomplishments of the Interstate Commission on the Delaware River Basin. They are cited here as a record of effective co-operation among governmental units of all levels in this region, and might be duplicated in part from the record of the Interstate Commissions on the Ohio Basin and the Potomac Basin.

INTERSTATE-REGIONAL PLANNING

The first advisory committee organized to assist Incodel in developing a broad program of conservation and development of the Basin's resources was composed of the chairmen and directors of the State Planning Boards in the area involved and the assistant executive officer of the newly named National Resources Planning Board. Co-ordinate planning of Federal and state development programs is the objective.

Three parallel activities have been directed by this group during the past three years: (1) the advancement of comprehensive state planning studies for each state located in the Basin; (2) the compilation, mapping, and tabulation of pertinent data concerning existing conditions and trends in the Basin; and (3) the formulation of a program of current activities to be carried forward and stimulated by the Commission while longer-range plans are in course of preparation.

Highlighting these planning activities during the past year was the preparation of a program for the states, counties, municipalities, and citizens of the

---

[5] A summation of official activity in the four states on the single problem of water supply is included in *A Chronology of Water Supply Problems of New York City, Philadelphia, and Northeastern New Jersey*, prepared by the Interstate Commission on the Delaware River Basin, Philadelphia, 1938. Mimeo.

Upper Delaware Valley, looking toward the conservation and protection of natural resources, toward the protection and improvement of recreational facilities and scenic assets, toward protection and improvement of highways, toward more adequate and effective planning and zoning, and toward promotion and education.[6]

Field work undertaken by Incodel with the direction of its Advisory Committee on Planning has sought to translate those recommendations into action. For this purpose a council on intertown co-operation has been organized in the Upper Delaware Valley, and the logical planning process, "from the bottom up . . . ," is being popularized.

WATER QUALITY

An Advisory Committee on the Quality of Water in the Delaware River Basin is composed of the chief engineers of the Health Departments of the states of Delaware, New Jersey, New York, and Pennsylvania. For the first time, these administrative agents, who are the responsible officials in each of the state governments for the correction and control of water pollution, have been meeting together each month, pooling their knowledge and the resources of their departments in a unified, concerted attack on the problem of water pollution.

A Reciprocal Agreement for the Correction and Control of Pollution in the Waters of the Interstate Delaware River was drafted by the members of this Committee, approved by the Commission, and subsequently ratified, formally, by each of the four State Departments of Health.[7] In substance, the states have jointly agreed to a code of specifications to be followed by communities and industries of the Basin in respect to the treatment and disposal of wastes.

Companion to the above agreement, a construction schedule for municipalities on the interstate stream was devised and agreed upon, setting time limits within which all needed improvements shall have been made.

The administration of this schedule is calling for negotiation and voluntary co-operation on the part of municipalities within the watershed. This support has not been lacking. Through the co-operation of the neighboring states and their local subdivisions has come a coordinated system of water-pollution control developed by the governmental officials of the affected states for the benefit of the region.

WATER SUPPLY

Another advisory committee is considering the extremely vital question of the quantity of the water in the Delaware River and its tributaries. Practical planning for future water supplies for the metropolitan areas of New York City, northeastern New Jersey, and the Philadelphia region is essential. In the three metropolitan centers cited above, local sources have become inadequate or unsuitable, and new sources of water supply for domestic purposes have been under consideration for decades.

This need has not been so acute in New Jersey and Pennsylvania as in New York City, which in 1929 proceeded with plans it had developed to divert 600 million gallons of water from New York tributaries of the Upper Delaware River. This action brought on the now famed Delaware River Case, in which the State of New Jersey sought to enjoin

---

[6] The Interstate Commission on the Delaware River Basin, *The Upper Valley*, printed pamphlet, Series B, No. 2, 1939.

[7] The Interstate Commission on the Delaware River Basin, *Water Pollution*, printed pamphlet, Series B, No. 1, 1938; see also, An Act to Promote Interstate Co-operation for the Conservation and Protection of Water Resources in the Delaware River Basin, New York, *Laws*, 1939, Chap. 600, and New Jersey, *Laws*, 1939, Chap. 146.

the State of New York and the City of New York from carrying out their plans. Pennsylvania entered the case as intervenor to protect its own legal rights.

Two years and hundreds of thousands of dollars were spent by the disputants before a decision was reached.[8] The decree of the United States Supreme Court in that case set a new precedent for governing interstate streams, based upon the principle of equitable allocation of interstate waters. New York was permitted to divert 440 million gallons of water a day, providing certain conditions were met. The decree did not determine the quantity of water permissible for future use by the other two states, although it stipulated that the New York diversion did not constitute a prior appropriation or give New York any superiority of right over New Jersey and Pennsylvania in the use of the waters of the Delaware River or its tributaries.[9]

The water-supply problems of the Delaware River Basin were not settled by the Supreme Court decision. New York City, northeastern New Jersey, and the Philadelphia metropolitan area still have imminent water-supply problems to meet.[10]

The Incodel Advisory Committee on the Quantity of Water in the Delaware River Basin, composed of the chief engineers of the water policy and control agencies of the four state governments, has as its foremost task the development of an interstate agreement as to the rights and responsibilities of the four interested states in the water resources of the basin, particularly for use as domestic water supplies.[11]

The Supreme Court has said that the Delaware River can be utilized, under reasonable restrictions, for the benefit of all four states. The drafting of these reasonable restrictions is the subject of the negotiations now under way by the members of the Incodel Advisory Committee on Quantity. The Committee is not considering an equitable division of these waters in the sense of attempting to arrive at allocations of fixed quantities to each of the states concerned; it is attempting to arrive at a formula for agreement as to the conditions under which any state through its subdivisions can take water from this interstate stream for water-supply purposes.

It may not be possible to draft an all-inclusive, hard-and-fast rule or formula which will cover all possible situations; but it should be possible for the members of the Incodel Advisory Committee on Quantity, representing the responsible water-resources agencies of each of the states, to agree upon the general conditions under which diversions of water from the Delaware River Basin may

[8] 283 U. S. 336. Other cases which establish governing principles of law relating to interstate waters include: Kansas v. Colorado, 206 U. S. 46; Wyoming v. Colorado, 259 U. S. 419; Connecticut v. Massachusetts, 282 U. S. 660; New York v. Illinois, 274 U. S. 488; and Arizona v. California *et al.*, 283 U. S. 423.

[9] For a full discussion of the law of interstate waters and its application to the Delaware River Case, see Thaddeus Merriman and Frank E. Winsor, with appended discussion, *Journal* of the New England Water Works Association, Vol. XLV, No. 3, 1931.

[10] Duane E. Minard, counsel for New Jersey in the Delaware River Case, discussed the future of water allocation and developments in interstate agreements, in the *Journal* of the American Water Works Association, Vol. 29, No. 7, 1937. Based upon his knowledge of interstate water law and his experience in the Delaware River Case, Mr. Minard concludes:

"The real question that confronts us is broader than strict legal rights. A court is not the best place to decide questions of policy, or the allocation or distribution of interstate waters. Litigation may, or may not, stop a given project, but cannot fully solve such problems."

[11] The Interstate Commission on the Delaware River Basin, *A Survey and Report, on the interstate aspects of the proposal to utilize waters of the Delaware River as a source of metropolitan water supply for the State of New Jersey*, mimeographed, Series A, No. 32, 1939.

take place, and perhaps provide that some continuing co-ordinating control should be exercised by an interstate body to provide for unforeseen contingencies and to permit flexibility.

Such an agreement on the part of the representatives of the four states of the Delaware River Basin, and such a continuing administrative agency, would make it possible for the states to be protected from blundering into controversy because of suspicions or a lack of co-ordinating machinery: the neighboring sovereignties would be currently informed of prospective plans of action, so that progress could be made as public necessity demands without conflict, without economic loss, and without the tremendous cost of legal controversy.

INFORMATION AND RESEARCH

A fourth major field of operations has been under the leadership of an Advisory Committee on Information and Research, composed of representatives from leading educational institutions within the Basin and a limited number of technicians from Federal and state agencies. This Committee originated a program designed to establish Incodel as a clearing house of information and research on the Basin and its problems. A bibliographical classification system covering the literature of the Delaware River Basin has been scientifically prepared and installed, and is currently maintained.[12]

A summary-analysis of all hydrologic research being carried on in the Basin has been completed, with the result that a program for future research in this field and the agencies to which such research should be intrusted, has been formulated and is being carried out in co-operation with numerous Federal and state agencies with as much dispatch as possible.

CONCLUSIONS

The four states of the Delaware River Basin have agreed to act in unison toward a common end. This extension of state powers has not involved the creation of a superimposed governmental structure; it has not entailed the addition of a new set of governmental officials; new governmental machinery, established by marked increases in legislation, has not been necessary; no new fields of activity have been created.

The impetus, the groundwork of organization, financial and legislative support, technical and advisory services—every feature of the organization and operation of the Interstate Commission on the Delaware River Basin has been a product of joint action by the states, voluntarily working with one another and with such agencies of the Federal Government as are involved.

It is obvious that the success or failure of this experiment in voluntary regionalism depends wholly upon effective collaboration between and among the officials and agencies involved. One of the major features of this experiment is to confirm the interest, the devotion, and the competence of state officials to carry forward to a successful conclusion an interstate project for the benefit of the Basin, the region, and the Nation.

The weakness of voluntary regionalism lies in the weakness of the states' wills. Each of the state governments participating in this enterprise acts through individuals to whom it gives authority. If any state or any authorized representative of a state is not willing to bear a share of the Commission's work or to agree in the programs which have been co-operatively formulated, the work of all is to that extent crippled.

The Interstate Commission on the

[12] The Interstate Commission on the Delaware River Basin, *A Basic Classification for Literature Relating to the Delaware River Basin*, mimeographed, Series A, No. 27, 1938.

Delaware River Basin has attempted to advance this experiment in voluntary regionalism by taking into account the total resources of the area and the manner in which these resources are associated. As a public agency, dependent for continuing existence upon public acceptance as represented by appropriations through the four state legislatures, the Commission has purposely limited its activities to a solution of those specific and intricate problems of land and water use and control which are of regional importance, which are most urgently needed, and which will be immediately useful. The organization and its method imply that negotiations which lead to the formulation of policy will involve compromise on the part of all interested parties. But the Commission has held, and by reason of some success still believes, that with sound facts upon which to base conclusions there should be no insuperable difficulty in arriving at decisions both immediately and prospectively fair to all concerned.

Incodel has attempted to secure the best judgment available in the states and apply it to the problems involved in the use and development of the water resources of the interstate stream involved. In no case has that judgment been unduly influenced by political, sectional, or scientific prejudices. While there may be room for differences of opinion on the subject; the co-operating states have felt that *joint* action through their established officers and agencies was more to be desired than action by an independent superstate agency, whether established by the states themselves or by the Federal Government.

David W. Robinson has been executive secretary of the Interstate Commission on the Delaware River Basin, Philadelphia, Pennsylvania, since its organization in June 1936. He served as research assistant at the Cincinnati Bureau of Governmental Research during 1933–34, after which he became a staff member of the Council of State Governments.

Interregional Relations

By Elwyn A. Mauck

A MAJOR phenomenon in the development of the United States has been the process whereby thirteen struggling colonies have evolved into one of the great powers of the modern world. Their struggle for survival required co-operation, and co-operation necessitated the relinquishment of the right of autonomous decision and action. When their first co-operative system of government guaranteeing the sovereignty of the constituent states proved defective, delegates from most of the units assembled once again "for amiable argument," and the result was the proposal and adoption of a substitute system establishing "a more perfect Union."

The plan of government envisioned by the Fathers of the Constitution represented both an ideal and a working reality. It has endured for a century and a half, although not without tensions that have tested the bond of unity to the breaking point. In addition to the cohesive elements of the Union there have developed also strong centrifugal forces tending to split it into sundry interest groups. The result of the development of such forces has been conflict, usually hortatory but on one occasion sanguinary in nature. The fears of the framers of the Constitution that the large states would align themselves against the interests of the small proved groundless. The opposing parties became identified instead with geographic areas, and at times the resultant sectional struggles bade fair to destroy the Union.

Of the scholars who have investigated the impact of the areal conflict on the course of American development, Professor Frederick Jackson Turner stands in the vanguard. By his studies of the American frontier and more particularly by his collection of papers published in 1932 on the influence of sections in America, Professor Turner has made a most valuable contribution to the proper understanding of the forces behind sectional conflict.[1] He has stimulated much discussion in academic circles, but of the validity of his major thesis there is no longer any doubt. Many other scholars have contributed to the subject by offering additional data or suggesting modifications. In the future, students in history, political science, and many allied fields will find a fertile subject of discourse in the significance of differences arising between geographic areas.

Sectional Conflicts

The major sectional conflicts in American history are revealed quite readily. Within a decade of the inauguration of the Constitution sectional differences resulted in the formulation of the Virginia and Kentucky Resolutions and, a short time later, in the calling of the Hartford Convention. The most colorful and disastrous conflict was that which culminated in the Civil War. A cotton economy, or rather a cotton culture, geographically united, found itself challenged by opposing interests, and the dilemma was resolved in force and bloodshed. The history of tariff legislation has been a dramatic story of sectional conflict. Antagonisms could be reconciled only after representatives of strategic sections were satisfied that the interests of their constituents had been duly considered. The sectional question has become a subject of major importance in Federal grants-in-aid. It was a matter that received judicial cogni-

[1] F. J. Turner, *The Significance of Sections in American History*, New York, 1932.

zance in the maternity-aid cases,[2] where the United States Supreme Court rejected the reasoning of Massachusetts counsel that the legislation placed an undue burden on one section in order to pay grants in another. Since the decision, the growth of Federal grants for multitudinous purposes has multiplied the evil complained of manyfold.

The sectional conflict developed again in similar form in the agricultural program of the New Deal. Since the large consuming population was found in the East, the organs of opinion of that region became the most vociferous champions of the individualistic rights of farmers. In 1936 the United States Supreme Court declared the first agricultural act unconstitutional[3] on the grounds that it imposed a burden on one group for the benefit of another, or, in other words, because it transferred wealth from one section to another. Further contemporary evidence of sectional conflict is revealed in the controversy involving differentials in freight rates. It is asserted that the manufacturing interests of the East have secured favored treatment. The Interstate Commerce Commission is conducting sectional hearings at the present time in an effort to find a solution to the difficult problems involved.

Preservation of Unity

It is evident that if the unity of the Nation is to endure, areal conflict must be replaced either by the complete ascendancy of some regions or by compromise, conciliation, and co-operation. That the Nation has survived gives proof of the fact that mutual areal concessions have been made. Co-operation as well as conflict does exist among the geographic units. The ideal of union as expressed by the framers of the Constitution has been translated into reality. While the concept of sectionalism carries the connotation of conflict, the existence of which there can be no doubt, there is also abundant proof of the subordination of areal interests to those of the Nation. To the co-operative area, as a reality and as an ideal, there has been applied the term "region." Both sectionalism and regionalism continue to be realities, but the latter includes the ideal of national unity. Such unity is preserved only through the recognition that national interests are paramount and must be preserved through co-operative effort.

The superior position of the central government to protect the national interests has not always been conceded, but now it is universally recognized as essential to the general well-being. The interests of sections, states, and local communities have been relegated to a subordinated place. The terms "local self-government" and "states' rights" are still used, but they belong to political institutions founded a century and a half ago. Today they are frequently shibboleths employed to prevent the re-examination and abandonment of institutions that have become outmoded. Sections, not having clearly defined political boundaries, have not invented terms for similar purposes, but instead they have adopted those already well known. The term "states' rights" often is found useful, not in protecting the interests of a single state but in confusing the issue in sectional conflicts. Local leaders when asserting the rights of states are frequently acting merely as spokesmen for sectional interests.

Confusion Regarding Regionalism

The trend toward regionalism operates not only from the smaller units but also from the National Government through the process of decentralization.

[2] Massachusetts v. Mellon and Frothingham v. Mellon, 262 U. S. 447 (1923).
[3] United States v. Butler, 297 U. S. 1 (1936).

There are more than a hundred instances in which the National Administration has divided the country into regions for purposes of management.[4] The boundaries as now established by the various administrative agencies present a very confusing picture, but potentially, the greatest degree of co-operation among regions could exist under this system of subnationalization. Since all the units are under the direct control of the National Government, co-operation enforced from above would be capable of the greatest degree of effectiveness.

The present confusion of the administrative agencies of the National Government is matched by that of the academicians. A wide diversity of opinion exists among them in regard to the elements that should be considered in formulating regional boundaries. An apparent majority are of the belief that the country could be divided into a limited number of geographic and cultural regions and that governmental units could in general be established on the same basis. Others believe that the administrative regions must remain primarily unifunctional, since the logical boundaries for the various activities of government necessarily differ. Some students of the problem hold that a region should be marked by diversity rather than uniformity, for in such diversity could be found the greatest degree of local self-sufficiency. Under such a plan the need for close interregional relations would be minimized and the trend would be toward sectional distrust and antagonism. However, the general conception of the region is that of a homogeneous area, uniform in its characteristics, and distinguishable from others by its cultural and geographic features. This type of region accentuates interdependence and stimulates close co-operation.

REGIONAL INTERDEPENDENCE

Some practical aspects of regional interdependence and co-operation are shown in dramatic fashion by activities in the United States Congress. When Congress puts the national interest ahead of that of any subdivision, it is recognizing the existence of such mutual dependence. When certain members band together to pass "pork barrel" legislation, they also are co-operationists, although entertaining a limited point of view. When the legislators representing several regions unite in a somewhat more permanent union, such as the Farm Bloc union of Midwest and South of the early 1920's, they too are engaged in interregional co-operation.

It does not follow that all such conflicts or evidences of co-operation indicate the existence of purely areal problems to be solved solely on the regional level. In many cases the change required is that of public attitude. Thus, the establishment of tariff rates remains a national question irrespective of the amount of sectional conflict it contains. The establishment of railway freight rates must have its final authority in the National Government, as must such questions as Federal grants-in-aid, relief, and the agricultural program. The functions of regional agencies in these matters can go no further than conducting research and acting in an advisory capacity. The co-operative features can lie only in the voluntary efforts of the respective regions, but true coordination would remain the function of the central government.

REGIONAL ORGANIZATION

Interregional co-operation on the subnational level can be found only in the activities of the states, for the machinery of regional administration is too

[4] J. W. Fesler, "Federal Administrative Regions," *American Political Science Review*, Vol. XXX (April 1936), pp. 257–68.

meager and recent to furnish similar material. Much has been accomplished and much more is anticipated through such instruments as interstate organizations, agreements, compacts, and similar devices.

In regional development the initial step—that of creating planning boards—has been taken in only two instances. Such boards are now in existence for the New England Region and the Pacific Northwest. Both regional boards are composed of members of the state planning boards within the respective areas, with a representative of the National Resources Planning Board acting as chairman in each case. This evidence of interstate co-operation may be found useful in guiding the formation of interregional machinery. Committees composed of members of the respective boards could be established to direct the joint activities of the co-operating regions.

A plan more ambitious and specific in its purposes is embodied in the creation of the Tennessee Valley Authority. It is a tremendous undertaking attempting to rehabilitate the population of a huge river basin. The governmental machinery, although created by Federal authority, is fairly autonomous within the limits set by statute. Being the only regional unit in the area, its problems in co-operation have been primarily those involved in negotiations with local governments and private utilities; but its interregional influences will be augmented greatly if, by example, it stimulates activity leading to the creation of similar projects elsewhere. Such projects already have been contemplated for the Mississippi River Basin and other areas.

The National Resources Committee, in its studies of regionalism in the United States, made the tentative suggestion that the country be divided into ten or more regions for all Federal administrative purposes.[5] Central cities were to be designated in each of the regions, and the boundaries, although real, were to remain flexible, thus being expansible or contractable as the nature of the function warranted. It was recognized that boundary lines under this arrangement might interweave and overlap and cause confusion, but the Committee believed that conflicting jurisdiction and duplication of work could be avoided by careful co-operation of the respective regional units.

Professor W. Y. Elliott of Harvard University has outlined reforms considerably more drastic.[6] He has suggested the creation of regional units, to be called commonwealths, whose primary function would be the execution of Federal law. Each commonwealth, however, would have its elected executive and a single-chambered legislative body. Since apparently the commonwealth governments would exist to implement Federal legislation, the co-ordinating element would emanate from the central government, thus minimizing the need for co-operation in the field.

Professors Odum and Moore have suggested the creation of regional and subregional planning bodies to supplement existing national, state, county, municipal, and special boards.[7] The regional board would be composed of members of planning bodies within the area, several delegates at large, and a representative of the national planning board. The authors explain that a major function of the regional organization would be that of serving as buffer between the national and state planning bodies. In other words, the regional boards would attempt to secure co-

[5] National Resources Committee, *Regional Factors in National Planning and Development*, Washington, 1935.
[6] W. Y. Elliott, *The Need for Constitutional Reform* (New York, 1935), pp. 191–204.
[7] H. W. Odum and H. E. Moore, *American Regionalism* (New York, 1938), pp. 272 f.

operation among all the planning groups.

Fields of Co-operation

Whatever type of regional organization might be created, there would be no dearth of problems for it to solve. For some such problems, the ideal solution would lie in the co-operative effort of regions. Thus, any act on the part of man affecting the amount or direction of flow of rivers of the United States, the amount of sediment they carry, the purity of the water, or the navigability of the stream has a very direct effect on those living in neighboring regions. Irrigation, municipal water supply, sewage disposal, navigation, and hydroelectric power are necessarily subjects requiring interregional co-operation.

Not only in the matter of navigable rivers, but also in the utilization of products of mine, farm, forest, and factory, interregional co-operation should be established to secure their most equitable distribution. As long as regions continue to be differentiated by the basic commodities they produce, the efforts of co-operation would be directed at securing the greatest degree of freedom in their interchange. Better transportation facilities, local processing, and a reduction in the number of middlemen would be some of the problems to be solved co-operatively. A continuation and accentuation of regional specialization would be encouraged, although not to the extent of suppressing valuable counter movements. Thus, interregional planning would determine how far agricultural diversification should be stimulated for the stability it would offer the individual farmer, miner, or factory hand. Specialization for maximum utilization as weighed against the security of diversification would be a major problem confronting the interregional planners.

Not only commodities in the usual sense of the term, but also the commodity of labor has become an interregional problem. When advertisements of southern states invite northern capital to the region of "reasonable" labor, the problem is revealed in one of its more vicious forms. Although the potential force of human labor should be fully utilized, to invite its exploitation is a sad commentary on the insight and ethical standards of the political leaders who sponsor such policies. Migratory workers and itinerant families create problems whose ideal solution can be found only in the closest co-operation among regions. The conditions under which this group of people work and live (as portrayed in a recent "best seller"[8]) is a disgrace to modern civilization. If migratory workers are found necessary to our economic society, the regions should co-operate in stimulating an orderly flow and in providing the minimum standards necessary to decency in living. The current practice of filling the migrant's gasoline tank to encourage him to "move along" on his aimless journey solves nothing. While mobility of labor within an area would remain a problem of the regional government, mobility among different areas should be solved by interregional co-operation. Only in this way can the obligations of the region be defined and the needs of the migrant satisfied.

Another field requiring co-operative effort is that of protection of migratory game. The natural hazards of the semiannual journey between the feeding grounds of Saskatchewan and the marshes of Louisiana should not be augmented by indiscriminate slaughter. State laws and international treaties have been of great value, but since the flight of game is interregional, responsibility for its protection could be logically placed on the same basis.

[8] John Steinbeck, *The Grapes of Wrath*, New York, 1939.

Other fields of possible co-operation need not be listed, for they are ever changing and expanding. As the techniques of civilization evolve, regional interdependence is increased. The development of rapid transportation facilities promotes trade, and trade encourages specialization. Specialization means dependence. Modern communication facilities permit the receiving of information and the placing of orders in distant regions on a scale hitherto unknown. Regional interdependence is a reality, and interregional co-operation a growing necessity.

Alternative to Co-operation

An alternative to interregional co-operation lies in the continuation of the transfer of functions to the National Government. Some may deplore while others justify the trend, some may resist and others encourage it, but apparently nothing will stop the inexorable movement. It is the usual practice that whenever the state government appears inadequate to cope with a problem because of its size, the function is transferred to the Nation, even though it be primarily regional in nature. Such transference marks a step in overcentralization. The National Government is expected to solve problems in which it is not primarily interested. Most effective resistance to the movement toward overcentralization would lie in a demonstration of the adequacy of the states or regions to cope with the problems presented. Such a demonstration could be given through the co-operation of the units involved.

The establishment of machinery of interregional co-operation would be an ideal solution for the evils of sectionalism. Whereas sectionalism is based on self-interest, bred often in ignorance and distrust, the machinery of interregional co-operation would provide for open discussion and agreements based on mutual understanding and compromises. Only through adequate machinery and full and free discussion could the various functions of government flow to their natural or logical levels. The diverse nature of regions is a reality, national unity is the ideal, and interregional co-operation offers the avenue of progress.

Elwyn A. Mauck, Ph.D., is assistant professor of political science and research associate of the Institute for Research in Social Science at the University of North Carolina, Chapel Hill. He was a staff member of the Institute of Public Administration (1934) and of the New York State Commission for the Revision of the Tax Laws (1935–36). He is author of "Financial Control in the Suburban Areas of New York State" and of articles in the field of public administration.

Relation of Federal Regional Authorities to State and Local Units

ANONYMOUS [1]

WE HAVE long had a number of common levels of government in the United States, namely: Federal, state, county, town, township, borough, city, precinct, and district. A new type of district, somewhat intermediate geographically between the state and the county, has developed more recently. These districts (levee, irrigation, water conservancy, drainage, mosquito abatement, soil conservation, and others) are organized chiefly for the protection and use of land and water resources. Most such districts possess taxing power over the included lands.

Now a still newer type, the regional level of government, is receiving attention, especially for planning and action in the conservation and use of natural resources. The idea of regional administration is not new, having come down through the Egyptian and later civilizations, as pointed out by Hodge.[2] In this country, regional agencies would lie between Federal and state in scope and authority. At present, there actually is but one Federal regional authority, the Tennessee Valley Authority, with an area covering parts of seven states.

The regional plan of administration is commonly employed by numerous Federal agencies nationwide in scope, as the War and Navy Departments, the Farm Credit Administration, the Forest Service, and many others. It is the plan encouraged by the National Resources Committee for planning bodies, as the Pacific Northwest and New England Regional Planning Commissions. It also has resulted from interstate compacts, such as the seven-state compact covering the use of water and power from the Colorado River.

THE TENNESSEE VALLEY AUTHORITY

The Tennessee Valley Authority, created by the Congress in May 1933, is a combination of a Federal executive agency and a business corporation. It is unique among Federal executive agencies, not only in being largely regional instead of national in scope, but also in having multiple and normally unrelated functions instead of a single series of technically related objectives.

The T.V.A. is concerned primarily with a natural geographic, economic, and cultural area, the Tennessee River watershed, although certain of its activities extend far beyond the boundaries of that area. It does not have taxing power, but is dependent for funds on Federal appropriations and the sale of bonds.

The Authority is required and/or authorized by the Congress to pursue six major and differing objectives: [3] naviga-

---

[1] This article is written by a thoroughly competent person whose name, by reason of his present connections, cannot be disclosed.—THE EDITOR.

[2] Clarence L. Hodge, *The Tennessee Valley Authority: a National Experiment in Regionalism*, American University Press, 1938. Bibliography, pp. 249–63.

[3] The Tennessee Valley Authority Act: Public No. 17, 73rd Cong., H.R. 5081, as amended by Public No. 412, 74th Cong., H.R. 8632. U. S. 74th Congress, pp. 20, 1935. For discussion of the Authority, its powers and its work, see, in addition to Hodge, *op. cit.*, the following publications of the T.V.A.: *Annual Report*, 1934 to date; *The Unified Development of the Tennessee River System*—a special report to Congress, 1936; *To Keep the Water in the Rivers and the Soil on the Land: The Story of TVA*, 1938; *Recreational Development of the Southern Highlands Region*, 1938.

tion promotion,[4] flood control, national defense, electric power production and promotion, fertilizer improvement and demonstration,[5] and soil-erosion and water control. Through Congressional authorization to the President, by him transferred in Executive Order No. 6161, on June 8, 1933, T.V.A. is empowered to make studies, develop plans, and suggest action for the general economic and social betterment of the area. Because of the multiple and diverse scope of the interdependent objectives, they are set forth in detail below, the parenthetic numbers referring to the sections of the T.V.A. Act as amended in 1935.

1. *Navigation promotion:* To improve (1) and promote (4 j, new 9 a, 18) navigation in the Tennessee River and its tributaries by providing a nine-foot channel in the river from Knoxville to its mouth, and to maintain a water supply for the same (1, 4 j, new 9 a), and to acquire or construct navigation projects (4 j).

2. *Flood control:* To control destructive flood waters in the Tennessee and Mississippi rivers drainage basins (1, 4 j, 18) and, in the operation of any dam or reservoir in its possession and control, to regulate the stream flow primarily for the purposes of promoting navigation and controlling floods (new 9 a).

3. *National defense:* To maintain and operate the properties in the vicinity of Muscle Shoals, Alabama, in the interest of the national defense (1); to alter and improve existing plants and facilities and to construct new plants (5 f); to maintain Nitrate Plant No. 2, or its equivalent, in stand-by condition for the production of explosives in case of war or a national emergency (5 g); to establish and operate laboratories and experimental plants and to undertake experiments to enable furnishing nitrogen products for military purposes (5 h); and, on request of the Secretary of War or of the Navy, to manufacture for, and sell to, the United States, explosives or their nitrogenous content (5 j), the Government of the United States reserving the right, in case of war or national emergency, to take possession of all or any part of the property described, for the purpose of manufacturing explosives or for other war purposes (20).

4. *Electric power:* To produce, distribute, and sell electric power (5 l), primarily for the benefit of the people of the section as a whole (11), from dams erected for navigation and flood-control purposes (new 9 a, 13, 18); to sell surplus power so produced, above its own needs and those of other Federal agencies (new 9 a, 10, 12 a), preferentially to states, counties, municipalities, and co-operative organizations of citizens or farmers, with specified resale rate schedules (10, 11, 12 a), but also to corporations and partnerships (10), although sale to industry shall be a secondary matter (11), in order to avoid the waste of water power and to assist in liquidating the cost or aiding in the maintenance of Authority projects (new 9 a), and to build or acquire the structures necessary thereto (4 j, 9 a, 10, 12 a, 17); to deliver without charge, on request of the Secretary of War, the power necessary to operation of all locks and other facilities in aid of navigation (5 k); to make studies and experiments to promote the wider and better use of electric power for agricultural and domestic use, or for small or local indus-

---

[4] J. Haden Alldredge, et al., *A History of Navigation on the Tennessee River*, 75th Cong., 1st Sess., House Document No. 254, 1937. Bibliography and references cited, pp. 152–81.

[5] Carleton R. Ball, *A Study of the Work of the Land-Grant Colleges in the Tennessee Valley Area in Co-operation with the Tennessee Valley Authority*, under the auspices of the Co-ordinating Committee of the United States Department of Agriculture, the Valley-States Land-Grant Colleges, and the T.V.A., 1939.

tries (10); to co-operate with state governments or their subdivisions or agencies, with educational or research institutions, and with co-operatives or other organizations, in the application of electric power to the fuller and better-balanced development of the resources of the region (10); to advise and co-operate with states, counties, municipalities, and nonprofit organizations in acquiring, improving, and operating electric-power facilities, and to assist them by extending credit (12 a), and to issue bonds to provide funds therefor (15 a); to pay to the states of Alabama and Tennessee 5 per cent of the gross proceeds from sale of power generated in said states (13).

5. *Fertilizer improvement:* To improve and cheapen the production of fertilizer (5 d, 11) and, for this purpose, to establish and operate laboratories and experimental plants to furnish nitrogen and other fertilizer products for agricultural purposes in the most economical manner and at the highest standard of efficiency (5 h); to co-operate with national, state, county, and local experiment stations and demonstration farms, for the use of new forms of fertilizer or fertilizer practices during the experimental period of their introduction (5 c); to distribute fertilizer products equitably, by sale or donation, through the agency of county demonstration agents, agricultural colleges, or otherwise, for experimentation, education, and introduction of the use of such products in co-operation with practical farmers so as to obtain information as to the value, effect, and best methods of their use (5 e); and to arrange with farmers and farm organizations for large-scale, practical use of the new forms of fertilizers under conditions permitting an accurate measure of the economic return they produce (5 b).

6. *Soil erosion:* To co-operate with national, state, district, or county experiment stations or demonstration farms, with farmers, landowners, and associations of farmers or landowners, for promoting the prevention of soil erosion by the use of fertilizers and otherwise (5 c).

7. *Aid to displaced families:* To advise and co-operate in the readjustment of the population displaced by the construction of dams, the acquisition of reservoir areas, and other operations, and may co-operate with Federal, state, and local agencies to that end (4 l).

8. *Unified development of the Valley area:* To promote the agricultural and industrial development of the Tennessee Valley area, through the operation of properties at Muscle Shoals (1). [The President is authorized] to make such surveys and general plans to aid further the proper use, conservation, and development of the natural resources of the Tennessee River drainage basin and adjoining related territory, and to provide for the general welfare of the citizens, as may be useful to the Congress and the states, in guiding developments through the use of public funds for the general purpose of fostering an orderly physical, economic, and social development of said areas (22), and to co-operate with the states affected, their subdivisions or agencies, or co-operative or other organizations in making surveys, plans, or necessary experiments or demonstrations (22).

[The President] shall recommend, as the work progresses, legislation for the especial purpose of achieving, in the Tennessee River drainage basin, (a) maximum flood control, (b) maximum navigation development, (c) maximum power generation consistent with flood control and navigation, (d) proper use of marginal lands, (e) proper reforestation of all suitable lands, and (f) the economic and social well-being of the people of the basin (23).

Interdependence of the right objec-

tives: The six mandatory objectives are highly interdependent, in a physical sense. The first five require a controlled and dependable flow of water, neither flood-high nor drought-low, throughout the year. Only a unified program, under a single planning and administrative agency, can accomplish this.[6] On erosion control depends not only the prevention of silting of reservoirs and consequent injury to the whole program, but also the ability to hold back and store water in the land where it falls. Of the two permissive objectives in economic and social improvement, one is specific and the other general. The planning and unified development of the Valley area is completely dependent on the gradual achieving of the six mandatory objectives.

T.V.A. Relations with State and Local Agencies

Official relationships between the Tennessee Valley Authority and various units of state, county, district, and municipal governments are numerous and varied. Some are governed by informal agreements, some by formally signed memorandums of understanding, and some by detailed legal contracts, depending chiefly on the activity covered. The Authority co-operates also with about thirty other Federal agencies. The T.V.A. is unique in that it established extensive co-operative relations, both Federal and local, from the very beginning.[7] Furthermore, it has developed an unusual degree of initiative on the part of local units of government and also an unusual degree of citizen participation. In its third annual report, the Authority has defined its regional responsibilities and described its relationships with state and local agencies in language worth quoting:

Control of the Tennessee River is under the authority and direction of the Federal Government. Although this report deals with the progress which the TVA has made toward assuring and promoting such control, it should be pointed out that the development of the Tennessee Basin is the work of several agencies. The TVA operates in fields in which national interests are directly involved and in which nothing short of national action can be effective. The roles of the states, and of cities, counties, districts, and voluntary associations within the states, are enhanced, not diminished, in importance, by this recognition of interest and jurisdiction. Co-operation, not destructive competition; Federal responsibility in Federal and interstate matters, with local initiative and self-reliance in matters of (p. 2) a local nature—these are policies by which the development of the Valley is being and should continue to be guided.

The planning of the river's future is intrusted to the TVA. The planning of the Valley's future must be the democratic labor of many agencies and individuals, and final success is as much a matter of general initiative as of general consent. The TVA has no power or desire to impose from above a comprehensive plan for the social and economic life of the Valley.[8]

The different mandatory, authorized, and permissive objectives of the Authority have been listed and described. Now the relations developed in achieving each objective are presented. This is the functional approach. The number of agencies, including counties, runs into hundreds and the number of agreements into thousands.

1 and 2. *In navigation and flood control*

In the purchase of land for reservoir and dam sites, in the construction of dams, and in the maintenance and operation of these properties, there obviously are few official relations except

---

[6] See *The Unified Development of the Tennessee River System,* and *The Story of TVA,* both *supra* note 3.

[7] See Ball, *op. cit.*

[8] *Annual Report,* 1936, pp. 1–2.

in recreation and health, discussed later.

When rural villages must be moved; state or county highways relocated; state, county, or city bridges replaced or raised; city levees or flood walls modified or sewer outlets and water supplies safeguarded; or municipal wharfage facilities permitted on Authority-owned water-front property, the official relations are governed by contracts. The Authority provides a structure similar to that destroyed or a better type if the local unit pays the difference in cost.

3. *In national defense*

No Authority relations with local units have developed in national defense. The phosphate research discussed below, as well as that on nitrogen, however, is immediately applicable to national defense, as is improved health through malaria control.

4. *In electric power development*

The Authority relations with municipalities and county or district co-operatives in sales of electric power are established by detailed contracts. These prescribe the wholesale rate and the retail rates for different customer classes. They specify the municipality's investment in its electric system and an amortization charge to liquidate any indebtedness; that the city shall pay its electric-power department, at retail rates, for all municipal power used; and that the power department shall pay from operating revenues into city funds an amount equal to the city property tax on the plant at value stated and a further sum equal to the county and state property tax thereon unless such taxes are levied by and paid to the state and county.

5. *In fertilizer improvement and demonstration*

In 1934, a three-way memorandum of agreement was signed by the United States Department of Agriculture, the seven Valley-States Land-Grant Colleges, and the Authority. It covers complete co-operation and co-ordination of the related agricultural work of these agencies and provides for a co-ordinating committee of three representatives. Under it, the Authority has established relations with state agencies in laboratory research, station greenhouse and plot experiments, and farm test-demonstrations with phosphates, as well as in erosion control, forestry, wild-life studies, and so forth.

When station experiments and/or test demonstrations are undertaken, a master contract is signed with the state college. For each project instituted thereunder, a project contract is signed. In case the Authority contributes any funds, a special budgetary contract specifies the financial obligations.

Phosphate research: Since 1933, research has continued on chemical and physical characteristics of phosphate rocks and manufactured phosphates, and on the compatibility of phosphatic fertilizers with limestones and slags, under agreement with the Tennessee Agricultural Experiment Station.

Station experiments: The Authority furnishes its experimental fertilizer materials to any state experiment station on request. The stations test them in greenhouse pots, field plots, and fields for possible harmfulness and actual and relative values on different crops and soils, and submit annual reports of progress and results. In 1938, experiments were in progress in thirty-seven states and Puerto Rico.

Farm test-demonstrations: Test demonstrations of the effect and value of Authority phosphates are conducted in representative counties in nineteen states, in co-operation with the agricultural extension services of the state colleges. With aid from county and community committees of farmers, community test-demonstration farms are located, the farm operator agreeing to a five-year program to conserve soil and water, increase fertility, and improve farm income. Assistance and supervision are given by state, district, and county extension workers.

6. *In erosion control*

Activities such as soil survey, studies of water runoff and soil movement, terracing, adjustment of farm-management practices, increased use of soil- and water-holding crops, and shifting of row crops from steep slopes to more level lands, are comprised in the program of erosion control, as well as on test-demonstration farms.

Soil survey and classification, fundamental to water and erosion control, are conducted co-operatively with the state colleges, in the Valley counties of six states.

Runoff and erosion studies, co-operative with the states, were established on Virginia farms in 1936 and on Tennessee Station and Substation plots in 1937. At the Alabama Station, artificial rainfall is applied to different soils on two mechanically tilting plots to any desired slope up to 30 per cent.

Terracing of farm lands is promoted by six of the Valley-state colleges and associations of farmers, with advisory co-operation from the Authority in helping associations to lease or purchase large power outfits and operate properly these and the farmers' own terracing implements. The Alabama Station in 1935 made co-operaive studies of cost records in six states.

Farm management studies are conducted on the test-demonstration farms mentioned above, with special studies on types of livestock farming in Virginia.

Use of reservoir lands: A protective border above high-water mark is purchased in order to insure protection of the shore line. The Authority co-operates with the state colleges and associations of farmers in growing soil-protecting leguminous crops, primarily for seed purposes.

7. *In relocation of displaced reservoir families*

Two-thirds of nearly nine thousand families affected by the end of 1938 had already been relocated. The State Land-Grant Colleges co-operatively prepared lists of farms for sale, made appraisals on request, pointed out mistakes to be avoided, accompanied prospective purchasers to listed farms, advised on farm-management plans and needed equipment, and helped relocated families to get acquainted with new neighbors and organizations. Community committees of farmers collaborated.

8. *In unified development of the area*

The activities in planning, experiment, and field operations under the permissive objective of unified development of the area may be allocated to nine groups, as follows: agricultural industries; archaeological studies; ceramic investigations; forestry development; health, sanitation, and safety; recreational facilities; regional planning studies; vocational training of employees; and wild-life conservation and use. Co-operation with state and local units has occurred in all.

Agricultural industries: Co-operation in developing and promoting new or improved implements and processes has included state college experiment stations and extension divisions, engineering experiment stations (Tennessee), State Departments of Vocational Education, and the Georgia School of Technology. Equipment has included a lespedeza harvester, a seed cleaner, a seed scarifier, a low-cost spreader, a small-scale plow and seeder, silage-treating apparatus, and community electric-refrigeration units. Processing and marketing of farm products have included hay drying, tobacco curing, heating sweet-potato storage, flax processing and spinning, feeding new-process cottonseed meal; surveys of oil-extracting plants and markets for quick-frozen fruits, methods and equipment for quick freezing, and quality of product.

Archaeological studies: The flooding of reservoir areas covers permanently the sites of aboriginal occupancy. An archaeological survey was begun in Norris Basin in 1934 and has progressed successively, using relief labor, to the other basins. The Universities of Tennessee and Alabama received artifacts from those states. The University of Kentucky received the skeletal material, its anthropologist being released to direct the survey. The Ceramic Repository of the University of Michigan received potsherds from all sites for study and report. The University of New Mexico collaborated in comparing specimens from living Tennessee junipers with logs from the prehistoric sites, for dendrochronologic purposes. Two studies have been published, with special chapters by the co-operating institutions.

Ceramic investigations were made to promote industrial development of the southern kaolins. The North Carolina State Geologist co-operated in tonnage estimates. The United States Bureau of Mines now operates the laboratory co-operatively.

Forestry development comprises watershed protection, water and erosion control, better land use, and industrial development. Co-operation with state college extension foresters in six states covers planting of Authority-grown seedlings on private farms within the watershed. Fire control and prevention education by fire districts in the watershed counties are carried on under formal agreements with State Departments of Forestry.

Health, sanitation, and safety: The Tennessee Valley Authority protects the health of its large groups of damsite workers and of the surrounding communities and prevents malaria from its increasing reservoirs. General programs of health and sanitation and special malaria surveys and control operations are conducted co-operatively with the Public Health Service, state, county, and municipal departments of health, and Tennessee University College of Medicine. The Authority co-operates also with county sheriffs in state-law enforcement at T.V.A. camps, where its safety officers are made county deputies.

Recreational facilities are promoted on T.V.A. land and water areas, and a scenic and recreational survey of the area was made, both in co-operation with the National Park Service. T.V.A. co-operated with the Tennessee State Planning Commission in a study of Tennessee parks and recreational areas and in drafting conservation legislation, and with the State Department of Conservation in providing land for and planning a state park. State Highway Departments co-operate in surveys of highway planning for recreational traffic.

Regional planning studies include many of the activities discussed herein, especially navigation, flood control, power development, fertilizer demonstration, erosion control, soil survey, forestry, recreation, and wild-life development. Topographic mapping is basic, and the T.V.A. exchanges mapping data with State Highway Departments and co-operates with them and county Highway Departments in highway relocation and traffic surveys. It co-operated with the Alabama State Planning Commission in map construction and in plans for Guntersville, and assisted the Hamilton County Regional Planning Commission in county land classification and flood protection for Chattanooga.

Vocational training of employees: In its educational activities the T.V.A. co-operates with the Valley-States Departments of Education. In training of construction and office employees, contracts are made with county Boards of Education. At Knoxville, the University of Tennessee co-operates. In agricultural training of reservoir-clearance employees, state college extension divisions and county teachers of vocational agriculture work with both adults and youth in discussion groups and farm and home demonstrations. There is co-operation with county Boards of Education also in providing school facilities for children of damsite workers, in surveys of needs after construction completion and reservoir flooding, in high school facilities, and in evacuation of reservoir-area school buildings.

Wild-life conservation and use: In developing natural and recreational resources, the Authority co-operates with Federal and local agencies in establishing suitable areas for fish and game. It has agreements with the Alabama and Tennessee State Departments of Conservation for development of fish, game, and fur resources, including two fish hatcheries, on T.V.A. areas in those states.

Political Regionalism and Administrative Regionalism

By Donald Davidson

TO THE general reader anxious to gather comfort from the studies of experts, nothing is more encouraging than the present disposition of political science to lift the anathema from discussions of regionalism, for the social scientist who is willing to talk about regionalism is, by that act, willing to speak American, as the followers of Marx and other European guides seemingly are not; and by implication, he is also willing to admit that more than one kind of American can be spoken. Such a comfort is worth having in a time when the general reader has been all but overwhelmed by popular advocates who think and write in a different context and can see but one design wherever they look. It is a little discouraging, perhaps, to find that "regionalism" is excluded from the compendious index of the Beards' *America in Midpassage,* which includes everything else under the sun. But the great studies of the National Resources Committee, which emphatically do make a place for regionalism, and the special or general studies of other agencies and individuals more than balance the account.

Among social scientists, certainly, the discussion of regionalism has proceeded far enough to distinguish some general agreement on the following fundamentals: (1) the existence in the United States of marked regional differentiations which arise from various causes, some old, some new; (2) the existence of large-scale social and economic problems, differing in kind and degree, which have a regional outline; (3) the inability of separate states to deal adequately with such problems; (4) the demonstrable inequalities caused by attempts to meet these problems by Federal legislation; and (5) the historic fact that nonsolution or inadequate solution of such problems leads to sectionalism, which is political regionalism in its gross and active form.

Political Regionalism

The gross form of political regionalism appears when a major regional grievance remains unsatisfied over a considerable time and the region concerned is left "without recourse." If the issue is brought into the arena of national policy and if the region is left in a solid minority, with a majority vote concentrated in other regions, then we have the extreme result: secession, as in the sixties; or threatened secession, as upon many occasions; or at least long continuing disturbance and bad feeling.

But political regionalism, if it is a sin, is not to be imputed to the minority region alone. The majority regions, for all their insistence on the merits of their "national" view, derive a profit which is denied to the minority region. The national view, so-called, may bring advantage to one part of the Nation and disadvantage to another part. Hence, as Turner has pointed out, regional leaders invariably disguise specifically regional aims and attempt to give regional policies the coloring of national policies. Political regionalism, though locally motivated, aims at Federal policy. Federal policy is always being influenced by the interplay of regional aims, and often turns out to be political regionalism falsely generalized.

There is no real disagreement as to the ends to be obtained by a national policy which would take this situation into account. Economic inequalities between regions hurt just as much as the economic inequalities between "classes" about which we now hear so much. The only disagreement among serious-minded people will be as to the method of righting such disparities or forestalling their appearance. Since the search for a method has just begun, it is highly important that all reasonable suggestions be received hospitably. At the same time, they should be discussed critically. We cannot afford to reject out-of-hand anything that looks practicable, or to commit ourselves too deeply to any device that may prove deceptive.

The present concern of social science with administrative regionalism evidently arises out of a desire to avoid the harsh results of political regionalism. With our economy already in a delicate condition from many complex causes, we cannot risk even a mild attack of political regionalism. And since the Federal Government, now more than ever, has enlarged its scope and become an economic rather than a political government, political scientists naturally turn to the Federal Government itself and ask whether its functions cannot be adapted to regional needs. The idea of administrative regionalism harmonizes on one side with the growing feeling that the industrial economy is too rigidly, too awkwardly, centralized, and ought for its own health to be decentralized; and on the other side with a notion, still not clearly outlined, that autonomous desires of regions may be defined through regional planning boards and other legal or extralegal agencies which will act in an advisory and informative capacity.

Administrative regionalism, then, is an effort to achieve better organic relationship between the Federal Government and the states (or groups of states) by regionalizing some of the functions of the Federal Government and by encouraging the growth of nonadministrative agencies which transmit, so to speak, the collective will of regions.

Old and New Administrative Regionalism

Here it seems wise to make a distinction between the old and the new form of administrative regionalism. The old administrative regionalism is represented in those divisions (now large in number) which the Federal Government has set up to carry out explicitly Federal functions, as, for example: to take the census, to collect revenue, to administer the Federal Reserve System, or to administer the various "alphabet agencies" of the New Deal. Various students have pointed out that the establishment of such territorial jurisdictions is in itself evidence of the regional character of the Nation, and that improvement in Federal administration would occur if some consolidations of jurisdiction could be made. Such observations have weight and merit, but they do not bring us any nearer to a solution of the problems of political regionalism. The Federal agencies of the kind referred to were not set up with any idea of relieving the specific pressures that cause political regionalism. Though they may touch regional problems, they do so from the strictly Federal point of view, under the assumption that a given Federal operation has exactly the same result in one region as in another. They do not assume the validity of the regional approach as such, but leave us in the realm of an enlarging Federal power and a diminishing state power.

The new administrative regionalism differs from the old in its assumption that Federal authority may be applied constructively in one region without at the same time applying it in all regions. It acknowledges inequality of operation and attempts to turn inequality into a benefit. It also differs from the old administrative regionalism in its ingenious method of applying Federal authority, so as to have the advantage, at a strategic point, of national rather than merely regional resources. Thus an old difficulty is apparently surmounted. The trouble with Federal legislation has always been like this: that the protective tariff protected the North but not the South; that the gold standard was good for the East but bad for the West; that the Negro slave was recognized as property not only in the Southern states but in all other states. The new administrative regionalism seems to afford a way of legislating for one region alone. The way to do it is to apply locally (and subtly extend) powers already clearly within the Federal province.

Tennessee Valley Authority

Among possible examples of the new administrative regionalism, the Tennessee Valley project offers the richest field of study, for its implications are now fully developed, and it seems to be a model of what the new device is expected to accomplish. It stays within the technical limits of constitutional prescription, and yet it has far-reaching aims which transcend a conventional interpretation of the bounds of Federal authority. Ostensibly the Tennessee Valley Authority works within the unimpeachably Federal sphere of navigation and flood control. It is charged with the maintenance of a nine-foot navigable channel on a river where steamboats are about as numerous as mule-wagons on city streets. "The Board is hereby directed (the act solemnly says) in the operation of any dam or reservoir . . . to regulate the stream flow primarily for the purposes of promoting navigation and controlling floods." As a secondary function the Board is empowered to construct dams and transmission lines for the disposal of electric energy "in order to avoid the waste of water power, to transmit and market such power as in this act is provided, and thereby . . . to assist in liquidating the cost or aid in the maintenance of the projects of the Authority."

The steps by which the by-product, electric power, has become the major product are well known. At this writing, the Tennessee Valley Authority by the use of apparently quite constitutional methods has eliminated a private power monopoly from competition in its regional area. A fundamental economic resource in a well-defined region is in the hands of a regional unit of the Federal Government. The "yardstick" furnished by the T.V.A. may be useful in national policy, but the real meaning of the T.V.A. as a Federal-regional device is in its action upon the depleted or "backward" economy of the Tennessee Valley and perhaps even of the upper South in general, which it is expected to "develop" or at least improve.

The development is to come in part, but only in part, from flood control, soil conservation, and reforestation. These are "good" reasons, legitimate Federal reasons, for the establishment of the T.V.A. Beyond these good reasons are the real reasons, foreshadowed in certain vague phrases in the act and frequently cited by social scientists who expect the T.V.A. not only to justify itself in the Federal sphere but also to help in removing some of the old and pressing causes of sectional irritation. The real reasons are that the T.V.A. will rectify the economic disadvantage into which the region has fallen and that it will prove to be a model for similar intervening Federal-regional agencies, which will cope not with identical difficulties elsewhere but with regional difficulties peculiar and pressing enough to deserve this "unequal" benefit of Federal law. The device, if it works, is expected to transform "sectionalism" into "regionalism" (in the beneficent sense described by Howard Odum), and to do so without endangering national unity on the one hand or imposing rigid unification on the other.

Undoubtedly the T.V.A. can accomplish—has already in part accomplished—the instrumental tasks for which it was created: it can improve land use, control floods and soil erosion, and manufacture and distribute power. But can it also relieve the economic disadvantage of the Tennessee Valley region (and in some measure of the upper South) without either doing harm to some distant region or changing to a marked degree the regional "culture" which it is supposed to conserve?

SHORTCOMINGS OF T.V.A.

In answering this question we should not fail to note that the regional experiment has become a national issue, not in terms of the beneficial functions that it exercises within its region, but in terms of what it means for national power policies. Members of Congress who debate over the T.V.A. do not seem to know about "administrative regionalism"; they do not vote T.V.A. appropriations with much sense of the value of the T.V.A. as a *regional* experiment. This warping of emphasis is due in part to the fact that the "power issue" is in national politics anyhow; but it is also due in part to the fact that the T.V.A. cannot *legally* be represented as having a specifically regional purpose.

Next, the conception of the T.V.A. embodies an analogy which may or may not apply in the Southeast. It is conceived and framed in terms of the industrial economy of the Northeast and the Middle states, and not of the largely agrarian economy in which it is set up. The inference is that the T.V.A. will confer upon the Tennessee Valley area the same benefits that would accrue to the upper Hudson Valley if a similar agency were established there. The T.V.A. proposes to transform a low-income, agricultural area into an area with a higher cash income or at least a larger real income. The economic imbalance is to be righted in terms of new industries, pay rolls, dividends, improved farming methods (including labor-saving machinery in house and field as well as diversification of crops), and in general a typically modern use of natural and human resources.

As one examines this broad inference he begins to suspect that the new administrative regionalism, no less than Federal legislation of the past, will reflect the psychology, economics, and generalized wishes of whatever regional group happens at the moment to possess Federal power; or, to put it differently, that the new administrative regionalism may be simply another expression of political regionalism.

The regional psychology of the T.V.A. conception is not native to the South. The T.V.A. was not created in response to a Southern crusade—although some Southern Congressmen had long agitated for a final disposition of Muscle Shoals. There was no popular outcry in the South for a T.V.A. The sponsor of the T.V.A. Act was a Middle Westerner, Senator Norris, who was crusading against electric utilities. What President Roosevelt contributed to the conception, we do not surely know; but the idea of a planned economy, popular among New Deal liberals of the Northeast, had something to do with the sudden launching of the great enterprise, which was created by Congress within two months after the first inauguration of President Roosevelt. The five states concerned had no opportunity to debate the project or to contribute ideas and leading personnel, or by any direct means to make known their opinion, if they had any; the project was superimposed (however benevolently) upon them.

Furthermore, the conception of the T.V.A., while proposing to remedy regional disadvantages, ignores the great underlying causes of those regional disadvantages. There is nothing in the T.V.A. program, immediate or ultimate, which promises to alter the relative economic positions of the dominant industrial Northeast and the all but completely "colonialized" and "agrarian" Southeast. Soil control and erosion programs are a concrete good in themselves, of course. But the market price of Southern farm products does not increase merely because they are grown on non-eroded land. The price of Northern manufactures (even of labor-saving machinery) does not decrease when they are bought by farmers on non-eroded lands where houses and barns are being supplied with electricity from government-owned plants. The promise of cheap fertilizer is interesting —and would be more interesting if we had not been assured that Tennessee phosphate lands are to be considered a "national" (perhaps even a military) reserve. But what is there in the T.V.A. program to change the relative position of a region where from 60 to 80 per cent of the farms reported their products in 1929 in the lowest cash-value column?

Industry is expected to "balance" agriculture by adding cash and thus relieving the strain. Against this promise we must set the established fact of extraregional ownership and control of industry, business, and even much farm land. There is little to indicate that administrative regionalism, in the form of the T.V.A. or any other body yet suggested, will reduce the already heavy percentage of absentee-landlordism in Southern industry; or encourage the rise of new industries, Southern-owned, which will sell goods at prices commensurate with Southern ability to buy; or protect such industries, if they should arise, against being eaten up by national (that is, Northeastern-controlled) monopolies. Yet economic imbalance in the region probably cannot be righted unless such things are attended to. Slight gains derived from cheaper power rates and larger pay rolls will probably help a little, but may be more than offset by the fact that the population will be drawn farther away from the agrarian economy and involved more deeply than ever in the chain of increasing purchases and increasing debts.

The program, in short, may benefit urban entrepreneurs and selected industrial groups, while the region as a whole feels, at closer range than before, the impact of an exploitative system. It is possible to argue that the T.V.A. is not a subsidy of the region, but actually another subsidy of the exploitative forces which have already set the region at a disadvantage.

Meanwhile, the play of other forces that tend to cause political regionalism goes on unchecked. The surplus population of the biologically lusty Southeast gets driven from rich land to poor land by the advance of labor-saving machinery, corporate farming, and absentee ownership; and its natural tendency to migrate to other regions is no longer facilitated—is indeed positively checked —by those regions, which are less receptive than of old. The industrialists of the Southeast begin their fight against differential freight rates and complain against the Federal wages-and-hours law, which, in their eyes at least, is rank sectionalism in a Federal disguise. And other specifically Southern problems of race, public education, suffrage qualifications, and the like remain confused and unsolved.

Analysis of New Administrative Regionalism

The nature of the new administrative regionalism becomes fairly plain if it is viewed in such a context. A device like the Tennessee Valley Authority is not an agent of a region which of its own will and out of its own resources has won a degree of antonomy or semi-autonomy. It is not a new unit of government, standing in a clearly defined middle ground between the states and the Federal Government. It is an agent of the Federal Government, or, more concretely, of the Federal Government of 1929-39—a "crisis government" desperately concerned with making an economic system work. That government apparently conceives the economic system to be irredeemably of a large-scale industrial type and has entered upon its reforms as if only that one type were possible in the United States. Conceding that the system causes inequalities to appear along "class lines," it has undertaken to repair the inequalities. But the same economic system is largely to blame for gross regional inequalities, which cut across class lines.

The new administrative regionalism cannot repair regional inequalities if it looks principally at class inequalities, and simultaneously retains, and even bolsters up, the identical economic system which causes stress lines to take a regional outline. Such a policy will probably have one or the other of two results: Either the regional economy of the Southeast (as our present example) will be completely changed and made an indistinguishable part of the one big national economy—in which case regionalism in very truth will become merely administrative, for the "conquest" of the Southeast begun in the eighteen-sixties will then have reached completion; or the effort to achieve such fusion will not succeed but will instead stimulate the rise of a competing regional economy, intent upon self-sufficiency and separatism—or political regionalism in its most active form. The rise of regional "industrial councils" and other concerted regional movements, as well as the growth of interstate "tariffs," seems to indicate that the second rather than the first result is now being produced.

OLD ADMINISTRATIVE REGIONALISM PREFERABLE

Such an analysis leads to the conclusion—undoubtedly speculative—that administrative regionalism most clearly demonstrates its value as it remains in the older sphere of action and does not too boldly enter the new one. As a unit of a Federal system of flood control and river management, with incidental benefits in conservation of land and forests, the T.V.A. is solid and reasonable—exactly what it appears to be in the descriptions set forth by the National Resources Committee in its publication entitled *Drainage Basin Problems and Plans*. But for checking or transforming political regionalism, such a device is far short of what we need. As long as the supposedly "national" economy is a sectional economy in disguise and remains exploitative in its action, the forces of political regionalism will jockey for power in the Federal Government, or, failing there, will endeavor to set up protective boundaries or their equivalent.

If this be true, it follows that some consideration of the economy itself must come into the argument. That question cannot be argued here. Suffice it to say that rebellious regions like the South and the West would be less rebellious if they could not accuse the Federal Government of subsidizing and protecting the economy which despoils them, while at the same time it frustrates their own efforts at self-protection and thus deprives them of all recourse.

Donald Davidson is professor of English at Vanderbilt University, Nashville, Tennessee.

State Centralization in the South

By Paul W. Wager

GOVERNMENT in the South has never been intensely local. Unlike the compact settlements of New England out of which there developed the town as the dominant unit of government, scattered settlement and the plantation system in the South led to the pre-eminence of the county. Except for the feeble and transitory existence of the parish in Virginia and the Carolinas, there was, prior to the Civil War, no government closer to the people than that which was quartered at the county seat. In South Carolina, not even county government got firmly established.

There were no townships in the South until they were forced upon North and South Carolina by the "carpetbaggers" in 1868. In neither state did they survive as active governmental units after the end of Northern domination. The rural South thus never became adapted to a unit of government smaller than the county, though the counties are smaller on the average than they are in the North.

Since the county is only one step from the state, Southerners view any encroachment upon the county by the state with about the same degree of concern or indifference as the people of New York or Michigan view encroachment upon the township by the county. Local government is thus somewhat of a sectional concept. With present means of transportation, both Northern townships and the smallest of the Southern counties are physically obsolete. But a local unit of government has psychological as well as areal dimensions. It survives because it is rooted in the mores of the people. Could the boundaries of political units be expanded as readily as the sphere of social and economic activities, local government might preserve its vigor and usefulness; but when traditional boundaries are held rigid, preventing local units from becoming effective service areas, these units will seek financial and administrative assistance from higher levels of government. It is this vertical expansion that is designated "centralization." If it has proceeded further in the South than in other parts of the Nation, it is probably because there are fewer layers of government to penetrate.

Road Administration

North Carolina startled the Nation when in 1931 its General Assembly passed an act transferring 45,000 miles of county, township, and other local roads to the state for maintenance. By this bold step more than 150 county and district road organizations were abolished, the road-building machinery of the local units was transferred to the state with compensation, and the burden of reconstructing and maintaining all roads outside of incorporated cities and towns was shifted from property owners to automobile users.

At the same time that the state assumed control of the roads, it also took over the prisoners from the county jails and road camps. The original transfer involved 3,713 men, but the average number in the state camps is now about 6,000. Some of the camps were those formerly used by counties, but in most instances the state built new ones. There are at present about ninety, well scattered over the state. These camps are a vast improvement over the typical county jail. The prisoners are no longer in idleness, but are engaged in healthful, outdoor work. It is pick-and-shovel work, but not too arduous. The food is varied and plentiful. The barracks are sanitary, there are shower baths and comfortable beds. There are limited opportunities for recreation and educational advancement.

On the whole, state maintenance of all highways in North Carolina has met with popular approval. Most of the disapproval has been voiced in the rich counties which enjoyed good roads under the old regime. It is possible that the state has had less money to spend per mile in these favored sections than was spent before, but in most of the rural sections the roads are uniformly in better shape than they ever were under local maintenance.

Only two other states have ventured to follow North Carolina's lead—Virginia and West Virginia; and Virginia cautiously provided that any county might vote to remain outside the state system. At first several counties elected to remain aloof, but the writer is informed that all but two have subsequently come into the fold. Neither of these two states has followed North Carolina's example in relieving the counties of their prisoners along with the roads.

All the other Southern states have two road systems—a primary system of arterial highways maintained by the state and a secondary system of tributary and local roads maintained by the counties or special road districts. The primary system is normally supported entirely from gasoline and motor-vehicle revenues, while the secondary system is dependent on property taxes and such portion of the gasoline tax as the state can be induced to surrender. The amount returned varies widely. In South Carolina one cent per gallon is returned to the county, in Tennessee two cents, and in Florida three cents.

Many miles of road were surfaced before being absorbed into the state systems. The counties have felt that they were entitled to compensation, and a number of states are relieving them of their road debt. Thus, in 1927 the Tennessee Legislature voted to reimburse the counties of that state the amount of the road bonds they had incurred, together with 5 per cent interest until retired.[1] The last legislature reduced the interest rate to 3.5 per cent.[2] Georgia in 1936 assumed $26,637,000 of county road debts, retiring one-tenth of the total annually.[3] The state is also absorbing the county road debt in Texas.[4]

While most responsible highway officials agree that the county is the smallest unit of government that should be utilized as a road district, even this degree of centralization has not been fully attained in the South. In numerous Texas counties the roads of each of the four precincts are under the direction of the board member from that precinct. In Louisiana, it is the exception when the roads of an entire parish have been consolidated into a unified system and are supported by a parish-wide tax. In fact, this has been fully accomplished in only eight parishes, and in a modified way in sixteen others. Moreover, the number of road districts has increased each year since 1921, and six parishes have fifteen or more road districts.

School Support

For twenty years or more the consolidation of rural schools has been going on in the South, so that today the large central school is more characteristic than the one-room school which is still so much in evidence in many parts of the country. Moreover, the number of school buildings far exceeds the number of school districts. The county has long been the most usual unit of admin-

---

[1] Tennessee *Acts of 1927*, Chap. 23.
[2] *Ibid.*, 1939, Chap. 188.
[3] Georgia *Laws of 1933*, Chap. 126.
[4] Texas *Laws of 1935*, Chap. 326.

istration, and in many instances it is now the smallest taxing unit.

In North Carolina the state meets the entire operating cost of an eight-month term in both the elementary and high schools, white and colored. Incidentally, its tax sources include no tax on property except about a half-million dollars from intangibles. Forty-odd communities, including two counties, levy a local tax to pay for a ninth month, to supplement the teachers' salaries, or to provide extra courses. All counties levy a modest county-wide tax to cover capital outlays and to liquidate any existing county-wide school debt. Many counties have assumed all district indebtedness.

In South Carolina the state pays the entire salary of teachers and contributes to the cost of transportation and other specific items, but it has not assumed the entire operating cost of the schools. Neither has the state relinquished the property tax. There is still a five-mill levy by the state.

In Louisiana school maintenance is on a parish-wide basis, with a generous supplement from the state. No parish is required to levy more than eight mills per dollar for school purposes; any additional revenue needed is supplied from a state equalizing fund. The latter is derived from a small property tax and the state's highly productive severance taxes. About half the aggregate cost of the schools is now borne by the state.

In Texas the state is now contributing a flat twenty-two dollars per pupil, and to many districts additional sums through an equalizing fund and a rural aid fund. In the aggregate, the state is bearing approximately 40 per cent of the load.

School appropriations by a recent session of the Arkansas legislature consisted of $4,000,000 to the common school fund, $1,000,000 to an equalization fund, and $600,000 to a revolving loan fund.[5]

In Georgia, not only are appropriations made for the public schools out of the general fund, but the legislature has allocated one cent of the six-cents tax on gasoline to this purpose. To share in the equalization fund derived from the gasoline tax, the city or county must first have levied a tax of at least five mills for maintenance purposes. State appropriations in recent years have represented about 30 per cent of the total cost of the public schools.

In Alabama the Minimum School Program Act provides that every county and city must levy a seven-mill property tax in addition to a state-wide tax of three mills for schools. The latter is distributed back to local schools on a per capita basis. The proceeds of the seven-mill tax are levied, collected, and spent locally. If the proceeds of these two property taxes are not sufficient to support all elementary schools for a period of seven months and all high schools for nine months, the state pays the difference from the Minimum Program Fund derived from other taxes.

The last session of the Tennessee Legislature appropriated $7,000,000 annually for the elementary schools and $950,000 for the high schools.[6] This permits a contribution of ten dollars per pupil in average daily attendance and leaves about $2,500,000 as an equalization fund. The entire $7,000,000 for elementary schools must be spent for salaries.

Virginia's appropriations for the public schools also aggregate over $7,000,000 annually. About three-fourths of the total is distributed on a per capita basis, and the rest is earmarked for specific purposes. The equalization principle has not been carried so far as in most states. About two-thirds of

[5] Arkansas *Acts of 1937*, Chap. 283.
[6] Tennessee *Acts of 1939*, Chap. 16.

the cost of the public schools is borne locally.

Shifting school support from the locality to the state has been motivated largely by two desires—to equalize educational opportunity and to relieve the tax burden on property. While most of the Southern states still levy a tax on property, the larger and larger school appropriations are derived mainly from other sources, hence the larger measure of state support has invariably meant less dependence on property taxes. The percentage of the cost of public elementary and secondary schools derived from property taxes in each Southern state in 1935–36 is indicated in Table 1.[7]

TABLE 1

North Carolina	15.1
South Carolina	56.0
Florida	57.6
Texas	58.5
Mississippi	65.8
Louisiana	67.9
Alabama	68.2
Georgia	69.0
Kentucky	70.7
Virginia	70.8
Arkansas	76.7
Tennessee	80.9

A large measure of state support inevitably means a considerable degree of state control. The state aid is usually conditioned on the meeting of state standards. The state sets the length of the school term, prescribes the course of study, selects the textbooks, establishes the minimum salary for teachers, prescribes the form of reports to be made, and reviews the local school budget. There is little room left for local discretion.

POLICING

Increased centralization is demanded in the field of crime control. Every Southern state now has either a state police force or a state highway patrol. In Alabama, Arkansas, Louisiana, and Texas the state troopers have been armed with full police power. While they are mainly highway patrols in the other states of the South, they may be, and often are, deputized for police work other than traffic control. North Carolina operates a state-wide police radio system, and Virginia has installed not only a radio system but also the latest teletype receiving sets in the police cars. Texas has reorganized its state police force, absorbing into it the famous Texas Rangers. It has been outfitted with the most modern equipment and given the status of a state department of public safety. In Kentucky, Louisiana, and North Carolina, state bureaus of criminal identification and statistics have been established; and the Governor of Tennessee has recently appointed a crime commission to study conditions in that state and bring to the next legislature recommendations for improved facilities in crime control.

PUBLIC WELFARE

Everywhere throughout the South the administration of the social security program is being assumed primarily by the state. This is due in part, of course, to the necessity of meeting Federal standards, but it is due even more to the poverty of the local units. If the state must provide all or a major part of the funds, it will naturally insist on supervising their expenditure.

In at least Florida, Louisiana, South Carolina, and Texas, the grants for old-age assistance are entirely from Federal and state funds; the local units do not participate. In Georgia the counties contribute only 10 per cent, and in Tennessee one-eighth. On the other hand, in North Carolina and Alabama the counties normally contribute 25 per cent. In North Carolina there is a state

---

[7] Advisory Committee on Education, Report No. 4, *Federal Aid and the Tax Problem*, p. 41. Superintendent of Documents, Washington, D. C.

equalization fund of $85,000 so that the poorest counties are not required to contribute as much as 25 per cent.

In all the states, the state department sets the standards by which the benefits are distributed and fixes the qualifications of personnel. The county is usually utilized as the unit for local administration, though this is not the case in Florida, where the state is divided into eight administrative districts. Each has a district board and district supervisors. Even in the states with an organization in each county, there are many state specialists and supervisors. In West Virginia, state welfare authorities may take over the administration of public assistance in any county failing to comply with Federal requirements.

The state department usually has a voice in the selection of county boards and county superintendents of public welfare. In Arkansas it selects a board of five from fifteen nominations, three of which are made by each of five county officials. In North Carolina the board has three members, one appointed by the State Commissioner, one by the County Board of Commissioners, and the third member by the other two. In South Carolina the County Board of Public Welfare consists of three members appointed by the State Board or State Director upon the recommendation of the county delegation in the legislature. The county director or superintendent in all states must possess the qualifications fixed by the state board. The state also requires that the case workers and field investigators be especially trained for the work.

The adoption of the social security program has no doubt drawn the states into the field of relief much faster and much further than they would have gone without this stimulus. But now that they are in, there is a tendency for them to go even beyond the requirements of the act. For instance, South Carolina in 1937 appropriated $200,000 to supplement county funds for direct relief. In the same vein, Florida has removed a constitutional provision prohibiting any direct state appropriation for relief. For a number of years there has been a growth of state institutions for special classes of dependents and delinquents, though perhaps in no Southern state do these institutions have adequate capacity. In Virginia, district infirmaries have replaced many of the former county homes for the indigent, and most of the county almshouses have been closed in Alabama and Georgia.

Control over Local Finance

Local governments in the South are having their financial affairs subjected to more and more state supervision and control. One of the first steps in state control has been the requirement that counties operate under a budget, and by 1936 budgets were required in the counties of all Southern states except Georgia, South Carolina, and Tennessee. In most states the budgets are not reviewed by a state agency, though a recent act in Alabama requires every county to send a certified copy of its budget to the newly created Division of Local Finance within thirty days after adoption. Budgets are reviewed as to legality upon petition in Oklahoma. Mississippi and West Virginia regularly review and validate all county budgets, and most of the states review school budgets.

State departments have encouraged and assisted in the installation of accounting systems in Alabama, Arkansas, Florida, Kentucky, Louisiana, Mississippi, North Carolina, Virginia, and West Virginia, though the accomplishment in the respective states has by no means been uniform. Perhaps the best record has been established in Alabama. An act of 1935 gave the State Comptroller authority to set up uniform systems of accounts in all counties of that state, and by October of the next year the work was completed.

Twelve of the states in the South provide for some form of central examination of county accounts.[8] Auditors are sent out by the state in Alabama, Arkansas, Florida, Louisiana, Kentucky, Oklahoma, Tennessee, and Virginia, but in most of these states the force is too small to make a systematic audit in each unit. Oklahoma has had a staff of only five, Kentucky of nine, Tennessee of twelve, and as a result only a few counties have been reached. All parishes in Louisiana are visited semiannually, but the audits are necessarily superficial. The most comprehensive work has been done in Virginia, where a staff of thirty-nine in a single year made 378 county audits and thirty-four installations of improved accounting systems.[9] North Carolina has made no audits, but the Local Government Commission approves the contracts with private accountants and dictates the scope of the audits.[10]

The most extreme forms of state control have been restrictions in respect to debt. Two states, Louisiana and North Carolina, require state approval before the issuance of any local bonds. The Louisiana measure was passed at the instance of the late Senator Huey P. Long in 1935 and is credited with having been politically inspired. The legislature created a state Bond and Tax Board of five members, to which all parishes and other taxing districts must apply for permission to issue bonds or incur other debts, or to levy taxes or spend other revenues in payment thereof.[11]

In North Carolina, not only has the Local Government Commission the authority to approve or disapprove any proposed bond issue, but in case an issue is to be floated the negotiation and sale are made by the Commission, and the Commission sees to it that provision is made to meet principal and interest payments as they fall due. All sinking funds must be invested and safeguarded in a manner satisfactory to the Commission. The services of the agency have resulted in the refunding of many issues with more favorable maturities and interest rates.

While no other Southern state has gone so far in controlling indebtedness as Louisiana and North Carolina, other states subject certain types of bonds to control by state agencies. For instance, school-bond issues in Arkansas and public-utility issues in South Carolina are passed upon by the state. Florida and Texas supervise county highway debt service.

Kentucky has recently provided for a local finance officer in the State Department of Finance to aid local units in handling their debt problem. Every six months the county judge of each county must report to this state officer the condition of the county's sinking funds, and it may turn over such funds to the State Sinking Fund Commission to invest and manage. Under certain conditions it must do so.

Within the last year Alabama has created a new Department of Finance containing a Division of Local Finance to collect information concerning the finances of local units of government and to advise with the local officials in respect to the management thereof. In one respect its powers are more than advisory. It requires from each subdivision an annual statement showing the amount and character of its public debt. In the event of default for ninety days or more in the payment of an ob-

---

[8] Frank W. Prescott, *County Finance in the South* (Arnold Foundation Studies in Public Affairs, Vol. VI, No. 1), p. 26.
[9] *Ibid.*
[10] North Carolina *Public Acts of 1931*, Chap. 60.
[11] Louisiana *Acts of 1935*, 2nd Extraordinary Session, Chap. 6.

ligation, the Division may, if requested by a bondholder, take charge of the revenues and expenditures of the unit until the default has been cured or a plan of orderly liquidation worked out.

Conclusions

None of the few counties in the United States which have been granted home rule and its concomitant—police power—is in the South. Southern counties are universally mere wards of the state. As long as their functions were simple and the volume of expenditures small, there was little paternal guidance. The state let them pursue their own course, set their own standards, and wriggle out of the difficulties which befell them. But the services demanded today of local governments, rural as well as urban, are complex and costly. This, in the light of the disparity in the capacity of these units to support these services and the consequent invitation to take financial fliers, made it inevitable that the state should come to their aid.

There can be little doubt that the shift in responsibility from the locality to the state diminishes the citizens' interest and participation in government. Support by the state also tends to obscure the identity of the taxpayer and the beneficiary of public services. Both these results are bad.

It is desirable that local self-government be preserved. It is also desirable that communities as well as individuals once more find pride in being self-supporting. If these twin virtues of self-government and self-support are to be preserved, the trend toward state centralization may need to be checked. It cannot be checked unless new and stronger units of local government are erected. This could be accomplished by reducing the number of political subdivisions, by eliminating as far as possible the overlapping layers of government, and by so simplifying the internal organization of local government as to facilitate direct popular control. But these improvements do not come easily. They are fought by entrenched interests. They are resisted by the overly cautious. They are retarded by the inertia and indifference of the many and by the cupidity of the few. The rehabilitation of local government is a positive undertaking; it requires exertion, patience, organization. Acceptance of state administration and control is a negative course; it is to follow the path of least resistance. Either course of action may lead to temporary solvency for local units; but one is an advance, the other a retreat. One weakens the foundations of democratic institutions, the other strengthens them. In a world in which mankind is threatened with the loss of the personal and political liberties which have been won through a thousand years of struggle, the right of local self-government should not be so little cherished. If county and city governments as now organized are not proving effective tools of democracy, the tools need to be sharpened, not thrown away.

Paul W. Wager, Ph.D., is associate professor of political science at the University of North Carolina, Chapel Hill, and consulting economist for the Land Committee of the National Resources Planning Board. He is the author of "County Government and Administration in North Carolina," and is one of the sectional editors of the National Municipal Review.

Fiscal Aspects of State-Local Relations

By George W. Spicer

NOWHERE is the relation between state and local government more intimate and inextricable than in the realm of fiscal affairs. Nowhere has the flow of authority and supervision from a lower to a higher level of government been more rapid and widespread than with respect to fiscal affairs. There was a time when local services were supported largely, if not wholly, from local revenues; and when the major part of state revenue was even collected by local officials. It is true that the sources of local revenue have usually been determined by the state, and that fiscal officers in localities, such as assessors, collectors, and treasurers, have been prescribed by constitutional or statutory law; but within this framework the local authorities were originally free to move without restriction.[1]

That was the day of a simple agricultural society when governmental problems were few in number and simple in nature, and when each local governmental unit was essentially self-contained. Economic and social life was then organized largely on a local basis, and the functions of self-government were of local interest only. It is obvious that these conditions have long since passed. Just as economic, social, professional, and occupational interests have transcended local and, to a less extent, state lines, so governmental functions in response to these changes have come to concern wider and wider areas and larger and larger populations. Poor schooling in one district affects the character of life and citizenship in the state as a whole, thanks to modern mobility of population. The problems of public health with which government now concerns itself on a large scale cannot be confined within the boundaries of counties and cities, nor can those of public welfare and relief. Underassessment of taxes in one county or city affects taxpayers in other areas, and public borrowing by local units affects the entire state. The credit of the state cannot be separated from that of its subdivisions any more than the financial stability of a central bank can be safeguarded against financial folly on the part of its branches. Each unit acts and reacts upon the other, for no government can operate within a vacuum.

Overlapping Functions

With these rapid and far-reaching changes in our economic and industrial life, accompanied by rapid means of transportation and communication, it is no longer easy to determine what is a local function and what is a state function. Such functions as schools, public safety, and highways illustrate this point. None of these is any longer exclusively locally controlled or locally financed. Thus there seems to be no clear-cut line between state and local functions. Many are both local and state, and demand a high degree of coöperation.

Moreover, these same changes have caused a shift in the available sources of revenue from the local units to wider areas. The general property tax, which was until the end of the nineteenth century the main source of both state and local revenues, is now not adequate even to support the increased or expanded services demanded by the local communities. In the meantime the state has developed new and elastic sources of revenue such as the inheritance tax, the

---

[1] See L. D. White, *Introduction to the Study of Public Administration* (New York, 1939), p. 170.

income tax, the sales tax, gasoline and motor-vehicle taxes, liquor taxes, and others, which are administered directly by it without reliance upon local agencies as formerly. With the general property tax insufficient to meet the needs of the local units, the state, with its more flexible sources of revenue, has developed certain financial aids to local government. The quite natural result of this has been that various forms of state supervision and control have been invoked. To some extent outright absorption of local functions has taken place.

Among the factors of state supervision of local fiscal affairs are: (1) state supervision of local assessments, (2) state limitation of local tax rates, (3) state limitation of local indebtedness, (4) state control over local budgets, (5) state financial aid to local governments, and (6) state supervision of accounts, auditing, and reporting. It is not intended here to undertake a lengthy discussion of any of these factors. There is already a substantial body of factual material on most of them. It is rather our purpose to consider each factor briefly in relation to the problem of state centralization and local self-government.

State Supervision of Local Assessments

Oliver Wolcott made the observation in 1796 that, although the valuations made by Virginia commissioners of revenue were just in respect to the relative value of different parcels of land within a given county, they were very inequitable in comparison with the valuations of other counties.[2] After a century and a quarter, it is interesting to note, the first part of this observation was distinctly not true, while the latter part was increasingly true. In the Report of the Commission on Simplification and Economy of State and Local Government in 1924, it was stated that "the gross inequality in the distribution of the tax burden, both as among political subdivisions of the state and among individual property owners, has long been a sore spot in our body politic."[3]

Although the constitution of the state required property to be assessed at its "fair market value," no attempt was made to comply with this vague standard. The assessors in each locality adopted their own standards, and these were legion. The farmer in Brunswick County paid five times as much state taxes as the farmer in Carroll County on a farm of the same value. For the purposes of taxation, the average automobile in 1920 was worth $428 in Halifax and $36 in Buchanan. In Dinwiddie in 1921 the average horse was worth $98 and in Grayson $26. Cattle were worth $49 each in Henrico and $11 in Floyd. A sheep was worth $7 in Clarke and $1 in Buchanan. A hog was worth $12 in Warwick and $1 in Buchanan. A watch was worth $23 in 1920 in Nottoway and $1 in Grayson, and a clock was worth $16 in Henrico and $1 in Floyd. The primary reason for this undervaluation was, of course, to evade the state taxes on real estate and tangible personal property.

The inequality between individual taxpayers was even more flagrant. The assessments ranged from .4 per cent of the true value to 160 per cent of the true value. In Amherst, where the average ratio of assessed value to true value was 29.4 per cent, the ratio of the individual assessments ranged from 2 per cent to 140 per cent of true value. In Brunswick, where the average was 55.3 per cent, the individual assessments ranged from 5 per cent to more than 250 per cent. In the cities the inequali-

[2] See S. C. Wallace, *State Administrative Supervision Over Cities in the United States* (New York: Columbia University Press, 1928), p. 60.

[3] See p. 122.

ties were equally severe. This injustice was all the more onerous because property owners were subjected to the same local rate, which was from four to sixteen times as great as the state rate of 25 cents on the $100.[4]

The remedy

In an effort to avoid these injustices and other tax evils, Virginia, along with several other states, abolished the tax on real estate and tangible personal property for state revenue purposes through the process of separation of tax sources. This principle was, perhaps unwisely, written into the state constitution in 1928. While it has done much good in reducing inequalities, it has by no means eliminated them.

In Virginia much more was accomplished through the organization of a well-integrated tax department in 1927 under the sole direction of a State Tax Commissioner who has certain supervisory and control powers over the locally elected commissioners of the revenue. Under the segregation plan the commissioner in each county and city assesses property for both the state and the local government. With reference to the former, the local officer serves as a mere agent of the state and is subject to review by an examiner of records appointed by the State Tax Commissioner. If returns on state taxes have not been properly made, the taxpayer may be summoned for examination and explanation. The tax code also allows the State Tax Commissioner to withhold the salaries of local commissioners for neglect of duty or failure to make the required reports. The State Commissioner may also report to the circuit court any incapacity, misconduct, or neglect of duty on the part of local commissioners, and thereby institute ouster proceedings against such officers. Certain inequalities still exist, however, as between individual taxpayers.

The foregoing facts can be largely duplicated in the history of many other states. To correct the gross undervaluations of competing assessors, state boards of equalization were first set up, beginning as early as 1820,[5] followed by state tax commissions, beginning with Indiana in 1891. The establishment of this commission marked a new era in the central regulation of assessments. Its power was not confined to the adjustment of differences in valuation as among the various taxing units (as in the case of the boards of equalization), but extended to the supervision of the original assessments made by the local assessors.[6] Tax commissions are now found in forty-one states, and centralized supervision over local assessments is apparently on the upgrade.[7]

The authority of some of these commissions is limited to advisory powers of control, such as the right to advise, to inspect the work of local officials, to collect information or require reports, to prescribe forms, and to make regulations. Others have mandatory powers to insure equitable assessment, or to exercise original jurisdiction to the same end, such as the reassessment of specific pieces of property on the commission's own initiative after notice and hearing, the right to order local boards to reassess property, and in some cases the power to appoint or remove local tax officials.[8] The last-named power was held unconstitutional in Virginia in 1931.

Professor White reports in the work previously cited that in substantially over half the states sufficient authority has been conferred upon state officials

---

[4] Figures taken from previously cited Report, pp. 122–27.

[5] Wallace, *op. cit.*, p. 61.

[6] *Ibid.*, p. 62.

[7] See L. D. White, *Trends in Public Administration* (New York, 1933), p. 61.

[8] *Ibid.*, pp. 60, 61.

to insure an equitable system of tax assessment, although the power is not always effectively exercised.[9]

In view of the preceding facts it can hardly be maintained that the exercise of this power involves any serious derogation of local self-government. In most cases the state is merely protecting its own interest against local misgovernment. Even its own revenue is at stake in the majority of instances.

State Limitation on Local Taxes

In the matter of state limitation of local taxes, there is an almost endless number and variety of restrictions.[10] Most states limit the rates that may be levied; a few limit the per capita amount that may be raised; others restrict the amounts that may be raised by property taxes; and a few accomplish the same purpose through restrictions on budget increases. The limits vary for different governmental units within the state, and for different purposes. A few states (among them, Indiana, New Jersey, Colorado, and Rhode Island) provide for administrative supervision over local tax rates, giving to an administrative agency the power to revise local levies in excess of the general limits. In New Mexico the State Tax Commission has the power to revise local budgets and levies without regard to limits. In fifteen states the limits are embedded in the constitution.

In the majority of states the levies for debt service and schools are not within the general limits, though such levies may be subject to specific limitations. In some states additional taxes for certain specific purposes may be levied subject to approval by the voters in a referendum on the question.

[9] L. D. White, *op. cit.*, p. 63.
[10] For facts and figures, see William O. Suiter, *Municipal Year Book*, 1936, pp. 328–39.

From the standpoint of local self-government, the most serious form of tax limitation is that product of the recent depression known as over-all or blanket limitation. The practice of creating new tax units and the resultant piling up of tax levies through overlapping jurisdictions led to a demand for limitations on rates of the blanket type, that is, limits that restrict the aggregate rate on the same property irrespective of the number of jurisdictions involved. The depression produced widespread agitation for limitations of this type, the leadership coming from those having large vested interests in real estate. Eight states, Georgia being the latest addition, now restrict taxes upon this broad basis. In Indiana and Washington the limitation is statutory, but in the other six states it is written in the constitution. The rates vary in these states from 1 per cent in Ohio to 4 per cent in Washington.[11]

Tax-rate limitations, especially those of the over-all type, seem to have accomplished little good anywhere. They frequently wreck the local units' revenue system and force them to curtail local services beyond all reason. This in turn has encouraged excessive borrowing, defaulting, and the resort to various juggling devices to evade the limitations. It is noteworthy that most of the states adopting over-all limitations have resorted to the sales tax.

In these circumstances local taxpayers are prevented from deciding what services they want and are willing to support. Surely this is no contribution to the effectiveness or the responsibility of local government. Such limitations seldom, if ever, are based on expert opinion or careful planning with a view to the general welfare. They are rather the result of popular hysteria inspired by adverse economic conditions and the propaganda of large real estate interests.

[11] *Ibid.*, p. 331.

It is difficult to see any advantage to the average homeowner in such restrictions. Indeed, there would seem to be no advantage to anyone save the large real estate interests, and it may well be doubted if even this is permanent.[12] Happily, this tax-limitation movement, which for a time threatened to eliminate property taxation, seems now to be definitely on the wane.[13]

STATE LIMITATIONS ON LOCAL INDEBTEDNESS

Closely linked with tax limitation is limitation of local borrowing. Herein lies one of the chief evils of the former device. Where both tax limitation and debt limitation are invoked, the result is likely to be, as previously suggested, defaulting, serious curtailment of necessary local services, hasty and thoughtless resort to new taxes, or subterfuges of evasion.

Nearly all states have laws on the subject of debt limitation, and a majority have constitutional limitations. These latter grew largely out of the prodigal use of local credit to finance various types of local improvement in the latter decades of the nineteenth century. The statute law on the subject is confined mainly to the last twenty-five years.[14] In all states having general laws on the subject, the limitation is stated in terms of the assessed valuation of the taxable property in the locality.

In the light of the foregoing discussion of assessment supervision, it is clear that this is a most inaccurate measure of borrowing capacity. This has been amply demonstrated in recent experience.

Formerly such restrictions were purely constitutional or statutory, with no control by state administrative officials over local authorities. Instead, restrictions were specifically stated in the constitutions or statutes and were enforced in the courts. In the past twenty years, however, according to Professor White's recent study,

> there has been considerable tendency to substitute effective state [administrative] control of the incurring of local indebtedness for the mere requirements of registration or certification of legality which had developed in the last quarter of the nineteenth century. . . . The present tendency is to limit this freedom by state administrative action.[15]

This would seem to be a wholesome development, provided the discretion of the state administrative officers is properly limited to safeguarding the solvency and financial stability of the local governments, and does not extend to the control of local policy. Such sweeping control as that granted in Indiana, Iowa, and New Mexico, for example, seems both unnecessary and unwise from the standpoint of the general welfare.[16]

STATE CONTROL OVER LOCAL BUDGETS

Closely related to, and to a considerable extent overlapping, tax and debt limitations, is state supervision of local budgets. While budget legislation in general is a recent development, more than half the states now require that all or a part of their local subdivisions operate under budgets. As early as 1909, Indiana and Washington required their

---

[12] For a fuller discussion of the effects of tax limitation see group of articles in the *National Municipal Review* for November 1935.

[13] *Ibid.*, pp. 631 ff.

[14] Lane W. Lancaster, "State Limitations on Local Indebtedness," *Municipal Year Book*, 1936, pp. 313–27.

[15] L. D. White, *Trends in Public Administration, op. cit.*, p. 257.

[16] See F. G. Bates, "State Control of Local Finance in Indiana," *American Political Science Review*, XX, No. 2 (May 1926), pp. 352–60; The "Indiana Plan" in Iowa (Editorial), *National Municipal Review*, May 1937; Carl R. Dortch, The "Indiana Plan" in Action, *National Municipal Review*, Nov. 1938, pp. 525–29.

local governments to prepare their budgets in accordance with state-prescribed forms. In all but a few of these states, budgetary supervision is confined to a review and checking of the form of the local budgets so as to guarantee their conformance to state laws. In such states as Indiana, Iowa, and New Mexico, however, state administrative officers are granted discretionary powers with reference to the purpose, the wisdom, and the amounts of specific items in the local budgets.

In Indiana the state has almost exclusive final authority over the budget levies of every local unit. Any ten taxpayers may appeal from the action of either the local legislative body or the recently created County Tax Adjustment Board to the State Board of Tax Commissioners. Under a 1937 act of the legislature all local budgets are automatically referred to the State Tax Board for review if the County Tax Adjustment Boards fail to set a rate within the tax limits of $1.25 outside and $2.00 inside incorporated cities and towns, with certain exceptions.[17]

In Iowa the State Board of Appeal, composed of the state comptroller, auditor and treasurer, will authorize deputies to hold hearings on a local budget if one-fourth of one per cent of the voters in the taxing district file a petition of appeal. The State Board may approve or reduce the budget but may not make increases.

In New Mexico the State Tax Commission has the power to reduce local budgets without local petition. Its jurisdiction extends to budgets of all local units, and it may disapprove any budget item with no appeal from its decision when made.[18]

In these three states local communities are deprived of virtually all responsibility for their financial programs. The state capital, not the county seat or city hall, is the final seat of authority for the determination of the wisdom or policy involved in local expenditures and indebtedness. The local residents continue to pay the bills, but the ultimate financial decisions rest with officials irresponsible to them.[19] This would seem to be carrying state control farther than is desirable for the best interests of either the local government or the state. Judging from a recent criticism of the much publicized "Indiana Plan," results have not been altogether satisfactory in Indiana.[20]

State Financial Aid to Local Governments

A different, and in some of its aspects a relatively new, form of state centralization is to be found in the various methods of affording state financial assistance to the local units of government, especially the increasing use of locally shared state revenues. Reference has already been made to the shift in sources of revenue from those that lent themselves to local administration to more flexible sources which can be effectively administered only by the state. Since few of the modern taxes can be successfully administered by local units, and since local expenditures are steadily increasing, it is inevitable that the cities and the counties, especially the latter, will lean more and more heavily upon the state for financial aid. There are three channels through which this assistance can be extended: (1) state grants-in-aid for the support of specified functions; (2) sharing of state-collected taxes, in whole or in part, with local governments; (3) state assumption of local functions. These may be used singly or in combination.

---

[17] Dortch, *op. cit.*, p. 526.
[18] Wylie Kilpatrick, *State Administrative Review of Local Budget Making* (Municipal Administration Service, No. 3, 1927), p. 8.

[19] *Ibid.*
[20] Dortch, *op. cit.*, pp. 528–29.

The state grant-in-aid in its original conception was a grant to be matched by the locality for the purpose of stimulating needed local expenditures and thereby raising standards of service. The matching feature, although still used, has become less important in recent years. It was found that matching encouraged extravagance, and that many poor communities remained backward because of their inability to meet the matching requirement. Consequently minimum standards of expenditure have been set up, which in the poor localities are maintained largely at state expense.

The grant-in-aid dates back to the early Colonial period in our history. As early as 1646, Virginia, for example, enacted a law providing for the training, at general public expense, of two children of poor parents in each county.[21] The general development of the grant-in-aid as a device for controlling and directing local functions, however, is of comparatively recent date. Although grants-in-aid and locally shared state taxes are closely related, it has been customary to distinguish them. Usually the former is distributed to local units without great regard to the local origin of the funds and is usually the result of a complex of endeavors on the part of the state to relieve local tax burdens, to fulfill state responsibilities in the support of certain functions, to gain and exert controls, and at the same time to improve the quantity or quality of services offered.[22]

State-administered locally shared taxes differ from grants-in-aid in that the amounts received by the localities depend solely upon the yield of the specific taxes rather than upon state-determined standards of expenditure and performance. Locally shared taxes are usually distributed to local units in some rough proportion to the amount of money derived from the localities, and are accompanied by few specifications for the use of the funds. In general, with the exception of motor-vehicle taxes, they are not distributed in support of any particular services, but may be used for general purposes.[23] Among the more important of these taxes are: gasoline taxes, taxes on motor vehicles, income taxes, sales taxes, corporation and public utilities taxes. Recent studies indicate that those taxes are growing in both number and amount, that the source of the increase is largely new types of taxes, and that as the amount of revenue from them increases, state restrictions upon the localities increase.[24]

Thus is raised in a new form the problem of state centralization. With centralization of tax resources and the distribution of state-collected taxes to the localities, it is almost inevitable that there will follow more rigid state control over those local functions supported by state taxes. Although locally shared taxes appear to have been resorted to in recent years largely as a means of resistance to such controls as ordinarily accompany grants-in-aid, as well as for property tax relief, both schemes lead to centralization and away from the traditional type of local self-government. A recent study points out that "as the number of controls imposed on local government functions increase, shared taxes may evolve as grants-in-aid, the grant system being either an alternative or preliminary to actual state assumption of functions."[25]

[21] Hening, *Statutes at Large*, Vol. I, p. 336.
[22] Russell J. Hinckley, *State Grants-in-Aid* (Special Report No. 9, New York State Tax Commission, 1935), p. 12.
[23] Ruth G. Hutchinson, *State-Administered Locally-Shared Taxes* (New York: Columbia University Press, 1932), p. 34.
[24] See Raymond Uhl and A. V. Shea, Jr., "State-Administered Locally-Shared Taxes," *Municipal Year Book*, 1936, *passim;* Hutchinson, *op. cit.*, and Hinckley, *op. cit.*
[25] *Ibid.*, p. 42.

Method of distribution

The most important, as well as the most difficult, problem in connection with the sharing of state revenue with local governments is that of the method or measure of distribution. There has been no single uniform method, partly because there has been no single purpose of sharing such revenue. Among the methods used are the percentage or matching method, the equalizing grant, and the return of a fixed portion of a specific tax to the community from which it is supposed to have come. If one may assume that the promotion of the general welfare is the proper test for distribution, it would seem that the equalizing-aid device is the most effective and the most economical. This method is, of course, designed to insure the distribution of funds to local communities according to their financial needs. The present tendency seems to favor a wider use of this method. Even this method, however, involves difficulties and dangers against which careful safeguards must be erected if gross abuse is to be avoided. The difficulty of determining the relative needs and financial abilities of local governments is extreme. This has been especially true where the basis of distribution was the local assessed valuation. Obviously, there can be no equalization of aid based upon locally controlled assessments. The first step towards equalization of state aid is the equalization of local property valuations.

Implications of state control

An even greater danger arises in those localities where the support of public services comes almost entirely from the state. If there is not rigid control over expenditures in these communities, they are likely to become parasites upon the state body politic. A recent writer has pointed to towns in New York State receiving three-fourths or more of their income from the state, in which highway pay rolls contain the name of every able-bodied man in the town and some women.[26]

It seems clear that adequate control in those cases where the revenue comes primarily from state sources will leave only the shadow of local self-government.

Herein lies the crucial problem of state-local relations. It seems inescapable that state control will increase as state aid increases. As one solution for this problem, it would seem both wise and equitable for the state to demand that local units embody sufficient taxable wealth and population to carry at least a substantial fraction of the financial burden; and poor and thinly inhabited areas unable to meet this condition might well be taken over and administered directly by the state. This would not involve any impairment of the principle of local self-government, for the reason that local self-government in such areas is impossible. In no other way, it would seem, can wasteful expenditures and the perpetuation of governmental parasites be avoided. If this is done, it may be possible to avoid the third method of extending financial assistance, namely, state absorption of local functions.

It may be stated incidentally at this point that space limitations will not permit consideration of such other important fiscal aspects of state-local relations as the supervision and installation of local accounts, state auditing of local accounts, reporting, and so forth. These devices are designed to aid the localities as well as to safeguard the state, and do not necessarily involve any serious encroachment upon local government by the state.

[26] Mabel Newcomer, "Locally Shared State Revenues," *National Municipal Review*, Dec. 1935, p. 681.

Conclusion

Any conclusions to be drawn from this discussion must of necessity be expressed in the broadest and most general terms. The problem of the proper relationship between state and local government will require much careful thought and research before it can be adequately solved, if it ever can. The most that can be done here is to set down a few guideposts:

1. It must be recognized, first of all, that the problem is one of insuring to citizens the opportunity of intimate participation in their own public affairs on the one hand, and of providing a type of government capable of rendering efficiently the services demanded by citizens and of solving the problems of a twentieth-century society, on the other; to the end that truly democratic government may be maintained.

2. It must be recognized that the excesses of local self-government, as well as of state centralization, have seriously obstructed progress to this goal. Unnecessary and obsolete taxing and administrative units have complicated and hampered the problem of securing effective local government. The abolition of perhaps a majority of those is an essential of proper state-local co-operation. The trend towards centralization has also been aided and abetted by the weakness and incompetence of local authorities in the face of new responsibilities.

3. A certain measure of state supervision is not only inevitable, but essential to the general welfare. The fortunes of local government are so inextricably entwined with those of the state that complete financial autonomy is impossible.

4. Minimum standards of fiscal procedure and functional performance should be set and maintained by the state, with an opportunity on the part of local units to exceed these standards, and with responsibility on the local officials for results.

5. Every effort should be made to improve local administration from within. Among the possibilities here are: (1) internal reorganization under a single executive head through the grant of home rule or the passage of optional forms of legislation, and (2) consolidation of counties, either geographical or functional. Each of these proposals has its advocates, and actual experience with each has been had in one or more states. For example, the county-manager and county-executive plans have had five years of successful experience in Virginia.

6. It should be remembered that efficient and responsible local administration is more important than state centralization. If democracy is to work at the apex of our governmental pyramid, it must first be made to work at the base. No structure is more secure than the foundation on which it rests.

7. Consideration might well be given to the creation of a single central agency to serve primarily as a liaison between the state and local governments. The normal responsibility of such an agency would be to assist, to co-operate with, and to furnish information to, the local units, using control and regulatory powers as a last resort to remedy conditions affecting the general welfare.

8. Finally, there can be no arbitrary separation of state and local responsibility for providing and supporting public services. They must co-operate, or both will suffer. Centralization or local self-government must and will conform to the needs of the time. As Professor White has well said:

> The social profile shows centralization progressing at various rates of speed and reaching a "saturation point" at different stages. No specific demarcation of the useful limits of centralization can be sug-

gested which has any promise of stability. One may suggest as tests or standards the effective attainment of prevailing social ideals and objectives; the preservation of community and personal sense of initiative and responsibility; and the preservation of adequate democratic control.[27]

[27] White, *Introduction to the Study of Public Administration, op. cit.*, p. 185.

George W. Spicer, Ph.D., is professor of political science at the University of Virginia, Charlottesville, and formerly held the same position at the College of William and Mary. He is a member of the Committee on County Government of the National Municipal League, and has served as chairman of the Virginia Commission on County Government, consultant on studies in local government to the Legislative Council of Kentucky, and president of the Virginia Social Science Association. He is author of "Constitutional Status and Government of Alaska" (1927) and other works.

Politics of Integration in Metropolitan Areas

By Victor Jones

THE politics of integration are the most important aspect of the problem. Experts can suggest any number of devices for complete or partial integration. Technicians can draft statutes or charters and are prepared to supervise their installation. The difficulty, or the dilemma if the term is preferred, lies in securing legislative or electoral approval. Venerable and accepted symbols are present on all sides to serve as material for the rationalization of opposition, sincere or otherwise, to integration. There has been little success up to now in transforming the unfavorable stereotypes held by a large number of suburban dwellers, rural and small-town folk outside metropolitan areas, legislators from these groups, and jurists who construe constitutions, statutes, and charters.

The configuration of attitudes in a metropolitan area toward a proposal to integrate local government is both static and dynamic. It tends to be static in that attitudes are rationalized around traditional conceptions of local self-government. Migrants to the metropolitan area hold on to their conception of the local government pattern of their home village or small city. On the other hand, the heterogeneity of the metropolis presents a variety of stimuli to cause the voter to react in several possible ways to an integration proposal.

Diverse Interests

Proponents of integration have failed to recognize the diversity of interests which might be used as bases of appeals for affirmative votes on integration proposals. They usually divide the electorate into voters of the central city, the suburbs, and, where constitutional amendments or statutes are required, the rural and village districts of the remainder of the state. These groups are treated as if they were homogeneous, although supplementary appeals are sometimes directed to the electors as businessmen, professional men, laborers, or farmers. It is an error, however, to plan a campaign on the assumption that all residents of metropolitan areas outside the central city are of one mind.

There are many kinds of suburbs, even within the broad classifications of industrial and residential. The residential suburbs may be predominantly composed of laborers, middle-class commuters, or wealthy families; industrial suburbs may be under the influence of a single large corporation or they may contain many small and medium-sized plants. Suburbs differ from one another according to their relative social and economic coalescence with the central city. Historical traditions are thick in suburbs which were originally founded as isolated towns or villages, only later to be overwhelmed by the movement of population from the big city. Other suburbs have never enjoyed a distinct communal existence, having been created as real estate promotion schemes.

In addition to distinctions which may be used to characterize municipalities as a whole, innumerable groupings of the residents representing wide differences in economic status and power, religious affiliations and attitudes, cultural contacts and background, party affiliations, occupational interests, and racial and national loyalties, work within and across the boundaries of counties and municipalities. The politics of a large city and its metropolitan area are, it has been well said, "as much of a tangle and as full of movement as a canful of angleworms."

What groups in the metropolis have a special interest in the integration of local governments? What groups are opposed to integration? What support have the advocates or the opponents of integration secured from groups "downstate" or "upstate"? How have these groups rationalized their interests and around what symbols have they built their rationalizations? And finally, what techniques of appeal or persuasion have they resorted to, and how successfully have they employed these techniques?

Business and Professional Groups

In many instances, agitation for a metropolitan government or for annexation to another municipality is provoked by objections to specific situations such as unpopular officials, objectionable tax rates, or embezzlement of funds. With the passage of time or a change in the situation, the movement is exhausted. Many people feel that these proponents of integration are attempting to grind their axes.

Although chambers of commerce are not primarily concerned with the organization and administration of local government, movements for integration are most frequently initiated by businessmen's organizations or by civic groups dominated by business and professional men.[1] They have initiated and sponsored integration movements in several metropolitan areas, such as Pittsburgh, Cleveland, St. Louis, and Philadelphia.

The Pittsburgh Chamber of Commerce, for example, has for over three decades urged the inclusion of the outside area and population within the city of Pittsburgh. Until 1921 the traditional type of municipal expansion by annexation was promoted and encouraged by the Chamber. Its activities were persistently opposed during that time by the League of Boroughs and Townships of Allegheny County. Between 1921 and 1923 the Chamber was on record as favoring the creation by the legislature of an *ad hoc* public works district to cover a large part of the county. The proposal was not vigorously pushed, however, and nothing was accomplished. Since 1923 the Chamber has in the main co-operated with other groups, including the League of Boroughs and Townships, in a long, and as yet unsuccessful, campaign to federate the local units into a county-wide government to be known as Metropolitan Pittsburgh.

The exceptional interest of Pittsburgh business leaders during the twenties in the creation of a metropolitan government was partly due to their chagrin at seeing the city ranked as the ninth in population—below Cleveland, Detroit, Boston, Baltimore, and St. Louis. A full-page advertisement in a local paper in 1928 declared that the problem facing the city and its suburbs was to arouse a "metropolitan spirit" and to undertake a "comprehensive program . . . which shall strive to place Pittsburgh and the Pittsburgh district in a position to meet and surpass any and all competition." [2]

The desire of the Chamber for a metropolitan government that would further business interests is indicated by its work for the proposed charter submitted to the legislature in 1935. The Chamber took an active part in its preparation. The State Senate passed the bill in essentially the form it was introduced, but the House amended the bill to provide for the taxation of utility property.

---

[1] For a more extensive discussion, see the author's forthcoming study of the integration of local government in the larger metropolitan areas of the United States, to be published by the Bureau of Public Administration, University of California, Berkeley.

[2] *Pittsburgh Post-Gazette*, Nov. 1, 1928.

The Senate, on the demand of the Chamber of Commerce and the Metropolitan Plan Commission, refused to accept the amendments, and the proposed charter died in conference. The same groups, supported by the League of Women Voters, the Civic Club of Allegheny County, the Pittsburgh Real Estate Board, and the Building Owners' and Managers' Association, brought about the defeat of a proposal on the ballot to establish a county public-utility administration as provided by an act of the 1937 legislature.[3]

The faction of the Republican party under the leadership of Andrew W. Mellon and W. W. Atterbury, formerly president of the Pennsylvania Railroad, sponsored the movement for a metropolitan government for Allegheny County which was defeated at the polls in 1929. The chairman of the Metropolitan Plan Commission, which drafted the proposed charter, was J. T. Miller, secretary-treasurer of a suburban water works of which R. B. Mellon was president.

Various groups

There are many associations besides chambers of commerce which draw their membership from business and professional men and women. Among those that at some time or other have pressed for a more integrated local government in the metropolis are: the Citizens' Bureau, the Real Estate Board, the City Club, and the United Taxpayers' League in Milwaukee; the Citizens' Association and the Civic Federation in Chicago; the City Improvement League in Montreal; the Civic Club of Allegheny County, the Allied Boards of Trade,[4] and the Taxpayers' League of Allegheny County in Pittsburgh; the Citizens' League in Cleveland; and the Commonwealth Club of California in San Francisco.[5]

The activity of most of these associations has likewise been sporadic and their interest in integration specialized. Taxpayers' leagues are obviously concerned with tax reductions, and they support consolidation schemes when they think economies can thereby be effected. They also tend to use every opportunity to attack the integrity of officeholders, and they often find such an opportunity in a campaign for integration.

The Civic Club of Allegheny County, the Philadelphia Bureau of Municipal Research, the Cleveland Citizens' League, and the Milwaukee Citizens' Bureau have, on the other hand, shown interest in all phases of the government of their respective metropolitan areas. These associations are largely responsible for the publicity given to the problem over long periods of time. In the heat of the campaign preceding an election other groups climb on the band wagon, but in the long months of preparation, both in the metropolis itself and at the state capital, these are the associations that have kept persistently at work.

Some businessmen, industrialists, and professional men are opposed to governmental change of any kind. The best example of such a group is the Philadelphia Board of Trade, which in 1937 opposed city-county consolidation for Philadelphia, along with four other proposed amendments to the State Constitution. The Board declared that

each and every amendment is framed pri-

---

[3] *Pittsburgh Sun-Telegraph*, Nov. 3, 1937.

[4] Composed of forty-two civic and businessmen's organizations in the county.

[5] A general survey of local government in the San Francisco Bay area is now being prepared by the Bureau of Public Administration, University of California, Berkeley. Among the topics included in the study is the political problem of securing public and legislative approval of alternative types of metropolitan government and of co-operation between existing units of local government.

marily in the interest of selfish partisan political advancement, pernicious in purpose and so menacing as to afford dictatorial control and relegation of the public ballot to rank as a mere perfunctory ceremony.[6]

Under the leadership of Ira Jewell Williams, a corporation lawyer and an old-time Philadelphia Republican leader, and with the support of manufacturing and textile-mill interests, a state-wide attack was waged on the proposed Philadelphia city-county consolidation amendment and all other propositions on the ballot.

Another type of business interest likely to be opposed to integration is that engaged in selling services or materials to governmental units. The Ohio road material and equipment interests opposed the county home-rule amendment of 1933, which permits integration, and have worked against county reform throughout the state.[7]

Labor Groups

Organized labor and unorganized workers, even in the central city, often are suspicious of movements to integrate local government in the metropolitan area. In the first place, they suspect on sight anything initiated by, or under the auspices of, a chamber of commerce. Under the general policy, by no means confined to organized labor, of rewarding one's friends and punishing one's enemies, labor leaders fail to see why they should support part of the chamber-of-commerce program when at the same time the chamber is espousing the open shop or opposing labor legislation at the state or national capital. In the second place, they fear that any movement designed to reduce taxes will result in a curtailment of governmental services desirable or necessary to the laboring class.

[6] *Philadelphia Inquirer*, Oct. 29, 1937.
[7] *Cleveland Plain-Dealer*, Oct. 17, 1933.

Another reason why organized labor is often opposed is that suggested schemes of metropolitan government frequently provide for a short ballot and the council-manager form of government. The ideology of labor—in and out of trades unions or labor parties—is still largely that of Jacksonian Democracy. It is believed that appointees in responsible positions are more likely to be controlled by business, industrial, and financial leaders than by labor.

The two labor men on the 1935 Cuyahoga County (Cleveland) Charter Commission were divided on the question of a county director with powers corresponding to those of a city manager. Max S. Hayes, editor of *The Citizen*, Cleveland Federation of Labor journal, voted for the manager plan, and W. J. Corrigan, labor attorney, voted against it. Corrigan raised the cry of "dictatorship" and referred to the example of East Cleveland, where councilmen had to be recalled before the people could get at the manager.[8]

The *Toledo Union Leader* recommended the rejection in 1935 of the proposed home-rule charter for Lucas County because it provided for a county manager and made the prosecuting attorney an appointive officer. This stand was taken despite the fact that the president of the central labor body and two other labor leaders were members of the charter commission. The charter was defeated. At the same time, however, the first Toledo city council under the manager plan, adopted the year before, was elected by proportional representation, and labor secured two of the nine seats.

Another point of concern with labor is the possibility that certain employees will lose their positions as the result of integration. Here is a sharp clash of interest between labor and chambers of commerce and taxpayers' groups, for the

[8] *Cleveland Plain-Dealer*, March 21, 1935.

latter hope that integration will reduce the total number of employees and lower the cost of government. In Milwaukee, on the other hand, organized labor did not oppose the transfer of city parks to the county, because they saw therein an opportunity to organize the county park employees. This they proceeded to do immediately after the transfer was effected.

Labor has not uniformly opposed the integration of local government. The formation of Greater New York was indorsed by labor leaders in 1896 before a legislative committee. Representatives of the Gilders' Union and of the Hack Drivers Association expected consolidation to have a favorable effect on the housing and transit situation. Since 1919 the Chicago Federation of Labor has been on record, in general terms, as favoring the integration of local government in Cook County. The Milwaukee Socialist party, with close ties to organized labor, has for several years urged the integration of local government in that area.

More assistance from organized labor might be secured if the proponents of integration would seek the views, advice, and participation of labor leaders during the early stages of preparing the proposal and drafting the legislation.

Politicians in the Woodpile

It is often said that politicians, from a desire to hold on to their offices and emoluments, present insuperable obstacles to integration. They prefer, moreover, to act as big frogs in small ponds rather than to be small frogs in a big pond. The fear that integration will result in a loss of deference is not, however, confined to public officeholders. Leaders in all kinds of suburban groups, such as boy scouts, chambers of commerce, leagues of women voters, and luncheon and service clubs, are motivated by the fear of being swallowed into the general membership of the respective groups of the metropolis.

Politicians will openly oppose integration only if they think it "good," or at least "safe," politics to do so. If the dominant political party is opposed to integration (and it can easily be brought around to this position by influential suburban party leaders, the natural reluctance of party men to touch the patronage machine, and the downstate or upstate leaders' distrust of integration), it can usually manage to approve the movement locally and yet kill it by maneuvers in the rest of the state. Most integration movements have to clear the hurdle of an amendment to the state constitution or the proposed scheme must originate in or be approved by the state legislature. The part played by the state and local Republican leaders in the mutilation and ultimate defeat of the 1929 metropolitan Pittsburgh charter, although they openly espoused it, is probably the best example, in the field of metropolitan government, of death by embrace. Eight years later, when the Democrats were in power, despite the declaration of their leaders, including the Governor, that the 1937 proposed constitutional amendment to reconsolidate the city and county of Philadelphia was strictly a party measure, they campaigned lackadaisically upstate, and the amendment was defeated.

On the other hand, the reorganization of Nassau and Westchester counties (New York) was initiated, under pressure, and carried through the legislature and a successful electoral campaign, by the regular Republican organizations. Politicians, like other men, look suspiciously upon any potential threat to their job-security and personal income, but they are deference-hungry. It is less difficult for politicians to support reorganization and integration movements when a sizable portion of their constituents, as in Nassau and Westchester counties, pay deference to the exponents and practitioners of economical, efficient, businesslike administration. One key, then, to secure genuine party support and leadership is to alter the unfavorable or indifferent attitudes of the electorate, or to create new attitudes that can be evoked by old or new symbols and transferred into votes.

Suburban politicians almost always strike a responsive chord when they accuse the "machine" politicians of the central city of designing to pull, directly or indirectly, the clean, graftless, orderly suburb into the social chaos of the big "boss-ridden" city. The central city is accused of attempting to ease its financial condition by "forcibly annexing" the taxable resources of the thrifty and graft-free suburbs. (To the suburban opponent of integration, any form or degree of integration is "forcible annexation.") The suburbanites know that many of the facilities of the central city may be used by them, making it unnecessary for the suburbs to be taxed to maintain similar facilities.

Surburban officialdom is, as a rule, well organized, and finds a ready ear at the state capital for its cries of Wolf! Wolf! It has succeeded in many states in freezing an undemocratic impediment to integration into constitutions and statutes. The assent of a majority, and in California of all, of existing units of local government is required to integrate municipalities into a metropolitan government. This is done upon the theory that the home-rule principle means that the corporate integrity of each and every unit of local government must be preserved—irrespective of its population or of the degree of its economic and social coalescence with other units in the metropolitan area. The theory as applied in this manner allows a very small part of the total population of an area to veto any scheme, even though it is acceptable to a large majority of the electorate of the whole metropolis. The device cannot be considered democratic which allows, for example, fewer than 15,000 people who live in the smaller thirty-one of the sixty units of Cuyahoga County (Cleveland) to veto a plan which is approved by a majority of the electors representing the 1,201,455 inhabitants of the entire county.

ATTITUDES OF PEOPLE OUTSIDE METROPOLITAN AREAS

People who live outside metropolitan areas distrust the big city even more, if possible, than does the most confirmed suburbanite. After all, the suburban resident is a daily or occasional commuter, and knows the city. Time and again, the rural and village voters have denied the right to a majority of voters in a metropolitan area to decide upon issues vitally affecting no one save the metropolitan resident. Unscrupulous opponents of integration (such as suburban politicians, county politicians, public-utility men, contractors, and supply dealers) have told the rural and village voters that a large number of farmers would be brought under an expensive and cumbersome form of city government if the local governments of metropolitan areas were integrated. City-county consolidation has been described to them as a subversive scheme to destroy the American constitutional system! Judging from the fate of several integration proposals, the majority of upstate voters believe such statements.

MAKING INTEGRATION MARKETABLE

The proponents of integration, then, must prepare a marketable article and undertake to sell it. Campaigns must be well planned, the details carefully executed by technicians, and the proposal systematically and persistently sold to the public and to politicians. This calls for the use of various propaganda techniques. They are used by the opposition—thus far with almost complete success. It is not proposed to replace debate and discussion with deception and demagoguery; but it is quite clear that insistence upon the administrative and fiscal need for integration, in however great detail it is presented, is not sufficient to change popular allegiance to old concepts of local government. An academic presentation of the case for integrated local government will have no effect upon them. Counterattacks must be made frontally and by flank upon the symbol-reinforcing propaganda of the opponents of integration.

To be successful, the proponents of integration will have to reorganize the attitudes which are now elicited and reinforced by appeal to such symbols as *local self-government, home rule, the little red schoolhouse, "Keep our government clean!" government close to the people,* and, negatively, *centralization, forcible annexation, autocratic and un-American, fascism, dictatorship,* and *corrupt city*. Each of these symbols is charged with high emotional voltage, and, by comparison, many of the symbols used by the proponents of integration arouse only a flicker of response. Symbols such as *economy, efficiency,* or *Pittsburgh . . . 1,500,000 people* evoke in only a few people central and dominating attitudes which can be translated into affirmative votes.

Victor Jones, Ph.D., is research assistant in the Bureau of Public Administration and lecturer in the Department of Political Science at the University of California, Berkeley. He has published two bulletins in the Legislative Problems Series of the Bureau, entitled "Transients and Migrants," and "Relief and Welfare Organization in California." His study of the integration of local government in the larger metropolitan areas of the United States will be published shortly.

County Consolidation

By J. B. Shannon

EVERY epoch reflects some dominant intellectual note. Ours is an age of urbanization and industrialization. In many respects the twentieth century, now approaching its mid-point, represents a reaction to the nineteenth. For three hundred years, a wide dispersion of man over the unoccupied portions of the globe took place—centrifugal forces prevailed. A reverse process set in near the end of the nineteenth century as the frontier with its great open spaces came to an end and was succeeded by a new frontier centralized in city growth induced by the centripetal forces of technology.

The vast economic power manipulated by the Robber Barons soon remade the United States in terms of a centralized corporate industry. It was perhaps inevitable that government should soon reflect the same trends which dominated the economic life of the country. To cope with contemporary problems, to come to grips with national problems, it was necessary for government to create and use national institutions and to set up state-wide agencies rather than to employ existing local governmental bodies. Citizens in a frontier-agrarian civilization were able to deal with their most fundamental problems individually and locally, but this is not true of industrial people. The folklore of the business élite came by gradual transition to be the symbols of governmental reformers. Efficiency, system, orderliness, budgets, economy, saving, were all injected into the efforts of reformers who sought to remodel municipal government in terms of the great impersonality of corporate enterprise. The inevitable next step was to include county government.

The ideology of the Taylor Society was applied first to cities and then to rural institutions. Governmental institutions were to be remade in terms of the ideals of efficiency held by big business.

Studies of Government

As America became adult, she turned to the study of herself and her problems with the same serious-minded drive that she had earlier employed in exploiting her natural resources. As scholars in the field of government studied more intensively, they began to talk of a science of government. That institutions of local government should come in for keen scrutiny was inescapable. Early political scientists and publicists not only were influenced by the severely scientific German approach, but brought into their study of rural government their ideas of corporate management and the advances in municipal managership.

When the county was first studied seriously a quarter of a century ago, it is not surprising that it was dubbed the "dark continent of American politics." In the eyes of the scientist or expert, county government was an incorrigible thing. Ever since, county government has been looked upon as a sort of country cousin by its superior city relatives. As our agricultural population has proportionally declined, due in no small measure to the systematic exploitation of agriculture through a conscious national policy favoring industry—the tariff—this attitude of contempt for all things rural has continued to grow.

The most prevalent form of agricultural government was the county—an importation from England with a faint odor of feudalism about it. Originally an administrative agency of the central government, it became a mongrel thing, partly an institution of local self-government, partly an administrative subdivision of the state. Its powers of local action were jealously restricted by the state, but its choice of personnel was left to the local population, and central supervision was slight. The folk uprising known in American history as Jacksonian Democracy brought about the popular election of local officials. Indeed, by the middle of the nineteenth century, county government had become interwoven with the warp and woof of rural democratic mores.

County Changes

Technology has played havoc with county boundaries. Originally set up in a sort of helter-skelter fashion, partly to satisfy the factional needs of politicians, but more particularly to meet the convenience of citizens in a sort of rule-of-thumb fashion (that is, the ability of a citizen to reach by means of horse and buggy the county seat from the periphery of the area and return in time to get his milking done before sunset), the county no longer fits into the contemporary pattern. At the time of its creation, of course, this agrarian criterion approximated an accurate standard of convenience. Meanwhile, time and space have shrunk as a result of the development of improved highways and high-speed automobiles. Originally an agency for satisfying the needs of farmers, the county has ceased to have any clear meaning at all.

Counties vary in size from over 20,000 square miles in San Bernardino County, California, larger than any of a half-dozen states, to twenty-five square miles in Arlington County, Virginia. Population varies no less widely, from approximately four million in Cook County, Illinois, to less than two hundred in Loving County, Texas.[1] Counties find themselves with many times their former populations. For example, in 1880 Robertson and Harlan counties in Kentucky did not vary widely in population, having 5,814 in the former and 5,278 in the latter; but in 1930 Robertson had lost 42 per cent of its population with a bare 3,344 left, whereas Harlan had increased by 1,123 per cent to 64,557. The first county has nothing but a narrow agricultural base to sustain its government. Twenty-five years ago a spur of a railroad opened up the rich coal veins of Harlan, and wartime high prices did the rest. Thus the problems of that county have suddenly changed from those of a poor agricultural community to those of a rich industrial community.

Doubtless these features have been duplicated elsewhere. The result is that the American county is meaningless as a descriptive term. In some districts it has entirely lost its rural aspects and has been swallowed up by a municipality. In several cases counties have been lost in one metropolitan area. Here the county becomes an anachronism. Like Sieyès' second chamber, if it performs the same functions as the city, it is superfluous; if it obstructs the city, it is obnoxious. More probably it will do the latter.

In other words, in a dynamic economy in which successive layers of natural resources are exploited by changes in technology, the political boundaries which applied to one type of economic life may not fit at all in the next stage of development. Wide diversity of types of economic wealth and rapid fluctuation in the demand for the kind of economic goods it produces may swiftly alter the economic adequacy of an administrative area or of a local governmental institution. Political institutions whose resource base has been mined out, cut over, or eroded away are too frequently evident in contemporary society. Politi-

[1] William Anderson, *The Units of Government in the United States* (Chicago, 1934), pp. 16–17.

cally static boundaries suffer in an economically dynamic world.

It is here that the efficiency expert steps in. Looking at America's three thousand counties, he is likely to say, "Abolish them. Consolidate them." But this quick solution is not so easy when one probes deeply, for investigation is likely to reveal that consolidation is not a facile matter. More than surface thinking is required of the student when confronted with these confusing matters, for he is brought face to face with the whole problem of administrative areas, as well as with the problem of the allocation of governmental functions.

Decline of County Government

As already stated, the county is in part an administrative subdivision of the state and in part an agency of local government. By and large, the local government aspect is declining and state administrative integration is leaving the county with a bare minimum of powers: the authority to appropriate money, and the authority to fix a tax rate within maxima and minima determined by the state. State limitation of county debts and control over county budgets and the absorption by the state and Federal governments of (1) highway building, (2) public health service, (3) poor and old-age relief, (4) educational control and supervision, and (5) state police force and crime control, leave the county a shell in which the lifeblood of local government has gradually ebbed away.

If this trend continues, as it seems likely to do, since the agencies of government tend to follow the areas and contours of the problems with which they grapple, then the county will serve only as a convenient administrative subdivision. But if the county is to be an administrative device, certainly its personnel and actions should not be determined by popular election. Such practices violate the most elementary principles of sound administration. If this continues, the county deserves to and eventually will wither away as the Marxian state is supposed to, because of an atrophy of its functions in the new social order.

But why is the process of atrophy so little evidenced by actual consolidation? Though advocated for a quarter of a century, little consolidation has taken place. Such amalgamations as have taken place have been chiefly where municipal and county areas were approximately coextensive or where a rural county was absorbed by an adjacent metropolitan county. In Denver, Los Angeles, Philadelphia, Chattanooga, and Atlanta, steps have been taken in this direction. In 1919 the consolidation of James County with Hamilton County in Tennessee was regarded as a trail blazer. The absorption of Milton and Campbell counties by Fulton in Georgia has recently been described by experts as an act of charity on the part of the urban county. The County Judge of Rhea County, Tennessee, remarked a few years ago that the Chickamauga Dam of the Tennessee Valley Authority would bisect his county and flood its best lands, but the debt of his county was so high and the tax base so low that no county would want to consolidate with her.

The Emotional Element

The obstacles to consolidation are real and genuine. Human beings are essentially creatures of custom. Graham Wallas sagely observed years ago: "As soon as any body of men have been grouped under a common political name, that name may acquire emotional associations as well as an intellectually analysable meaning."[2] Thus habit or custom, reinforced by human inertia, makes it exceedingly difficult to change.

[2] Graham Wallas, *Human Nature and Politics* (New York, 1921), p. 102.

This is particularly true of rural areas. The rural county and its officials form a human institution. It is not always logical, it is seldom efficient, but it affords an opportunity to express many genuine human emotions. People are able to act in a practically face-to-face community. The citizen personally knows his own officials and can call them by their first names. He is more confident in his ability to make a choice locally than in a larger area. Some years ago a newly enfranchised woman voter vouchsafed the opinion that she was much better qualified to choose local officials than national and state officials, since she knew the former personally and could value their characters, while she dealt at a distance with national and state officials.

The sporting impulse is as eager for the biennial or quadrennial local electoral contest as it was for the excitement of a horse race at the old county fair. One can support and wager upon the contestants. The election affords an opportunity for an expression of human charity and kindness by the selection of the lame, the halt, and the blind for public office, and thereby soothes certain worth-while human emotions. Moreover, there is an element of personal wooing in the local electioneering which gives a feeling of significance even to the humblest, in striking contrast with "the fatalism of the multitude" in national elections, commented upon by Lord Bryce.

However ridiculous the county may appear to financial experts, however ineffective it may seem to administrative reorganizers, yet it satisfies a genuine human want, albeit it may prove an expensive luxury. In some respects the small county is an ideological survival in contemporary politics of the ancient Greek city-state, with an added element of equalitarianism. It is the family and the neighborhood writ large. The small size of the population and the extended degree of personal acquaintance make for a community organic in character, where individuality and human personality find numerous facets of expression. To point out that very frequently these matters are delusions does not materially lessen their democratic emotional appeal.

Against this ideal is set the conception of the efficient administrative bureaucracy—perhaps a survival of the Roman imperial idea. Efficiency, rather than democracy, is its chief end. It is democratic, however, in so far as it secures goods and services for its people. Its greatest emphasis is upon *for* the people rather than *by* and *of,* if the celebrated Lincoln trilogy may be employed once more. To this extent perhaps it is Aristotelian.

However, many less ideal considerations are involved. The vested interest of county officials is a powerful obstacle to consolidation. Oddly enough, the poorer the county, probably the more intense the opposition to elimination; for the fewer the job opportunities, the greater the necessity of holding on to existing jobs. In the South, where the county is more typical of local government than elsewhere, frequently the county is an agency utilized by the local mercantile-lawyer-banker-well-to-do-landlord governing class in exploiting farm labor and farm tenants, as well as the Negro. The closer the government the greater the tyranny, as organizers of labor have often discovered. To disturb the present relationship would be to upset the balance of class relations and cause a severe disturbance to the status quo.

INCOMPATIBILITY OF COUNTIES

Sometimes counties have followed in a rough fashion the areas of fertility of soil. Here the absorption of poorer counties by the more fertile land or wealthier counties would add to the tax burdens of the latter because of the need to provide greater services for the less fortunate county. In addition, the poor and more infertile counties represent a different set of mores from the wealthier counties. For example, the proposal to annex Union County, Tennessee, already split in several directions and its best soil flooded by the Norris Reservoir, to adjacent Knox County, with an urban center at Knoxville, brought the protest that it would subject the Union County people to the evil influence of the urban center where liquor was sold either legally or illicitly.[3]

Not infrequently the annexation to a larger urban center would bring clashes between the more emotional and the more formal religious groups in their indirect efforts to direct the moral and political behavior of the community. The lines of social cleavage may be fairly well drawn between the rich valley counties of a river region and the headwater hill counties. For example, in Kentucky a bluegrass county with very fertile soil, where, under the supervision of a group of well-to-do farmers every road in the county has been surfaced with concrete or asphalt so that automobiles may go anywhere in the county, would be reluctant to amalgamate with a neighboring less fertile county which borders on a small river, many of whose roads are well-nigh impassable. To consolidate these two counties would arouse all sorts of conflict. It would be bitterly opposed by the richer county as a charitable undertaking in which a poor relative was taken care of, and resented by the poorer county as a loss of identity in the larger and more socially aristocratic county.

These are intangible things, but they afford difficulties frequently insuperable. The plea of economy is too cold for many, and generally too remote for the majority who pay few if any direct taxes. Only by state-wide action is it possible to give intelligent administrative direction to any rearrangement of county boundaries.

MACHINE POLITICS

Further, any consolidation of counties will mix into machine politics. Every county seat is the site of a political machine, perhaps two or three machines, which are the very flesh and blood of political power in the state and the Nation. To cut off one of these nerve cells is a dangerous procedure. Where there is a considerable urban center, frequently there is intense rivalry between municipal and county machines in statewide contests. To alter county boundaries or to consolidate city and county governments would run athwart the wishes of the real wielders of power in many communities. Efforts to consolidate by popular or legislative action would probably result in a kind of gerrymandering of which Congressional districts show such excellent examples now.

CRITERIA FOR CONSOLIDATION

Finally, in a scientifically conducted consolidation, the matter of criteria for consolidation arises. Numerous suggestions have been offered. First of all, the test of area might be applied, as in the frontier period; but in terms of what transportation machine shall distance be measured—the automobile, the airplane, or what? This brings us face to face with the matter of topography, for obviously distance can be covered more swiftly on the plains of Kansas than in the Rocky Mountains of Colorado. But topography is further influenced by the presence or absence of good roads, so no easy yardstick is discoverable. Further, there is no conclusive evidence to show that a large area is more eco-

[3] Maynardsville (Tennessee) *Newsette*, Spring, 1939.

nomically administered than a smaller one.[4]

In the second place, population has been suggested as a possible measure of an administratively efficient unit. Here, however, area complicates affairs. For example, the sparsely populated areas of Wyoming or the Dakotas are scarcely comparable with the more densely populated areas of the Iowa farm lands.

A third measure has been suggested, that is, the adequacy of the economic base of the region to be administered. Here likewise the problem is not a simple one. What measure can be applied? The tax assessment test is notoriously inadequate either in its aggregate or on a per capita basis. The per capita wealth of a community is a far better measure than either of the above, but this leads to an investigation of the whole economy of the region. Despite its defects and complexity, this seems the most reasonable and feasible approach to the whole problem. It is to be remembered that no final conclusion has been devised in international relations for determining the exact boundaries of states. The failure of the Treaty of Versailles eloquently testifies to the difficulty. Of course, local boundaries such as those of counties are not complicated by economic tariff barriers, although a difference of tax burdens may affect the outlines of the problem.

In other words, what seems prima facie a simple problem amplifies itself into the very foundations of state life. How is unity in the midst of diversity, integration in the midst of decentralization, to be obtained? Reconciliation of these opposites is not easy. Probably the most intelligent approach is through the device of comprehensive social surveys.

[4] Edward B. Schmidt, *County Consolidation* (Nebraska Studies in Business, No. 36, Lincoln, 1937), p. 50–52.

Natural Subdivisions

To arrive at any conclusion, examination of a number of factors must be undertaken. One of these is the geographical natural subdivisions of a commonwealth or state. A watershed of a river is one of the most suggestive features for study. America has but recently become conscious of the need for utilization of her water wealth. The regional development of the Tennessee Valley area points the way to the multiple problems of the utilization of water. Projects like those of the Columbia and Colorado rivers suggest the probability that in both arid and humid districts rivers will come into their own again, even as they have been at the core of human activity throughout the history of man. As hydropower comes to be utilized as one of the forces of production, there is a possibility not only of a decentralization of industry but also of a decentralization of political power along regional lines.

River watersheds frequently include three or more fairly clear economic divisions. In the rugged mountains or hills where slopes are steep, minerals are present. Lower down, the water sweeps through agriculturally fertile valleys and then empties into a larger stream, gulf, or bay, where towns or cities of commercial and industrial importance are likely to be located. As the mineral or timber base of the upper region is exhausted, that section must be devoted to recreation and conservation purposes. In such districts, through necessity sparsely populated, there is a unity of economic life with its consequent tendency to develop a like cultural pattern which may well become the nucleus for formal organization into a unit of government. Not only may it be an administrative unit or an agency of local government, but it might well become a unit of representation in national and local government. This is especially true if the single member district system of representation is to be continued.

In other words, if the consciousness of kind is to grow—a condition precedent to real community interest and necessary for effective local government —the more ways the people come to feel the common unity the better. Little inducement to unity can be developed by belonging to the 76th legislative district, the 29th senatorial district, the 15th judicial circuit, and the 14th Congressional district. If areas of economic and cultural similarity can be discovered which in a fashion follow approximate natural frontiers, then a basic consideration in local government will have been achieved.

It will be objected, of course, that no such arbitrary natural subdivisions exist. This may be admitted in part without destroying the validity of the argument. The question resolves into a problem of scientific classification. No two leaves are alike, but there is a certain similarity among all leaves. This does not prevent the classification of leaves into maple and oak.

It is appropriate to point out the growth of rural electrification co-operatives, and the development of soil conservation districts by the Agricultural Adjustment Administration, as likely to give a new content to local government; but it would be pouring new wine into old bottles to try to revivify and reinvigorate the present counties. In too many cases rural electrification probably has already led to this result. With the hydroelectric rural co-operative age on its way, the seats of productive power should be the genuine centers of local government. If these administrative areas tend to coalesce with the judicial and legislative areas, the forces of habit will freeze them into a local custom and develop a communal consciousness which will be the basis of genuine regional local government. The more closely these core areas are linked to the cultural heritage of the people, the better it is for a swift evolution of regional consciousness. It is in the development of these new areas that progress must be looked for. When these new areas take on vitality, the old units will gradually atrophy and slough off, even as the township and the school district have done in the past.

THE FUNCTIONAL ASPECT

There is considerable evidence, however, that unless there is more balance between the farm and the metropolis, geography may have less and less significance in the state. Functionalism is certainly on the increase at present. It is not membership in the general citizenry of the community that is important to the average citizen. Rather it is his participation in his trade union, his farm bureau, his chamber of commerce, that is significant. These are the dynamic forces which dominate our politics, as evidenced by the presence of pressure groups. Unless class conflict is warded off, there is considerable evidence that local government will probably center around a plant or a productive unit rather than a geographical area.

It may be added that the prospect of alteration in county boundaries and consolidation of counties is likely to grow only when the social and economic dynamics make such alteration expedient. In Tennessee, where considerable legislation providing for county consolidation was passed during 1939, it had the powerful backing of Ed Crump, "boss" of Memphis. Living in an industrial center which is likely to have to pay taxes to maintain poor counties, Mr. Crump is in position to advocate county consolidation. It was his candidate for governor that advocated and subsequently pushed through such legislation, though it must be admitted that the prospect for the utilization of the opportunity offered is not encouraging.

This is perhaps symptomatic of what may be expected if the present concentration of population in urban centers continues. Inequality of tax base and consequent inequality of governmental services (for it is a truism that the state is becoming more and more a service agency) continue to lead to state-wide taxing and supplying of services. In turn, the heavy urban tax base will insist upon the elimination of unnecessary counties and the development of more efficient and effective administrative areas. When trade unions see the importance of modifying local government because of its functions in control of labor conditions, something more than the cold symbols of efficiency and economy may prove effective. Labor and possibly farm bureau pressure groups may be brought to unite. Then only can we expect rapid progress in any kind of consolidation. Realistic students must admit that at present the probability of such merger is rather slim.

It is a real challenge to social science to discover, by a careful investigation of the whole economy of areas, the genuine cultural and "natural" units which will tend to supplant the present outmoded areas. Research can bring these matters to the attention of powerful pressure groups. Thereby, the objective of more efficient and realistic administrative areas may be attained with some celerity. However, it is probable that until the scholar can show how the stream of power can be canalized and a proliferation of cultural regions harmonized into an organic unity, the change of political boundaries will be slow. Only when social scientists have made this achievement can they expect or deserve to expect the enlargement of the areas of local government. The road ahead is a long one, but it is a very definite challenge to the scientist to supplant accident by knowledge.

Trend toward Decentralization

In summary, it may be observed that the lines of difference between rural and urban government are being softened rather than sharpened. Suburbanization is blurring the distinctions between the two. As this is written, megapolitanism seems on the defensive in Europe. Huge metropolises are being evacuated. People of Paris and London, for example, may spend from three to ten years in the countryside. The present world war may well bring the much discussed industrial decentralization. If it happens in Europe, it will come to America as well. The development of a low-resistance conductor of electric power will tend to eliminate still further urban and rural differences. It is here that the balance between country and city—the equilibrium between the natural and the man-made—may be obtained. When and if this trend becomes dominant, it is probable that the existence of municipal and county governments in the same area will disappear. Counties and cities may well merge in a genuine local government, for the decentralization of economic power may permit the decentralization of political power.

J. B. Shannon, Ph.D., is associate professor of political science at the University of Kentucky, Lexington. He was formerly research associate for the Regional Planning Department of the Tennessee Valley Authority, and is the author of "Henry Clay, Political Leader," and of "Happy Chandler, A Kentucky Epic."

Municipal Government and Special-Purpose Authorities

By William T. R. Fox and Annette Baker Fox

ONCE again municipal government is meeting new demands by piecemeal adaptations of old forms. To the student of public administration preaching the virtues of integration, this must seem a backward step. Like the Port of London Authority from which their name is derived, the new authorities which have been created lack the independent tax-levying powers of the older units; they finance themselves through the power to borrow against anticipated revenues.

The recent increase in the birth rate of special public corporations on the municipal level has redirected attention to those extra layers of government in the larger urban areas whose jurisdiction includes (and may extend beyond) the area of the central municipality. The Bureau of the Census lists such units for sixty-two out of the ninety-four largest cities in its 1936 *Financial Statistics of Cities*. Most widespread and in many cases most ancient is the independent school district, which in ninety-nine of the 191 cities with population of 50,000 or more has undivided control over its own budget. Newest is the housing authority, which has been set up in 229 communities, including twelve out of the fourteen largest cities. Of the 175,000 independent units enumerated by William Anderson in his *Units of Government in the United States*, very few are in the category treated here. Yet each affects the lives of thousands and in some cases millions of persons. Table 1 includes sixty-one in the twenty-six largest cities.

Motives for Separate Incorporation

The earliest justification for such units was that the new function had to be kept "free" of politics and politicians; so separately incorporated school districts were created. Similarly, the transfer of the earlier private corporation or association libraries to public auspices was achieved with the understanding that they remain "out of politics" and therefore independent. Where, as with Philadelphia and Pittsburgh, the boards are partly or wholly self-perpetuating, the special unit may be freed not only from politics but from any form of public control.[1]

True or false, belief in the efficacy of independence persists and was used among other arguments to justify the independence of the housing authority. Proponents of any new governmental function, both lay and expert, tend to favor independence because it frees them from making administrative or political concessions necessary in an integrated administration. Legal independence is not, however, certain to prevent political pressure. With regard to education, Henry and Kerwin found indications that application of such pressure was just as frequent in the case of independent schools as in others.[2] In fact, an intensive study of the Chicago school system's relations with the municipal government showed that in the absence of legal integration, "the stage is set and will continue to be set for integration under other auspices—those of machine politicians and the financial overlords."[3]

State political bosses have sometimes

[1] Carleton Bruns Joeckel, *The Government of American Public Libraries* (Chicago: University of Chicago Press, 1935), pp. 89–90, 180–81.

[2] Nelson B. Henry and Jerome G. Kerwin, *Schools and City Government* (Chicago: University of Chicago Press, 1938), pp. 92–93.

[3] John A. Vieg, *The Government of Education in Metropolitan Chicago* (Chicago: University of Chicago Press, 1939), p. 255.

TABLE 1—Independent Agencies in Principal Cities of the United States

Cities	School	Housing Authority	Park	Library	Sewer	Public Works Authority	Miscellaneous
New York............		x					xxxxx[h]
Chicago.............	x	x	xx[b]		x		x[i]
Philadelphia.........	x	x	x	x		x[f]	x[j]
Detroit..............		x[a]					
Los Angeles.........	x	x					x[k]
Cleveland...........	x	x	x				
St. Louis............	x						
Baltimore...........		x		x			
Boston..............		x					x[l]
Pittsburgh..........	x	x	x			x[g]	
San Francisco.......		x					
Washington.........		x					
Milwaukee..........					x[c]		
Buffalo.............		x		x	x[d]		x[m]
Minneapolis.........					x[e]		
New Orleans........	x	x					x[n]
Cincinnati..........	x	x	x				
Newark.............		x					
Kansas City, Mo.....	x						
Seattle..............	x						x[o]
Indianapolis.........	x						
Rochester...........							
Jersey City..........		x					
Houston............	x				x		x[p]
Louisville...........		x					
Portland............	x			x			x[q]
Total...............	13	17	5	5	5	2	14

Sources: For schools, Henry and Kerwin, *Schools and City Government;* for housing, National Association of Housing Officials, *Housing Yearbook,* 1939; for libraries, Joeckel, *Government of American Public Libraries;* other data derived chiefly from Bureau of the Census, *Financial Statistics of Cities,* 1936. Because of the various sources, the definition of an "independent agency" may not be uniform throughout.

[a] By state law a "noncorporate" agency.
[b] Both Chicago Park District and Cook County Forest Preserve District.
[c] Milwaukee Sewerage District.
[d] Buffalo Sewer Authority.
[e] Minneapolis-St. Paul Sanitary District.
[f] Philadelphia Authority.
[g] Allegheny County Authority.
[h] Triborough Bridge Authority; New York City Tunnel Authority; New York City Parkway Authority; Port of New York Authority; Planetarium Authority.
[i] Chicago Exposition Authority (quiescent).
[j] Delaware River Joint Commission.
[k] Metropolitan Water District.
[l] Massachusetts Metropolitan District (park, sewage, and water).
[m] Buffalo-Fort Erie Peace Bridge Authority.
[n] Levee District.
[o] Port District.
[p] Navigation District.
[q] Port District.

parodied municipal reformers in their efforts to make a given municipal activity independent of the city hall and, incidentally, dependent on the state capital. Although no longer common, such an attempt was made in the Pennsylvania State Legislature in 1939 regarding the Philadelphia police.

Since the political boundaries of the metropolis never coincide with social and economic boundaries, a jurisdictional problem is created which is another cause for the incorporation of special units with powers extending beyond the area of the central municipality. Such are the Massachusetts Metropolitan District and the Chicago Sanitary District. Independent incorporation is probably the only solution for interstate problems of the type the Port of New York Authority was called upon to solve. In other cases, the creation of the metropolitan *ad hoc* authority has been a substitute for annexation of adjacent suburbs. Studenski calls it "essentially a makeshift" not answering conclusively the problem of integration of government in metropolitan areas.[4] Lepawsky sees them as more than substitutes for annexation, suggesting that "it is not impossible that the large *ad hoc* authority will develop into a compendious unit of metropolitan government incorporating many functions of a consolidated municipality."[5]

Corporate independence for newer activities of government is sometimes justified on a third ground—that it affords the administrative flexibility necessary to a function with unsettled techniques, and freedom from red tape necessary for efficient operation as a business enterprise. A proponent of the independent housing authority, who as an official of the Public Works Administration was instrumental in securing the passage of housing-authority legislation, says:

> The use of a housing authority as an instrumentality for undertaking and financing low-rent housing projects is a sound, feasible, businesslike way of approaching the low-rent housing problem. The authority can be managed by experts trained in this highly specialized and technical field. Its lack of power to tax, to exercise police power, to enact penal ordinances, to regulate the use of streets, to license—all are factors which meet with the approval of those who are concerned with the threat of rising taxes and overlapping governmental functions.[6]

An opponent of the authority form has argued that American experience with municipally operated waterworks is a sufficient answer to this type of claim.[7] Some students of metropolitan government acknowledge the efficiency of an authority as an agent for the construction of important public works but doubt its utility as an operating body, when the monotonous duty of maintenance may bring about a deterioration in the spirit and personnel of the authority.

Evasion of restrictions

A powerful motive for independence is the comparative ease with which an authority may be created or continued, in comparison with the difficulty in removing constitutional or legal restrictions binding the general municipal corporation. In approving the creation by the state of an independent Sewer Authority, a Buffalo City Council resolution frankly stated that "the City because of its constitutional debt limitation

---

[4] Paul Studenski, *The Government of Metropolitan Areas in the United States* (New York: National Municipal League, 1930), p. 341.

[5] Albert Lepawsky, "Development of Urban Government," *Urban Government* (Washington: National Resources Committee, 1939), p. 32.

[6] E. H. Foley, Jr., "Legal Aspects of Low-Rent Housing in New York," 6 *Fordham Law Review* 1 (Jan. 1937), p. 11.

[7] Horace A. Davis, "Borrowing Machines," *National Municipal Review*, XXIV (June 1935), p. 331.

cannot finance this undertaking by bond issue." Likewise in Philadelphia, which was caught between the upper millstone of an already exceeded constitutional debt limit and the nether millstone of an order from the state to cease pollution of adjacent rivers, the Philadelphia Authority was created. Obviously authorized for its debt-incurring potentialities, this Authority is legally enabled to borrow for many types of public works. The Chicago Sanitary District is a much earlier example.

Frequently this circumvention of an apparently clear constitutional limitation on local debt has been justified by asserting that the independent corporation carries on a state function. The separate debt-incurring power of the Buffalo Sewer Authority was upheld in *Robertson* v. *Zimmerman*[8] on the ground that sewage disposal was a state concern. Yet two years later, in *McCabe* v. *School District, City of Troy*,[9] the highest New York Court stated:

If this city school district can be created as an entity, separate and apart from the municipal corporation, upon the theory that the state is thus making the city school district its agent, because education is a state purpose, so also may special districts be created in the same way for police, fire, and health.... Thus not only will the debt-borrowing capacity of cities be allowed to expand, but these separate districts will be able to incur indebtedness without any constitutional limit whatsoever.

The new Public Housing Law in New York State provides for a 2 per cent rise in a city's debt limit for housing purposes, thus partially removing the need for a separate debt-incurring body for public housing.

A strong argument made for independent authorities and the exemption of their debt from the limit of the municipality is that the authority's projects are self-liquidating and its debt backed only by its own revenues. However, special revenue bonds outside the regular debt limit have long been used in many states to finance municipal undertakings such as sewers and water supply. Nevertheless, this use of special revenue bonds by municipal corporations has often been narrowly circumscribed by the courts. Authorities, in their legal capacity as agencies of the state, have been more leniently treated, and the exemption of their debt from the municipal debt limit has been upheld.[10] Some students have questioned the justification of exemption on the basis of self-liquidating operations; housing authorities are not in reality self-sufficient, and certain other authorities' bonds have been purchased by regular governments when not assured a favorable reception in the investment market.

Similar to the problem of constitutional debt restrictions is that presented by a tax limit. Indianapolis took advantage of an already existing Sanitary District and had transferred to it the functions of garbage and ash removal, thereby maintaining the budget of the general government within the tax limit.

Other constitutional restrictions may result in the creation of special units. Cities seeking to subsidize a needed public utility and prevented by constitutional prohibitions against financial aid to private corporations, have with judicial approval organized public corporations to carry out that purpose.

None of the foregoing reasons is sufficient to explain the creation of the most recent authorities. Public Works Administration officials definitely encouraged the use of the authority form at the municipal level as helpful in exe-

---

[8] 268 N. Y. 52, 196 N. E. 740 (1935).
[9] 274 N. Y. 611, 10 N. E., 2d, 576 (1937).

[10] Cf. Lesser v. Warren Borough, 237 Pa. 501, 85 Atl. 839 (1912) and Tranter v. Allegheny Co. Authority, 316 Pa. 65, 173 Atl. 289 (1934).

cuting its program. States and municipalities, eager to do whatever was necessary to secure their share of Federal funds, promptly complied. Consequently these authorities have been called "borrowing machines." Thus, the Chicago Exposition Authority was created to develop land on the site of the 1933 Chicago Fair. This task was actually performed by the Chicago Park District when Federal funds were not forthcoming.[11]

PROBLEMS OF CO-ORDINATION

Special-purpose units, irrespective of the motive for creation, raise problems of administrative co-ordination, but there is no need to repeat here the long familiar arguments for integration. While co-ordination is possible under a disintegrated setup, separate organization may hinder and certainly does not promote co-ordination.

Sometimes special legal requirements designed to prevent friction reduce the significance of independence from the administrative point of view. School-bond issues may require authorization by the mayor or city council before issuance or before popular referendum may be held. The city of Cincinnati, Hamilton County, and the School District "facilitated by state law" have for years maintained certain joint enterprises in the matter of civil service administration, administration of sinking funds, and legal services.[12] Laws creating recent authorities in New York provide for controls by the municipal civil service commission and the city comptroller. The corporation counsel may serve the authority in some cases.[13]

The New York Public Housing Law, in contrast to housing-authority enabling legislation elsewhere, requires that new housing projects must be approved by the local legislative body and the municipal planning commission. Further, all public improvements in New York City must conform to the master city plan now being developed under the new charter. Similarly, by a recent Chicago ordinance a new Plan Commission is required to co-operate with the local housing authority and the city council in the location of housing projects and the elimination of substandard housing conditions.

Rarely do housing authorities make use of the municipal civil service commission, except in Michigan, where it is mandatory to do so, and in New York City. Housing officials hesitate to come under the jurisdiction of the civil service commission for reasons familiar to students of educational administration, viz., that the special function is administered at a level of efficiency much higher than that of the city civil service. Official studies of civil service administration, such as those of the Avery Commission in Chicago and the Philadelphia Charter Commission, sometimes confirm the impression of low efficiency.

Voluntary co-ordination of fiscal operations occasionally occurs. The city, the county, and the school district in Cincinnati plan their bond-issue programs together five years in advance so as to keep the charge on the taxpayer at a fairly normal rate. In Pittsburgh, Cincinnati, and Detroit the municipal planning commissions have effectively participated in the planning of the public-housing programs of their cities. Elsewhere, housing authorities have

---

[11] Arthur J. Todd, *et al.*, *Chicago Recreation Survey*, Vol. I, Chicago: Chicago Recreation Commission and Northwestern University, 1937, p. 49.

[12] S. Gale Lowrie, "Metropolitan Government in Cincinnati," *American Political Science Review*, XXX (Oct. 1936), pp. 950–55.

[13] See New York *Laws*, 1933, Chap. 145 (Triborough Bridge Authority); 1934, Chaps. 138, 162 (Henry Hudson and Marine Parkway Authorities); 1935, Chap. 349 (Buffalo Sewer Authority); 1936, Chap. 1 (New York City Tunnel Authority).

made extensive use of material prepared by the planning commissions, although frequently planning commissions lack the financial support necessary to play an active part in the local housing programs.[14]

In numerous cases co-ordination has been achieved through the use of interlocking directorates or joint personnel. In Syracuse the director of the housing authority is secretary of the planning commission. In New York the chairman of the housing authority has been head of the Department of Housing and Buildings. The library board in Buffalo includes the superintendent of schools and the corporation counsel. Five municipal officials in Philadelphia are ex officio members of the Fairmount Park Commission. A desire for co-ordination is reflected in the composition of the new Chicago Plan Commission, which together with its Advisory Board includes heads of all independent units.

Since no single function of government can operate in a vacuum, corporate independence does not obviate the necessity for agreements between services regarding the division of labor and joint policy in areas of common interest. Thus, an independent school administration must be concerned with the program of the agencies dealing with health, recreation, safety, library service, and the prevention of juvenile delinquency. Housing-authority programs must be related to parks, playgrounds, and school and street facilities. The special pleader for a particular independent function frequently sees the need for modifying the programs of other services to gear into his own program. "Co-operation" to some housing officials means just that. The need for integration of other services may become apparent to an aggressive administrator like Robert Moses, who is himself a one-man authority. He suggests the abolition of the New York City Housing Authority and the administration of the housing program by a board whose ex officio members would be heads of the city departments vitally concerned.[15]

Although legal separation engenders difficult problems of administrative co-ordination, these are not always insurmountable. An occasional forceful personality like Mayor La Guardia may gain control over the independent authorities with which he has to deal.[16]

THE CITIZEN AND THE SPECIAL UNIT

Turning now to the most fundamental question, what difference does the existence of special governmental units make to the citizens under their jurisdiction? The multiplication of governmental units does not in itself multiply the taxable resources of the community. However, it may markedly alter the tax bill and the distribution of the tax dollar between the independent and the integrated governmental functions. The independent budgets of the special units inevitably lead to competition. Finer, writing of a similar problem in English local government, declares:

> The greatest care has to be exercised to prevent a large expenditure along one line of local services, while another, which may even be an indispensable element in the efficiency of the better endowed one, is starved. All these problems of co-ordination are difficult enough within a *single* local governing authority, where there is already a community of feeling, and a related responsibility to one single electorate.[17]

---

[14] Harry W. Alexander, *et al.*, "Bases for Co-operation Between the Municipal Housing Authority and the Planning Commission," *The Planner's Journal*, IV (May–June 1938), pp. 62–63.

[15] Robert Moses, *Housing and Recreation* (New York, 1938), pp. 39–40.

[16] Langdon Post, "My Clash with La Guardia," *Nation*, Jan. 29, 1938, pp. 125–26.

[17] Herman Finer, *English Local Government* (London: Methuen and Co., 1933), p. 161.

Chicago's six tax-levying and debt-incurring units, each with its own budget, have created a fiscal chaos. Is it astonishing that the tangled web of this multi-unit financing bewilders the expert and leaves the general public uncomprehending and apathetic? Yet reform through consolidation is effectively blocked because it would reduce the debt limit to about one-quarter of what it is today.[18]

Illustrative of the competition for public funds is the current controversy between Park Commissioner Moses and public-housing advocates regarding whose funds should provide the recreational facilities necessitated by the construction of new housing projects. Unco-ordinated fiscal operations of overlapping units may not only impose a hardship upon the community pocketbook but may adversely affect the credit rating of each competing unit, especially where the authority form is used for an enterprise not really self-supporting.[19]

Twenty-five of the sixty-one special governmental units shown in Table 1 may levy general property taxes. Where such units obtain pegged levies, the effect may be to starve the general government if the tax rate already has approached the point of diminishing return. Although the new authorities cannot themselves raise funds through taxation, the general government may be moved to develop for them a source of revenue independent of the service rendered. New York City levied an occupancy tax to guarantee housing-authority bonds. That there are limits to the fiscal independence of a housing authority is recognized by Louis Pink, one of the earliest proponents of that form of administration, when he emphasizes the necessity for integrating the housing program with the long-term fiscal planning of the municipality. The new Public Housing Law in New York State explicitly provides for this type of financial integration.

Creation of an authority without the power to tax implies that the direct beneficiary of the new public work, not the general property owner, is to pay for the improvement. This may indicate a significant shift in the tax burden for some new governmental functions. As an advocate of a Chicago Metropolitan Improvement Authority has stated, "With modern improvements the modern slogan should be 'The User Must Pay.'"[20] This principle is, of course, not absent from the financing of older municipal undertakings, but it is typical of projects undertaken by authorities. The user may not always bear the entire cost, however, as when the personnel of a regular government agency is used in the administration of an "independent" authority, without a clear allocation of administrative costs. Or he may pay for more than he uses, as when park and recreational areas are financed through tolls collected by strategically located highway authorities.

DISABILITIES OF OVERLAPPING UNITS

Independent corporate status is a bar to maximum utilization of the resources of one unit useful to another. The Chicago Sanitary District and the Chicago Park District each maintain their own pumping stations apart from the municipal water system. The failure of the city of Chicago and the Park District to co-ordinate their highway construction means that the fine highways of one may terminate in rough, narrow streets under the other's jurisdiction. Independence

---

[18] Victor Jones, "Local Government in Metropolitan Chicago," *American Political Science Review*, XXX (Oct. 1936), pp. 935–42.

[19] Peter R. Nehemkis, Jr., "The Public Authority: Some Legal and Practical Aspects," 47 *Yale Law Journal* 14 (1937–38), pp. 31–33.

[20] John Ickes, "What is an Improvement Authority?" *Illinois Municipal Review*, Dec. 1934, pp. 244–48.

may mean that funds lie idle in the accounts of one unit while another unit must issue tax-anticipation warrants, as in Chicago in 1930.[21] The special unit rarely benefits from the civil service, retirement, or purchasing system of the general government. Full use of each other's resources must await extended negotiations and special agreements. Thus, to erect a library branch in a Chicago park required a special resolution of the Park Commissioners and approval of the sale of the property by the Circuit Court.

Overlapping independent units lack the formal machinery for joint consultation, and thus may provide ample opportunity for conflicts in public policy. In the case of authorities created to construct specific public works, the very act of setting up the authority reflects a prior determination of the major policy involved; but with such units as the school district and the housing authority, policy determination is implicit in every expansion and contraction of activity. Moreover, in their enthusiasm for their particular service, members of such authorities are in a position to advocate and even effect policies damaging to the community as a whole. Educational groups have sometimes campaigned for the regressive sales tax, and housing groups have recommended the dubious policy of tax exemption. The Chicago Park District has denied liability for injuries to persons occasioned by defects in its streets, even though the city government would be liable under analogous circumstances.[22] Such actions reveal a lack of responsibility to the larger interests of the community.[23]

Irresponsibility may be promoted by undemocratic methods of filling vacancies in the governing boards of the special units, such as in the case of self-perpetuating library boards. Alternative methods of appointment may leave the governing boards equally remote from public control, and result in flagrant disregard of the public interest. Appointment by county courts as in the case of the old Chicago South Park District, by state government officials as with the Massachusetts Metropolitan District Commission, or by election at the bottom of an already long ballot as with the Chicago Sanitary District, may result in bureaucracy, arbitrariness, and political interference. Even appointment by mayor and council does not insure responsiveness to the public, especially where the mayor lacks power of removal and where there are hold-over members from another administration. Power without responsibility may be seen in Chicago, where the citizens have learned to go directly to the City Hall when they are dissatisfied with the Board of Education, because of the invisible political connections between the two. Yet when an investigation into maladministration of school funds threatens, the Board (supported by political friends in the Council) claims that the Council has no jurisdiction over an independent district.

Extensive debt-incurring power not subject to the regular fiscal procedures designed to insure public control may ultimately embarrass the local government's fiscal planning program. The newer authorities, being set up primarily to borrow Federal funds, have been subject to Federal scrutiny, and this supervision apparently saved the Triborough Bridge Authority from a

[21] Simeon E. Leland, "Waste Through Multiplicity of Governmental Units," *Bulletin* of the National Tax Association, XXII (March 1937), pp. 162–68.

[22] Chicago Park District, *Second Annual Report,* Chicago, 1936, p. 254.

[23] Charles E. Merriam, Spencer D. Parratt, and Albert Lepawsky, *The Government of the Metropolitan Region of Chicago* (Chicago: University of Chicago Press, 1933), p. 137 and *passim.*

major scandal under a Tammany-appointed board. The Chicago Sanitary District in its "Whoopee Era" was able to borrow money from private bankers to construct a million-dollar bridle path. This government unit, composed of politically active members and operating behind closed doors, built up a huge patronage machine by expanding its activities in directions unforeseen by its founders and undesired by the citizens.

Thus irresponsibility thrives on a governmental three-ring circus which exceeds the span of attention of the thoughtful citizen. Under a regime of *ad hoc* authorities civic groups interested in one or another of the functions performed by the separate agencies fail to perceive the relationship of each to the whole. Nor do they fuse into a larger group demanding a high standard of government for every function.

William T. R. Fox, M.A., is instructor in political science at Temple University, Philadelphia. Annette Baker Fox is preparing a doctoral dissertation on the relationship of the housing authority to the municipal government.

America's Tax Dollar—A Key Problem in Governmental Reconstruction

By Albert Lepawsky

HOW much is this year's tax bill? What will the new tax do to business? How can this tax be "avoided" without actually "evading" the law? Will that tax hit one group harder than another? Such are the questions that have predominated in American tax circles; for American public finance has generally been more concerned with the *economics of taxation* than with the *government of a tax system*.

But newer types of questions are now being asked in the field of American taxation. What is the division of the American tax dollar between the Federal Government, the states, and the local authorities? How can intergovernmental tax competition be avoided? Can we establish some degree of revenue reciprocity and tax planning among the various governmental authorities of the country? How can we make tax administration less complex and less expensive for both government and business?

American business and American government have at various times received different degrees of emphasis, and this tug and pull between business and government has been especially pronounced in the realm of taxation. Actually, the two are inseparable facets of our total society; but if a choice must be made, it would be safe to suggest that at the present time America's tax problem is fundamentally a problem of *government* rather than of *economics*.

There should, of course, be no underestimation of that ever recurring problem of raising enough revenue without at the same time discouraging private enterprise. But we have reached the stage in our national development when the solution of the tax problem is not to be found merely in preserving corporate business and individual enterprise from pressures growing out of the demand for more governmental aid and public services. In an economy which, at least for the time being, has ceased to expand, these shocks to private business can be minimized but not entirely avoided; and they are magnified when government itself is inadequately organized to engage in the process of revenue-raising so that it may obtain the wherewithal to perform the public jobs called for by the times. It would therefore seem that the most fruitful attack on the tax problem, while taking into consideration the interests of commercial enterprise, must now be made with more regard for the needs of public administration and the possibilities of effective planning of governmental revenues.

American Government and the Tax Dollar

The primary difficulty about administering—let alone planning—American public revenues is the fact that the American tax dollar is split three ways, among the Federal Government, forty-eight states, and 160,000 local governments.[1] No single level of government may be called the controlling revenue authority of the country. Before the World War, in 1912, the local governments collected about 58 per cent of the Nation's taxes, leaving the Federal Government with 28 per cent and the states with 14 per cent. But by 1938 the local governments' share had shrunk, after several ups and downs, to 33 per cent;

[1] The most recent 1939 figure is 161,144, presented by the *Atlas of Taxing Units*, published by the Illinois Tax Commission.

185

the states had climbed slowly up to 26 per cent, and the Federal Government, with alternate rises and declines, had moved up to about 41 per cent. While in the United States only two-fifths of the Nation's revenues are under Federal control, in Great Britain, by contrast, over four-fifths of the revenues go to the central treasury, leaving one-fifth to other authorities.

Because of our comparatively decentralized system of government, tax planning, even if it should prove desirable, is going to be difficult on a national scale. Many in the United States resent the continued increase of the Federal Government's slice of the tax dollar at the expense of the states and the local authorities, but strangely enough, Americans still look to Uncle Sam for the solution of their tax problems just as they depend on him for their general fiscal salvation and for economic recovery.

This is the paradox of American public administration. In ordinary times, we resist national centralization in government; but when we are in a pinch, we look to the Federal Government for the solution of our ills. At the same time, we are grudging about giving it powers, particularly over the public purse, commensurate with the demands we make upon it; and when things change for either the better or the worse, we are inclined to upset the newer centralizing trends by sudden shifts in governmental powers and fiscal policies.

Tax planning, like general governmental planning, is a stupendous task, made infinitely more difficult by the fact that the various factors in the situation never remain constant. The oscillations in the revenues of the various levels of government in the United States are especially pronounced. In a short space of six years, between 1932 and 1938, the proportion of the tax dollar collected by the local governments of the country dropped from 54 per cent to 33 per cent, while the Federal Government's share rose from 23 per cent to 41 per cent—a centralizing trend that has already shown some signs of abating. (See Table 1.)

TABLE 1—TOTAL TAX COLLECTIONS, BY LEVEL OF GOVERNMENT, 1912 TO 1938 [2]
(In Millions of Dollars)

Year	Total Taxes	Federal Amount	Federal Per Cent	State Amount	State Per Cent	Local Amount	Local Per Cent
1912	$ 2,295	$ 633	27.6	$ 333	14.5	$1,329	57.9
1925	8,051	3,132	38.9	1,303	16.2	3,616	44.9
1930	10,425	3,627	34.8	2,080	20.0	4,718	45.2
1932	8,243	1,885	22.9	1,882	22.8	4,476	54.3
1934	8,841	2,986	33.8	1,996	22.6	3,859	43.6
1936	10,546	3,907	37.0	2,495	23.7	4,144	39.3
1937	12,162	5,140	42.3	2,815	23.1	4,207	34.6
1938	14,811	6,034	40.7	3,857	26.1	4,920	33.2

[2] All figures except for 1938 taken from Clarence Heer, *Federal Aid and the Tax Problem* (prepared for the Advisory Committee on Education, United States Government Printing Office, 1939), p. 31; 1938 figures taken from United States Treasury Department *Bulletin*, August 1939.

SHARING TAXES AND GRANTS-IN-AID

Assuming that we can stabilize our revenues at about the present level of 40 per cent Federal, 25 per cent state, and 35 per cent local (or at any other level that might prove desirable), and then start from that point and plan for the future, we have still to conjure with that confusing system of allocating the American tax dollar between one level of government and another, either through grants-in-aid or through locally shared state-collected taxes. For, after collection by the various levels of government, substantial revenues are assigned from higher to lower levels by

4.9 billions, they finally obtained a total of 6.5 billions in American taxes. Consequently, the actual division of American taxes is not really 41 per cent Federal, 26 per cent state, and 33 per cent local, but approximately 35 per cent Federal, 21 per cent state, and 44 per cent local. (See Table 2.) When the American tax pie is actually cut up, it is clear that Federal fiscal centralization is not really what it appears to be.

TABLE 2—SHARING AND ALLOCATING AMERICAN TAXES, 1938 [3]
(In Millions of Dollars)

	Federal	State	Local	Total
Taxes collected	$6,034	$3,857	$4,920	$14,811
Per cent of total	41	26	33	100
Revenues allocated to other levels	$805	$1,400	$32	$2,237
Per cent of collections	13	36	1	15
Revenues received from other levels	——	$665	$1,572	$2,237
Per cent of collections	——	18	32	15
Net revenues received after allocations	$5,229	$3,122	$6,460	$14,811
Per cent of total	35	21	44	100

means of either (1) grants from general or special funds, in aid of specific functions, made either by the Federal Government to the states and localities or by the states to the local governments, or (2) specified shares or percentages of revenue, derived by the state from certain taxes and assigned to the local governments, which are not necessarily earmarked for any specific functions of the localities.

Out of a total of 14.8 billion dollars in American taxes in 1938, 2.2 billions, or one out of every seven tax dollars, did not remain with the level of government to which the taxpayer made his payment. Actually, while the Federal Government administered and collected 6 billions in taxes in 1938, it netted only 5.2 billions; while the states collected 3.9 billions, they were left with only 3.1 billions; and while the local governments administered and collected only

Federal aid to the states alone totaled 633 million dollars in 1938, while Federal aid to local authorities totaled 172 million. But the process is not a new one. Beginning with the assignment of Federal funds to land-grant colleges in 1862, agricultural experiment stations were added to the grant-in-aid roster in 1887, state homes for soldiers and sailors in 1888, National Guard in 1903, forest funds in 1911, agricultural extension in 1914, highways in 1916, vocational education in 1917, public health services in 1918, vocational rehabilitation in 1920, employment offices in 1933, and social security in 1935.

State financial aid, either through grants or through shared revenues, stood even higher, amounting to 1.4 billion

[3] Figures and estimates adapted by the Federation of Tax Administrators from U. S. Treasury Department *Bulletin*, August 1938. See *Tax Administrators News*, Nov. 1939.

dollars. For several years it was believed that the states, at least, would have reached the high point in sharing revenues with their local authorities. But the figures are going to new highs. Out of 416 million dollars, which it is predicted the state of New York alone will collect in taxes during the year 1939, 279 million, or 67 per cent, will be paid to its local governments.

Put in terms of percentages, the American tax merry-go-round works as follows. Thirteen per cent of Federal revenues are granted back to the states and to the local governments. These Federal grants-in-aid provide at least 16 per cent of the tax revenues of all the state governments, while the Federal and state grants together, which are made to localities, furnish 32 per cent of the total local tax revenues. Thirty-six per cent, or over one-third, of the total state tax revenues are granted back or shared with their local authorities, and these state funds account for 28 per cent, or over one-fourth, of all local revenues.

The amount of revenues available to any governmental authority from grants and shares varies from year to year. As a consequence of this unpredictability, fiscal planning is made exceedingly difficult. Cities and other local authorities know they can expect grants-in-aid for various functions like education, roads, and welfare, but at the time they budget their own revenues and expenditures, they are not certain about the precise amounts that will be available to them. There are instances where money is shunted back and forth between various sublevels of the local levels of government—from county to city, from city to township, and even from local authorities back to the states.

The degree of central control accompanying the various types of allocated revenues depends upon whether the money comes in as a grant-in-aid (from general or special funds), as a shared revenue (from specific state taxes), or as any one of the varied combinations and devices of revenue allocation which have of late been growing up. The general tendency is in the direction of greater central participation, and in some instances interference with local administration, whether it be a question of state-local relations or Federal-state relations, or whether the device be a grant-in-aid, which assumes central supervision, or a shared revenue, which ordinarily does not assume central supervision but which inevitably imposes upon the localities earmarking of funds for specific purposes and also conditions in expending those funds. One of the fundamental questions of public finance that needs answering in the United States is whether the degree of revenue centralization called for by this system of shares and grants must necessarily lead to a greater degree of centralized supervision and interference with state and local administration, and if so, what are the actual effects, favorable and unfavorable, upon the services so supported and upon the consuming public.[4] What, specifically, is the effect of grants for capital improvements upon the subordinate government's task of maintaining or operating the project paid for by the grant? To what extent does the present system fill well-merited state or local needs for wider and richer sources of revenue, or to what extent does it encourage the acceptance of aid for projects that will later cost the subordinate authority more to maintain than it can afford?

Another problem of revenue-sharing and revenue-planning is the tendency to earmark specific tax revenues for specific functions rather than to establish a true exchequer or treasury from which governmental units may draw revenues as needed. State income tax proceeds are

[4] V. O. Key, *The Administration of Federal Grants to States.*

TABLE 3—AMERICAN TAXES, 1938 [5]
(In Millions of Dollars)

	Federal	State	Local	Total
Miscellaneous taxes	$ 37	$ 133	$ 30	$ 200
Customs	359	——	——	359
Motor-vehicle taxes	——	391	20	411
Inheritance taxes	417	145	——	562
Tobacco taxes	568	55	5	628
Liquor taxes	568	243	27	838
Gasoline taxes	204	772	5	981
Sales taxes	376	717	302	1,395
Pay-roll taxes	743	707	——	1,450
Income taxes	2,762	480	——	3,242
Property taxes	——	214	4,531	4,745
Total	$6,034	$3,857	$4,920	$14,811

frequently earmarked for education, sales taxes for relief and welfare, and sometimes liquor taxes go for schools. Funds for one function may be flush while another function may be "flat broke." Meanwhile, governments are hog-tied by statutory funds and earmarkings that destroy their power over their own budgets.

INTERGOVERNMENTAL TAX POLICIES

The various types of taxes that make up the American tax dollar at each level of government do not follow any clear lines of demarcation. Only three major sources of revenue fall exclusively within either the Federal level or the state and local levels of government. These are: the motor-vehicle license tax, which is principally a state-administered tax; and the local and state property tax and the Federal customs, both of which are shrinking in the total tax picture, thus making the possibility of a separation of revenue sources ever more dim. (See Table 3.)

The American constitutional system permits the Federal Government and the states to tax the same things, irrespective of the total load upon the individual. Latest available estimates show that 80 per cent of Federal taxes and 55 per cent of state taxes come from bases subject to both Federal and state taxation.[6] Twenty-three states levy general sales taxes, and some of the articles subject to these state taxes are also taxed under Federal excise levies. Twenty-six states tax cigarettes and tobacco, and so does the Federal Government. All forty-eight states secure revenue from gasoline and liquor, which are also taxed by the Federal Government. Thirty-four states levy personal or corporation income taxes, thus paralleling the Federal income tax revenues. All the states but one collect inheritance or estate taxes, paralleling the Federal Government, which encourages these state taxes by an offset provision.

Tax duplication of this sort is also to be found on subordinate levels, between the state governments and their local

---

[5] Figures and estimates adapted by the Federation of Tax Administrators from U. S. Treasury Department *Bulletin*, August 1938. See *Tax Administrators News*, Sept. 1939.

[6] See reports of the Interstate Commission on Conflicting Taxation, published by the Council of State Governments. See also the article in this volume of THE ANNALS on "Tax Competition Between States," by James W. Martin, who, together with Clarence Heer, did much of the research for the Interstate Commission.

subdivisions. The Nation's metropolis, New York City, is now resorting to new and relatively less convenient sources of municipal revenue, like the cigarette tax and the sales tax, and in the past few years it has tried to enforce even an income and inheritance tax. Many other cities, both large and small, are administering cigarette taxes, sales taxes, gasoline taxes, and gross income taxes.

Pending Problems of Revenue Administration

Any attempt to simplify this system of triplicate or duplicate tax administration will touch upon some of the most fundamental problems of American government—questions of federalism, states' rights, and local autonomy. From the administrative point of view, however, numerous questions can meanwhile be raised.

1. What is the added cost, if any, of maintaining duplicate administrative systems by separate levels of government enforcing the same type of tax upon the same individuals? Factual experience is not lacking for a research project on the concrete savings involved in intergovernmental tax adjustments of various degrees. After a few years of experience we should be able to estimate more accurately the savings and advantages accruing to the states now that they have access to the contents of Federal income tax returns under the duplicate "Green Slip" law. Perhaps we can learn lessons of value from the Australian system under which the states administer and collect income taxes for the national government, or the Canadian scheme where the Dominion has been carrying on for several years a joint system under which the Dominion government administers the income taxes of some of the Canadian provinces and charges them for their share of the cost of administration.

2. How much time and effort are lost by business in conforming with dissimilar tax laws? One sample of ninety companies reported that they were obliged to pay from a minimum of seven to a maximum of 117 separate types of taxes, and the number of governmental agencies to which these taxes were paid ranged from a minimum of six to a maximum of 7,350.[7] Further research on this subject would be helpful.

3. How large a proportion of our potential taxes is lost through avoidance made easy by governmental duplication? Sales on Federal reservations, military posts, and national parks avoid state taxes not only in the case of bona fide official transactions but also in the case of many private transactions that do not deserve the cloak of governmental immunity but cannot easily be distinguished from legitimate official transactions. Federal "tax islands" go to ridiculous extremes. The city of Birmingham, for example, has had difficulty in enforcing its brokers' license fees against bail-bond brokers, who insist upon immunity because they operate in the Federal courthouse. The Buck Resolution (H. R. 6687), attempts to solve the Federal reservation problem by making possible nondiscriminatory state taxation of nongovernmental transactions on such reservations.

4. How far do the immunities of interstate commerce complicate state taxation? Interstate parcel post shipments of cigarettes evade the taxes of twenty-six cigarette-tax states (with Uncle Sam unwittingly participating as party to the process by handling shipments C.O.D.) to a point where the state cigarette taxes now producing more than $75,000,000 annually are being threatened with extinction by an interstate bootlegging trade that is eating away the tax at the estimated rate of

[7] New York Trust Company, *The Index*, Feb. 1935.

$15,000,000 per year.[8] The complex technical formulae which have grown up to allocate to each state its share of the taxable income of corporations doing interstate business constitute a body of highly interesting but intricate tax calculus. If the present trends with respect to state sales taxes continue, there will soon be as voluminous, but no more definitive, a body of court decisions and legal opinions attempting to clarify the distinction between a transaction that is intrastate and one that is interstate. It is interesting to notice how New York City, since it enacted its sales and cigarette taxes, has had to pass through the same tortuous channels the states have been navigating in differentiating between sales consummated within the city, and therefore liable, and sales consummated outside the state, and therefore exempt.[9]

PROSPECTS OF AN AMERICAN TAX POLICY

Administrative considerations alone will not determine the answers to these questions of intergovernmental revenue relations. Any suggested policies of tax uniformity, reciprocity, or co-ordination will have to take into account the effects, actual and alleged, upon our traditional form of government with its strong adherence to the principles of federalism, state sovereignty, and local autonomy.

These principles have a power and a history of their own. Some of the present state practices in taxing activities that have their origin outside their own borders seem to be reminiscent of the sort of tax struggles that the Constitution, drafted in 1789, intended to outlaw. At the time of the Confederation, New York, for example, wanting to retain for its own farmers the market, dairy, and firewood business being done in New York City by thrifty Connecticut Yankees and Jerseymen, required every sloop coming down through Hell Gate and every Jersey marketboat to pay entrance fees and other clearances that soon stifled the trade.[10]

One hundred and fifty years later, we find the borderlines of several western states lined with rival ports of entry at which motor trucks must clear and pay a tax before being permitted to proceed upon a cross-country trip. A half-dozen states impose higher tax rates on alcoholic beverages coming from outside the state than those assessed on beverages manufactured inside the state. One would think he was living in a continent of internecine autarchies when he reads a state regulation entitled "Regulation imposing additional reciprocal taxes on wines brought into the state of ———, which are manufactured within the state of ———." When one state attempts to lure industry by creating artificial advantages like tax exemptions, other states are likely to try to meet competition in the same manner, with disastrous results for the Nation as a whole.

Under our form of government, it is not within the province of any level of government to step in with authority to terminate our interlevel, interstate, intergovernmental struggles for tax revenues and tax advantages. Yet American government—Federal, state, or local—cannot stand idly by while such telltale cracks begin to appear in the Nation's system of administering its public finances. It is, in fact, not doing so. While the Federal Government is taking (and granting back) larger slices of the American tax dollar, it is decentralizing

[8] See Federation of Tax Administrators, *Tobacco Tax Evasion Through Interstate Parcel Post Shipments*, a report of the Committee on Interstate Evasion of the National Tobacco Tax Conference.

[9] Sears, Roebuck & Co. v. McGoldrick, 279 N. Y. 184, and Compagnie Générale Transatlantique v. McGoldrick, 279 N. Y. 192, now on appeal to the United States Supreme Court.

[10] John Fiske, *The Critical Period of American History, 1783–1789*.

and localizing its entire system of internal revenue administration on a regional basis, to a point where it is getting as close to the people as many phases of state administration. By May of 1939, contested internal revenue matters no longer had to be taken to Washington in the first instance but were handled by the Internal Revenue Bureau's Technical Staff in ten regional divisions, each of which contained several local offices.[11]

States, too, are establishing local field officers to assist the taxpayer. In fact, the development of these administrative areas in the field of taxation is one of the most significant trends in the whole realm of regional reorganization and public administration.[12] State surveys of tax resources and state reorganization of tax administrative machinery, together with technical improvements in local property assessments[13] and alert local revenue programs,[14] indicate that creative skill in replanning the practical phases of public finance is to be found on each of the levels of American government. The smoothness with which the country—officials and citizens alike—recently accepted and adapted themselves to reciprocal income taxation of Federal and state and local governmental salaries, following a historic Supreme Court decision[15] and an Act of Congress[16] that reversed what was thought to be an unalterable maxim of intergovernmental immunity, is symptomatic of the country's readiness for revenue reform, even if it involves long-standing intergovernmental adjustments.[17]

All these developments have had their repercussions on a national scale. State and local tax officials, as well as Federal revenue experts, have been growing more conscious of the need for establishing reciprocal relations between governmental authorities and for exchanging technical information. Out of this recognition of the need for some degree of co-ordinated knowledge and joint effort, there have grown up such specialized organizations of public officials as American Association of Motor Vehicle Administrators, National Association of Assessing Officers, North American Gasoline Tax Conference, National Conference of State Liquor Administrators, National Association of Tax Administrators, National Tobacco Tax Conference, and a clearing house for the official tax field—the Federation of Tax Administrators.

MOVEMENT FOR A NATIONWIDE SURVEY

Other organizations have favored the establishment of an official nationwide commission to survey the whole problem of American revenues from the point of view of intergovernmental relations and to suggest alternative policies and feasible solutions. In 1925 the United States Chamber of Commerce considered the proposal for some agency with responsibility for "co-ordinating and systematizing the national and state taxation systems so that the overlapping, duplication, and inequities now existing may be reduced or eliminated."[18] In 1933 an Interstate Commission on Con-

[11] See *Tax Administrators News,* Dec. 1938 and May 1939.
[12] See *Report of Proceedings,* National Association of Tax Administrators, 1938, pp. 3–20.
[13] See Federation of Tax Administrators, "Official Surveys of State Revenues," Research Bulletin No. 31; also the various publications of the National Association of Assessing Officers.
[14] See especially *The Support of Local Government Activities,* a report of the Committee on Local Government Activities and Revenues of the Municipal Finance Officers Association of the United States and Canada.
[15] Graves v. O'Keefe, 59 S. Ct. 595, 1939.
[16] Public Salary Tax Act of 1939, Public Law No. 32.

[17] See David Saxe, "States Modify Intergovernmental Tax Policies," *State Government,* Sept. 1939.
[18] Chamber of Commerce of the United States, Referendum No. 46, April 1925.

flicting Taxation was established by the Council of State Governments to study intergovernmental tax problems, and in 1935 this was followed by a Tax Revision Council with official representatives from all levels of government.[19] In 1937 the Committee on Taxation of the Twentieth Century Fund recommended "that tax co-ordination be made a part of a comprehensive study concerning Federal, state and local fiscal co-ordination. This study should be carried on over a period of a year or two by a nonpartisan committee of from five to seven members appointed by the President."[20]

To this invitation for Federal leadership in surveying the tax problem there has been some response from Washington, but so far, no concrete action. In November 1937 Senator Davis of Pennsylvania introduced a measure for a United States Tax Commission to "make a continuous study of Federal and State Tax structures," and in May 1938 Representative Treadway of Massachusetts introduced a proposal for the creation of a Federal Tax Commission which would among other things "minimize double taxation by co-ordinating the Federal tax system with those of the state and local governments." The Secretary of the Treasury told the House Ways and Means Committee on May 27, 1939 that the Treasury had been giving consideration "to the problems created by Federal-state tax conflicts," and suggested "that Congress create a small temporary national commission to report on the various aspects of intergovernmental fiscal policy and propose a plan for the solution of the problems involved."

There is, of course, the danger that a nationwide survey or a nationally appointed commission may have a Federal bias; but proper safeguards for the appointment of competent persons having state and local as well as Federal experience can minimize this danger of undue partiality to the idea of centralization. Besides, we have our own correctives in this country against central domination, in the strength of our local allegiances, in the history of our state and sectional traditions, in the pride of the minority groups that constitute the majority of the American nation, and in the necessity for decentralized administration occasioned by our far-flung regions. We are, after all, a practical people, and we do not favor centralization or co-ordination merely for the principle of the thing. Workability will be the test, and there is no reason why we cannot, in the field of public finance and tax planning, by-pass slogans and mythologies and take the long practical look ahead.

[19] See the publications of the Commission and of the Tax Revision Council, published by the Council of State Governments.
[20] Twentieth Century Fund, *Facing the Tax Problem*, p. 450.

Albert Lepawsky, Ph.D., is executive director of the Federation of Tax Administrators, Chicago; research associate in political science at the University of Chicago; and consultant for the National Resources Planning Board. He has served as special agent of the United States Department of Commerce; research director of the Law Department of the City of Chicago; and assistant director of the Public Administration Clearing House. He is the author of several books and numerous articles in the field of government.

Deficiencies in State and Local Government Data

By Edward R. Gray

DEFICIENCIES in current data on state and local governments are of two varieties. First and most simply, there may be no data at all. Secondly, there may be information that is lacking in significance, comparability, timeliness, or accessibility. Nearly every type of information that should be available in an ideal reporting system, in which comparable data on the most significant governmental activities and financial transactions would be published promptly by centralized agencies, is now deficient in one of these senses, for at least some governmental units. To catalogue the few adequate reports would be easier than to enumerate the deficiencies and the places where no reports exist.

At present, some cities, counties, and other local governments have their own excellent centralized, informative, annual reports. In a few states, financial reports of at least some types of local governments are relatively comparable with one another, and the state compiles a reasonably adequate summary of them. Some states also have excellent centralized financial and activity reports. A few public and private agencies, including the Federal Bureau of the Census, compile annual financial data on a comparable basis for states and large cities. Organizations of public officials publish information of particular interest to themselves. Certain commercial firms analyze debt issues, state tax legislation, and some construction and public-service-enterprise activity. This list of relatively satisfactory compilations could be extended to include only a limited number of other current reports.

On the other hand, obvious deficiencies are enormous and challenging. Most local governments do not have adequate centralized reports. Most states do not attempt to have their local governments produce even financial reports on a comparable basis, or to collect and publish extracts from such reports. And where states do publish financial summaries of their local governments, these data are not comparable *between states*. Furthermore, nonfinancial information (on purchases, employees, construction, elections, physical plant, and other matters) is in a distinctly rudimentary stage, where it exists at all. Fiscal years end on many different days in the year. The few suitable reports that are published usually appear from one to three years after the period of the information, and are frequently expensive and inaccessible.

New Needs Increase Deficiencies

Yet the need for adequate current information is more urgently felt now than ever before. The World War's aftermath of economic disturbances increased the scale of social problems, brought about a redistribution of financial burdens among Federal, state, and local governments, and upset the rather rigid jurisdictional lines theretofore existing between the different "layers" of public agencies. Precedents established with difficulty and persistent effort in the past, such as co-operation between different governmental levels in agricultural education, have been followed rapidly and easily in other types of activity. Cities have become more independent of both states and counties, and the influence of the Federal Government has been more directly felt in state and local affairs. To understand the changes that have been taking place and the effect of innovations upon governmental organization in the country as a whole, current periodic statistical reports are essential. Statutes and ordinances state in general terms what is supposed to be done by each governmental unit or what they may do under certain circumstances, but the story of what is actually happening and to what extent permissive powers are used is known only when adequate current statistics are available.

Some of the more serious present deficiencies in periodic data on governments concern the data bearing directly upon new intergovernmental relationships. There is a time lag in supplying needed integrated information when new activities or organizations begin. Hence the present statistics reported by governments are based for the most part on functions and relationships which existed before the recent depression. Only slowly do such routine technical procedures as use of classifications of accounts and accounting systems for compiling public reports in perspective become altered to supply newer types of information.

Most of the periodic data about a government that are desired by persons outside the governmental unit itself can be expressed most conveniently in statistical form, using appropriate units for translating activities into quantitative terms. Within the governmental unit, financial records are devised primarily to insure accountability of finance officers and administrators for funds passing through their hands and to show that the separation of funds and the limitation of expenditures authorized by a legislative body in appropriation and revenue acts have been respected. So firmly is the principle of accountability intrenched at present, however, that the supplementary principle of facilitating financial reporting sometimes suffers, and the citizens are deprived of the summarized, analytical, statistical reports that best explain their government's functioning.

Present deficiencies in current governmental reports may be classified as: (1) inadequacies in basic records kept by governments performing the operations reported; (2) deficiencies in centralized collections of data from groups of reporting governments; and (3) hindrances to using reports of intergovernmental activities from different levels of government because of incomparability between the records of the respective governments.

Inadequacies in Basic Local Records

1. *No centralized source of data*

The absence of a centralized source in each governmental unit for information of similar character about the activities of the administrative agencies within the unit, such as cost of current operation, number of employees, and so forth, is probably the most serious single deficiency in present records of state and local governments. Until there is centralization in the records of a government for its financial transactions and for each type of activity, there will be no possibility of obtaining summary data for even that single governmental unit without effort spent locally in assembling and correlating material from the scattered sources. Worse still, comparability is prevented between the records prepared by any one state or city and those prepared by another state or city where a different degree of centralization may exist.

Sufficient centralization of reporting might be achieved merely through a consolidated periodic report, or through uniformity in summaries prepared periodically by the different administrative agencies on the similar phases of their respective work. At present, the number of separate reporting systems of independent or semi-independent boards and commissions for schools, parks, sanitation, highways, libraries, hospitals, welfare, and other activities, is astonishing to the uninitiated, and discouraging to anyone interested in a complete picture of a single government's work. Where multiple unco-ordinated agencies exist that together could furnish information about a single government, it is unusual to find that more than a few of the agencies recognize the value of periodic reports on their work. For example, if the total number of city employees is not available in one central office, it is improbable that monthly, or even annual, data on the number of employees are published by more than a few of the city's separate administrative services.

Federal and state grants to cities, and state supervision of local accounts, have frequently helped in centralizing particular types of records kept by local governments, but the reverse effect has sometimes occurred. For example, the Hatch Act of 1887 and the Morrill Act of 1890 specify that the custodian of funds received by states under the provisions of those acts shall be a school official, entirely independent of the State Treasurer. Similarly, a city's Public Works Administration accounts are not always kept by the city's chief accounting officer.

When a multiplicity of establishments exists in one government, the absence of integrated accounts and records can be defended only on the assumption that citizens can and will keep up with the numerous activities of the many different agencies and consolidate this knowledge into a comprehensive whole. This curious view of citizen omniscience is illustrated in another field by the appearance on single state and city ballots of numerous proposals upon which citizens are asked to express their well-considered views at the same time they make a choice from among a long list of state, local, and sometimes Federal, office seekers.

Probably there can be no great improvement in consistency or centralization of records within a governmental unit until the principle of centralization of administrative responsibility has made headway against the usual device of government by a multiplicity of independent, relatively irresponsible, *ad hoc* agencies.

2. *Lack of records for a geographic area*

A second deficiency in basic records of governmental units, which is somewhat similar to the lack of a centralized source of information in any one governmental unit, is the lack of easily synthesized information for one geographic area. In some regions the overlying and underlying governmental units of varying sizes and shapes sprawl in a crazy quilt of inconsistency and irresponsibility. As long as governmental units bear no particular relationship to geographic positions, and the number of governmental units piled on top of one another in the same area is largely accidental, it will sometimes be difficult, if not impossible, for any citizen to discover the exact extent of activities of the various governments under whose jurisdiction he lives. Complexity of the pattern of overlapping governmental units almost necessarily brings about a deficiency for that area in the basic records of any governmental function or activity. Even in the most prominent geographic areas having considerable economic unity, as, for example, in so-called "metropolitan districts," it is rarely possible to find satisfactory current data for any one governmental function carried on by several layers of governments.

3. *Absence of certain types of data*

A third deficiency in basic state or local government records is the nonexistence of certain types of data. The comparative recency of the demand for some types of information undoubtedly explains their absence in some communities, since reporting customs of governments do not quickly respond to change. For example, in a bibliography of state documents on state grants-in-aid published recently by a state tax commission, only 28 states were listed as having annual reports of a sufficiently comprehensive nature to let their citizens know the principal grants given by those states to their respective governments.[1] Contributing factors in paucity of some kinds of data, however, are reticence on the part of some public officials to include in reports the newer and more controversial features of their work, and lack of interest by the public in any government report, especially if published in a drab buckram-covered octavo volume, without pictures, and obviously written without imagination or perspective.

More important than all other reasons, however, is the overemphasis on pecuniary accountability in governmental financial systems. This overemphasis undoubtedly originates in the laudable attempt to discourage outright thefts of public funds, but such a negative advantage is not sufficient to explain failures to develop or adopt accounting and reporting systems to produce current summaries for policy formulation. The idea of accountability as proof of the honesty of the persons concerned with receiving and spending public money may be a forward step over the stage when officials took money from public funds for private purposes without any subterfuge or finesse, but balanced statements may prove nothing except the ingenuity of the bookkeeper, and are completely worthless to anyone trying to understand what the government is doing or what its efficiency or financial standing is.

As illustrations of the types of local-government data largely lacking at the present time may be mentioned: (1) balance sheets, showing, among other things, the trend in value of physical assets, investments, and types of outstanding liabilities; (2) the quantity and quality of administrative or functional activities carried on, measured in appropriate activity units; (3) cost analyses of such activities, in enough detail to permit at least some rough comparisons between different governments carrying on the same functions in somewhat similar ways; [2] (4) purchases of articles, reported by quantity and specification, with price range and average cost, to permit a comparison of purchasing experience between governmental units, and also to make possible estimates by industry, of types of commodities purchased in the market by governments as consumers; (5) expenditure data on an object basis, especially salaries and wages paid public employees; (6) total number of employees classified by governmental function and by general employment status, that is, whether permanent full-time, permanent part-time, or temporary; (7) amount of new construction and repairs on structures; and (8) results of elections and primaries, with respect to choice of candidates for various types of offices, and approval or disapproval of measures submitted to the electorate. Nonfinancial data are especially inadequate at present.

Before making available current re-

---

[1] That this illustration is not atypical is confirmed by the statement, in Carpenter and Stafford, *State and Local Government in the United States* (1936), page 326, that "of all municipal financial statistics the worst reported are those relating to state aid to local government and local sharing in state-collected or so-called 'state administered' taxes."

[2] H. F. Alderfer, in the *National Municipal Review*, Vol. 27 (April 1938), p. 194, remarks, in a discussion of state administrative control over local units of government: "In the matter of actual economy, there are few reliable or comparable figures which prove anything. It would be exceedingly difficult to say whether local or state administration was cheaper in dollars and cents."

ports on these subjects for which information is now largely nonexistent, the most important information from each field for current reporting should be considered, along with the appropriate definitions and units of measurement to be used, and, in some cases, the traditional data in the same or related fields which could be supplemented or displaced.

4. *Unneeded data*

A fourth deficiency in basic records is the counterpart of the absence of certain types of data, namely, the plethora of information of no particular general significance. The continuance of unneeded data is usually explained either by too great emphasis on pecuniary accountability, at the expense of information devised for policy determination; or, probably equally often, by a past special interest in a particular type of data, perhaps on the part of only one dynamic person who began the current collection of such data. Such cases exemplify in governmental activity Newton's first law of motion, which for this purpose might be restated: Every government procedure, activity, or periodical publication once begun continues indefinitely in the same manner unless impelled by some external force to change its accustomed form or content.

The content of many governmental reports seems to be a matter of historical accident, depending largely upon the hobbies of the persons responsible for reporting when the last retrenchment was made in appropriations for printing the documents, and upon the accretions from subsequent innovations in government activity. Similarly, whether data which are reported at all are reported currently or at long intervals, seems also to be determined by some historical whim. Monthly data are sometimes reported when no seasonal differences are expected and when quarterly, or even annual, data would be as suitable; while, on the other hand, information about activities that are subject to large seasonal variation in magnitude may be reported in annual totals or as of a single date once a year.

5. *Confusing variety*

A fifth important deficiency in local records is their unnecessary variety and frequent failure to follow well-established precedent, except in states that have imposed uniform accounting systems on their own local governments. Even these state-wide systems, however, are at variance with one another. Interstate and intercity comparisons are usually possible only after some outside agency that undertakes a centralized collection of current data on a comparable basis, has carried through to completion expensive field work, editorial supervision and analysis, and publication. Among the most important and most obvious types of incomparability at present may be mentioned: differences in fiscal years; differences in methods of allocating overhead or administrative costs to constituent activities; differences in definitions and use of terminology; and variations in the classifications and subclassifications devised to present details of an account or activity. Illustration of each of these irritating incongruities will readily occur to readers who have fought their way through an assemblage of footnotes that explain some of the deficiencies known to the relatively conscientious compiler of tabular material on state and local governments.

6. *Inadequate indexes*

A sixth deficiency in basic records, which at first sight may seem superficial, is important as a hindrance to the use of information that is physically available. This deficiency is the lack of adequate indexes to most government records. It is an unusual public document that carries any index at all, and even a table of contents is sometimes omitted from documents supposedly presented for public information. These quasi-mechanical omissions may have more significance than would appear on the surface, as they often indicate unsystematic, un-unified, and in many cases uncritical, methods of throwing together public documents, the author or compiler often merely following what was done in the previous year, and even sometimes justifying his shortcomings by extolling the virtues of "comparability."

7. *Lateness in publication*

A seventh major deficiency, and the last which will be mentioned in this list as applicable to the records of the individual states and local governments, is the lateness in publication of such documents as are published. No elaboration of this point is needed for anyone who has used government documents. Tardiness in making data available in published form may sometimes be equivalent to the suppression of information needed for policy-making and criticism of current methods. In most cases, postponement of publications is the result of the desire for accuracy in official records, or of the precedence given by compilers to their current administrative work, on the assumption that published records have only historical interest.

DEFICIENCIES IN CENTRALIZED
COLLECTIONS OF DATA

There are over 16,000 cities, towns, villages, and boroughs in the United States, in addition to more than 3,000 counties, nearly 20,000 townships and towns, nearly 30,000 school districts, and about 10,000 other civil divisions. Even if each of these governmental units had completely satisfactory reports of its individual activities, both appropriate for its own citizens and comparable with those of other similar units, there would still be need for centralized collections of at least the most important information in order to have a regional or national picture of trends, permit a comparison of the results obtained from different tax systems or administrative organizations, and show the place of governmental activities in the national economy.

Centralized collections of data from governmental units on one or more levels are now being made by a variety of different agencies. The Federal Government collects information from states and large cities annually, in addition to its decennial collection of financial information from all units of government. A small but growing number of states publish information from cities or counties or both, and a few include all local governments in their reports. Associations of public officials collect information about the activities with which they are most concerned. Commercial organizations, usually catering to investment bankers and investors, carry on extensive compilations of current data about governments.

Some of the deficiencies in these centralized collections of data are quite distinct from the defects in the basic records of the original governmental units reported upon, but some are of the same general nature as those discussed previously. Among the deficiencies common to both categories, may be named, without further comment: (1) concentration on traditional subjects, showing a subject-matter lag in supplying data on newer developments; (2) current reporting of relatively fixed or unimportant detail, while significant fluctuations are reported only occasionally; (3) lack of indexes to publications, especially lack of cumulative indexes covering a long period of time; and (4) lateness in publication, which is a failing common to almost all government-prepared data, in contrast to the relative timeliness of data collected by private enterprise, where profits depend on prompt publication of material.

1. *Limited scope*

The first and most obvious deficiency in centralized collections is their limited scope. Only eight states report information about city receipts and expenditures, with one additional state reporting tax receipts but not expenditures. While a few more states report the receipts or expenditures of their counties, and six states collect some data for other governmental units, the area covered by all the local governments represented in these states is only a small portion of the whole country. The Federal Government's annual compilation of financial statistics has never included cities with a population of less than 25,000,[3] and since 1932 has excluded cities of less than 100,000. Similarly, other centralized collections drastically limit the type and the number of local governmental units included in the compiled data.

The effective scope of data found in centralized collections is even more limited than appears from the enumeration of local governments and subjects covered in these collections. States that publish reports on the finances or the activities of their cities, counties, or other local governments have devised their systems, for the most part, without reference to comparability with the reports of other states. Subjects covered, classifications, and definitions show wide discrepancies. The result is that for interstate comparisons, a large part of the value of each state's collection is lost.

2. *Data from less appropriate units*

A second deficiency peculiar to centralized collections of government data is the failure to secure information about the most significant governmental units concerned with a particular operating function. For example, when figures on welfare activities of cities are compiled in a state where public assistance is administered through county agencies, the data for welfare expenditures in urban areas are deficient. The existence of overlapping units of government in the same area always creates the danger of such defects in collections of data from a limited number of different types of local government.

3. *No central source of information*

A third defect in centralized collections is the absence of a recognized central source of information for all general-purpose data on state and local governments. Until the time of the World War, the Federal Bureau of the Census was the pioneer in devising, developing, and carrying on the centralized collection of financial and nonfinancial data on state and local governments. When the drastic wartime reductions in the work continued through the succeeding decade, and temporarily became even more drastic in 1933, other public and private organizations began to take over the parts of the work of immediate interest to them. At the present time, therefore, a wide variety of agencies are collecting important data from state and local governments, and there is much duplication and confusion of effort in the field. Furthermore, some of the agencies which have stepped into the breach since the World War are of a temporary character, being financed with emergency funds of governments, profits made from reports, or temporary grants from philanthropic organizations. Nongovernmental collecting agencies probably have a relatively short expectancy of life, are not likely to correlate their results with other data, and in some

[3] The lowest population size of cities in the report for 1902. See Bureau of the Census, Bul. 20, 1905.

cases do not furnish sufficient information about methods used to enable the critical reader to know exactly the type of data reported. On the other hand, there are deficiencies peculiar to the centralized collection of governmental data by government agencies. Among these are delay in publication, insufficient analysis of results, relative inflexibility of program, and resistance to progress.

INCOMPARABILITY BETWEEN SIMILAR RECORDS OF RELATED GOVERNMENTS

It is rare that the records of the same intergovernmental action on the books of the separate governments concerned can be reconciled without considerable adjustment. Not only are there differences in classification and definitions, but funds or activities which play an important part in one government's existence may be of only incidental interest in the other governmental unit, and hence may be reported with accretions of other somewhat related data. Some discrepancies in the report of the same transaction by two governments are entirely logical. For example, from the viewpoint of a state giving aid to local governments for highways, education, or welfare, the state's administration of these grants is a part of the expenditures for that purpose; but to the local governments receiving the aid, the state's expenditure for administering the grants is not only unknown but is of no immediate interest. Again, if grants to local governments for a certain activity are to include reimbursement for the cost of administration of the local government in carrying out the program aided, the amount of these administrative costs will be reported separately from other administrative costs. But where there is a system of state allocations to local governments for general purposes, there is no immediate necessity for the local government to keep separate the administrative costs of each function, and the probabilities are that no such cost analysis will be attempted, and no data made available to the public.

On the other hand, interstate agreements covering treatment of river basins, ports, or parks are likely to be so slowly developed that information about such intergovernmental activities is often made relatively accessible as part of the campaign to promote the activities themselves. The present deficiencies in current information about intergovernmental relationships are, therefore, found principally in connection with the relationships of two or more units in different levels of government.[4]

POSSIBLE METHODS OF IMPROVEMENT

Several specific improvements that could be made in current reports of state and local governments are implied by the preceding enumeration of present deficiencies found in government reports. In addition, a few considerations that do not arise directly from the deficiencies discussed may be mentioned.

Restriction of current reports to data of enough general significance to warrant monthly, quarterly, or annual publication, would reduce the amount of detail now carried in government reports that

[4] Among the more prominent of these relationships, about some of which, however, adequate current data are already available, may be mentioned especially the following: (1) Federal-state relations with respect to social security, relief, highways, education, health, employment placement, promotion of agriculture, and the National Guard; (2) Federal-county and Federal-City co-operative activities with respect to public works, public safety, recreation, and terminal facilities for transportation systems; (3) state-county, state-city, state-township, and so forth, relationships with respect to education, relief, highways, agriculture, health, and public safety; and (4) city-county agreements and services with respect to fire and police protection, schools, water and electric supply, parks, and libraries.

has only limited interest. Furthermore, concentration on more important data would permit a wider range of valuable information to be published adequately at appropriate intervals.

General adoption by states of a uniform classification of financial accounts and definitions of terms would diminish present difficulties in compiling and interpreting comparative reports. Similarly, widespread adoption by cities and counties of a uniform classification of accounts, such as one recently recommended for cities by the National Committee on Municipal Accounting,[5] would remove several major difficulties in public use of municipal government data.

Lastly, simplification of governmental organization, both by consolidation of agencies within a governmental unit, and by simplification or integration of the various overlapping units in the same area, would be the most effective step in bringing about more comprehensive and significant reporting by local governments.

[5] *Standard Classification of Municipal Revenues and Expenditures,* Chicago, 1939.

Edward R. Gray is assistant chief statistician of the Division of State and Local Government, Bureau of the Census, Washington, D. C. He was formerly in charge of the Research Section in the Office of the Secretary of the Treasury, and was review officer of the Central Statistical Board. He has taught economics and statistics at Tusculum College and Duke University.

Readjusting Governmental Areas and Functions

By W. Brooke Graves

THIS volume undertakes for the first time to present a fairly comprehensive survey of the problems of intergovernmental and interjurisdictional relationships in the United States. In earlier times, when life itself was relatively simple and government was geared to the needs of a predominantly rural mode of life, relatively few problems of this character arose. Quite the opposite is the case today. On every hand, changes in political boundaries and new types of governmental machinery are being proposed or adopted, in an effort to accomplish the adjustments required if government is to serve adequately the people of our time. It is the present purpose to view this general situation in broad perspective, depending upon the preceding articles for the elaboration of the various devices mentioned.

Federal Relations with the States

Much popular misunderstanding exists regarding the problem of Federal-state relations. It is often assumed that this is some new question that has risen to plague the people of our time. As a matter of fact, the question of the relations between the central government and the political subdivisions is not peculiar to the American federal system, nor to the era in which we live. It rises in every country in which federalism prevails, and it has been intermittently a subject of controversy in the United States from the date of the independence of the colonies to date. It would be silly to suppose that any permanently satisfactory solution of it will ever be achieved; since the question has to be answered anew by each succeeding generation, it is important that some serious effort be made to find out what has been happening and what tendencies are being established.

It is well known that in a period of over a century and a half, great changes in the American federal system have taken place. It is plain that these have not often come about through the formal amendment of the Federal Constitution. Other and less direct methods have been used. The rise and growth of the grant-in-aid system, the uses to which the tax power, the commerce power, the postal power, and the treaty power have been put, and the influence of Federal legislative and administrative agencies upon the corresponding agencies in the states, have all contributed to the net result. The development of a variety of fiscal controls has been important. The Federal Government has assumed responsibility for expensive functions formerly performed by the states; it has developed the device of Federally collected, state-shared taxes; and it has liberalized the conditions attending grants-in-aid, even to the extent of giving unconditional grants.

Since the advent of the depression in 1929 extensive developments have taken place, first under President Hoover, and in more marked degree under President Roosevelt, all of which have tended to extend the Federal influence over both states and cities. In addition to expenditures for direct relief and the public works program, legislation of far-reaching importance in the fields of agriculture, labor, social security, and power development are shifting the balance in the American federal system at a constantly accelerating pace.

Federal departments and agencies have sought state co-operation in the form of legislation supplementary to or supporting that of Congress. With a unity of party control of both Federal and state governments rarely experienced in American history, such measures have been made a matter of party policy, and have been enacted on an extensive scale. While future changes may be made in some of this legislation, it is already quite clear that all or most of it will be retained in principle. It will be impossible to re-establish the old pattern of Federal-state relations—even if that should come to be desired.

Interstate Relations

The changes in the field of interstate relations have been quite as numerous and quite as significant; they represent an equally great departure from previously existing patterns. The provisions of the Federal Constitution touching upon interstate questions—while important—do not now provide, and have not for years provided, an adequate basis for the solution of questions affecting two or more states. Through the National Conference of Commissioners on Uniform State Laws, and other agencies, the states have for nearly fifty years struggled—not too successfully—to secure uniform laws on subjects of common concern. They have tried the interstate compact device, not so often as might have been expected, and have found it useful chiefly for the settlement of boundary disputes and for the allocation of the waters of adjacent sources of supply. Recent attempts to use compacts in solving labor problems and others of a controversial nature in the field of social and economic relationships have been singularly unsuccessful.

In the face of this situation the Council of State Governments has been busily engaged in the effort to create new machinery that would make possible the establishment of "a more perfect Union." We have seen the national conferences of state officials in specific fields, such as the governors and the attorneys-general, strengthened by the establishment of permanent secretariats and the development of more constructive programs. National conferences of state officials have resulted in such permanent organizations as the Interstate Commission on Crime, the American Public Welfare Association, and others. State commissions on interstate co-operation have been established in nearly all states, and the habit of consultation and co-operation between legislative and administrative officers of different states has been strengthened to a degree heretofore unknown.

The most serious recent problem of interstate relations has been the development of trade and tax barriers. For a century and a half, Americans prided themselves upon the complete freedom of trade in this country, and were wont to make derisive remarks about the lack of such freedom in Europe. Financial stringency, growing out of the depression, encouraged a competition for sources of revenue which resulted in the many overlapping and duplicating taxes described earlier in this volume—all with detrimental effects upon freedom of trade and commerce in the United States. Differences in wage levels, labor standards, and unemployment aggravated by the depression, induced the passage of numerous state laws favoring products produced within the state. These tendencies seem to have been arrested as a result of the Interstate Conference on Trade and Tariff Barriers held in Chicago in April 1939.

These numerous devices and remedial measures have all been undertaken with the twofold purpose of providing a workable alternative to further centralization in Washington and of making possible a more adequate discharge of state functions.

Regionalism

The Federal Constitution did not contemplate any type of regional arrangements, nor did the practice of American federalism for more than a century seek to develop anything of the sort. Then, as the organized territories assumed the position of statehood, as the population increased, and as the functions of government increased in number and in scope, there developed a need for administrative areas smaller than the Nation and larger than the states. Thus subnational regionalism came into existence.

Since identical administrative regions did not seem suitable for all Federal governmental functions, and since there was in existence no unifying influence, each department or agency established zones or districts of such size and in such numbers as it pleased. They varied all the way from three Army Areas to as many as 750 Employment Service districts in the Department of Labor. There were twelve Federal Reserve districts and twelve Federal Land Bank districts, but the boundaries were not the same. Although many followed state lines, others did not. It remained for the National Resources Committee, in its significant study of regionalism in 1935, to present a plan by which order might be brought out of chaos. The Committee found that the existing field offices tended to center in from ten to twenty cities, and proposed that these cities be established as subcapitals of the appropriate areas of which they were the centers.

Meantime, other types of regions or "areas" were in process of development—notably, interstate and metropolitan. The former have only recently been recognized. There are problems, such as those of river valleys, that affect the interests of several states, that yet do not directly concern either the Nation or other groups of states. We are in the process of developing new methods of solving them, and it is too early to predict which type of solution will be found most generally useful. The Federal Government has by act of Congress created the Tennessee Valley Authority, and proposals have been presented and considered for the extension of this type of agency into other comparable areas. In contrast to this, we have a sort of voluntary regionalism operating in the Delaware, Potomac, and Ohio River valleys, in the form of the Interstate Commission on the Delaware River Basin, the Interstate Commission on the Ohio River Basin, and so forth. In these cases the states concerned have by joint action undertaken to work out the solution of their own problems. Here is presented a clear-cut alternative between having the Federal Government do things for the states without any necessary regard for local sentiment, and having the states solve their own problems in their own way.

Just as the states have found it impossible to deal effectively with all the problems within their jurisdiction without regard to their neighbors, so the cities have been forced to face the fact that their own boundaries seldom if ever coincide with the social and economic life of the area of which they are the center. The growth of huge slum areas within the boundaries of the city proper, the decentralization of industry, and the growth of large suburban residential areas have given rise to the metropolitan area. Here, an area that is socially and economically a unit struggles under a multiplicity of overlapping and uncoordinated governmental establishments—cities, boroughs, towns, townships, villages, authorities, and special districts for schools, highways, and many other purposes. The city population looks with longing upon the wealthy suburban assessment rolls, while the suburbanites regard with suspicion and distrust the political machines which have so often misgoverned the cities. The situation is further complicated by the fact that these metropolitan areas frequently extend far beyond the boundaries of a single state.

STATE-LOCAL RELATIONS

Perhaps the most difficult problems of adjustment exist in the field of local government. Here, as is pointed out elsewhere in this volume, Americans live under layer upon layer of units of local government—about 175,000 of them in all. While overlapping, duplication, and waste have been greatly reduced at the Federal and state levels, they still flourish unrestrained in large numbers of local units. This multiplicity of dwarf-sized units, struggling under the burden of poor and inefficient management, combines to impose an increasingly heavy burden upon the American taxpayers. It seems clear that they cannot, and it is to be hoped that they will not, submit indefinitely to the continuance of this burden.

Numerous solutions of this problem have been suggested, and in isolated cases, adopted. The more important proposals are: (1) complete state centralization; (2) extension of state supervision (partial centralization); (3) county consolidation (state regionalism); (4) reduction of the number of the smaller local units and readjustment of boundaries; and (5) reorganization of the machinery of local government. Obviously, not all of these ideas are mutually exclusive, but might be combined in various ways, in a variety of patterns.

State centralization or supervision

The proponents of state centralization regard this as a natural solution of the difficulties into which local government has fallen. They argue, with much justification, that modern methods of transportation and communication have placed the state in a position in relation to the citizen, comparable to that occupied by the county in days gone by. It is contended that real estate, which is the chief source of local revenue, can no longer bear the tax burden necessary to support the numerous and extensive services demanded of present-day government; that road building is no longer properly a function of local government; that modern education cannot properly be subjected to the vagaries of local boards of education; that dangers to the public health are no longer confined to the limits of any particular community; that old-fashioned methods of poor relief have no place in an enlightened community; and so on, *ad infinitum*. North Carolina and Virginia have taken over the construction and maintenance of roads. North Carolina has taken over its schools. By thus absorbing local functions, the local units will atrophy and in time disappear. Many other states are moving more slowly and deliberately in the same direction. It may be noted that this device, together with new functions of government, would to a large extent compensate the states for losses of power sustained through Federal centralization.

To those who object to complete state centralization as violating the principle of local self-government, the principle of state supervision appears somewhat more acceptable. While they resent "state interference," they recognize the deficiencies of local government, and realize that here is a method by which the local communities can retain powers which they have long exercised. So the states, by statute and by appropriate administrative agencies, now frequently supervise local assessments, local tax rates, local budgets, and local fiscal reporting, audit local accounts, and exercise control over local indebtedness. In the field of education, the granting of financial aid enables them to extend control over school buildings, pupil transportation, and other phases of the school program; they enforce standards of teacher training through certification, and they control the content of the curriculum. In many other fields, local officials feel the regulatory power of the state legislature and the administrative departments of the state government.

County consolidation or reorganization

Still others propose county consolidation and the establishment of an intrastate regionalism. They point to the decrepit condition of the average county government, and contend that the county as we have known it no longer has any valid reason for existence. In addition to the fact that it has no structural setup adequate for the discharge of any very important responsibilities, it is, they claim, too small in size to meet the needs of interlevel government, and too large to serve as a unit of purely local government. However useful it may once have been, they say, it represents an anachronism in the world of 1940.

Others propose that instead of consolidating the counties or abandoning them, we ought to retain them as the basic units of local government. They point to the fact that the county seat today is not so far from the home of the average citizen as was once the town hall. If his business at the courthouse cannot be transacted by telephone, a short ride in an automobile over smooth, hard-surfaced roads will bring him there in person. They point to school districts in which there are no children of school age, or too few to permit the operation of a school system; to town and village lockups in which a prisoner is a curiosity; to road districts in which no road tax has been levied for years; to justices of the peace who have never qualified, or who, having qualified, have never heard a case. These units, they say, are the ones that ought to go, the county being strengthened and retained as *the* unit of local government in rural areas, as the city is the unit in more populous sections.

Whatever the ultimate solution of the problem of reorganizing the units of local government, there are two tests which must be met. First, the unit adopted must be large enough to permit the employment of competent, trained, full-time, salaried personnel. Most cities and a few counties now meet this test; many more counties might do so if their existing powers were augmented by those now exercised by smaller units. Counties which are too small to do so might still be consolidated. Second, the unit adopted must be small enough actually to meet the needs of the people for a unit of local government. The people must be brought to understand, however, that the extent and the efficiency of popular control over local government is determined not so much by the size of the unit as by its practicability under existing conditions. The county would appear to meet these tests more nearly than any other unit of local government now existing. In most states, the counties are frozen in the constitution; considering the difficulties involved in changing many of these constitutions, this fact provides an additional practical reason for using them as the basis for the reconstruction of local government.

Structural change

Finally, there is the proposal to reorganize the structure of the governmental machinery in the local units. The proponents of this plan contend that the trouble with local government lies not so much in the number or the size of the units as in a defective organization. The average county has no responsible executive; what it needs is some kind of executive officer—a county president, a county executive, or a county manager. The city-manager plan has been successful where tried; why not use it in boroughs and other small local units? The cities themselves, unable to cope with existing needs, turn hopefully to special-purpose "authorities," and vie with one another in their efforts to secure financial assistance from the Federal Government. Whether or not changes in the structure of local government organization would be sufficient to meet the present need, it should be apparent to anyone that any increase in the powers of the county would be foolhardy without them. When the county cannot properly perform the functions now intrusted to it, it would be useless to expect it to render additional services with the present structural setup.

The truth of the matter is that the kind of civilization that has been developed in the United States in recent years, with its high-speed machinery, its assembly lines, its railroads and automobiles and airplanes, its telephone and telegraph and radio, has made necessary the reconstruction of government all along the line. After years of study and debate, with almost countless investigations and reports, some measure of reorganization of the machinery of the Federal Government has been accomplished. Since 1917 the states have been in the process of reorganization, and the city-manager movement has been making notable progress throughout the country during the same period. In the countries of Europe, likewise, it has been necessary to adapt the machinery of government to the needs of modern life. It is high time that some intelligent and sustained effort be made to reconstruct the machinery of local government in rural America.

NATIONAL RESEARCH NEEDED

It has been the purpose of the preceding paragraphs to sketch in broad outline the more significant current trends in intergovernmental and interjurisdictional relationships in the United States. In the Federal-state, interstate, and regional fields, the developments discussed are actually happening, while in the state-local field, many of the proposals are still largely in the discussion stage. The most important fact is that tremendous changes are now in process in American government as we have known it—changes which are modifying long-established forms, structures, and procedures. These changes are occurring in response to public pressure for government service which the government as it has been is unable to provide; hence the groping for some new device or relationship capable of giving sufficient strength to existing agencies to enable them to function.

No one has any well-developed plan, and no one knows more than a very small part of what is happening along a dozen different fronts. Present efforts are being made by the slow and expensive methods of trial and error. Important consequences are incidental and even accidental. There is no plan, and it has been said, "Where there is no vision, the people perish."

The device of the national research commission, used successfully in recent years for other purposes, might properly be employed here. President Hoover had his Commission on Law Observance and his Commission on Social Trends, both of which rendered valuable reports. President Roosevelt has had commissions on social security, administrative management, the economic condition of the South, and other important subjects. Some have led to specific proposals of legislation, while others have not. We need to develop a plan to guide the course of events in the field of intergovernmental relations in the future, but before any plan can be made, we must secure much more basic information than we now have.

The President should be prevailed upon to appoint a national commission composed of the ablest and best-qualified persons in the country to undertake the study. They should be given sufficient time and adequate financial support. All existing published materials bearing on any phase of the problem should be gathered and examined, and original investigations undertaken where necessary to fill in serious gaps. The effort should be made to see the entire picture and to see it whole.

OBJECTIVES OF STUDY

We need to know exactly what functions of government *are* now being performed, at what levels—national, state, and local—and with what interrelationships, and to determine at the same time what functions *ought* to be performed by each unit. We need to know, by as objective standards as can be devised, the degrees of efficiency of the various functions in various parts of the country and at various levels. We need to clarify existing conflicts and uncertainties in the field of taxation, and to work out more satisfactory arrangements with regard to interlevel personnel relations. With such information at hand, it might be possible to determine optimal units for specific governmental purposes, and to get some intelligent guidance to the course of future developments in this field.

Such a study as is contemplated would start with the administration of governmental services, using approved methods of scientific inquiry. It would seek to be practical and to avoid the vague and highly theoretical approach which has often characterized the discussion of such relationships in the past. Many studies of similar character have already been made on a smaller scale. The National Resources Committee, in the regionalism study already referred to and in its urbanism study, has dealt with segments of the larger field. Excellent studies of local government have been made in a number of states, including New Jersey, New York, Ohio, and Pennsylvania, by public and private agencies. A growing body of special studies, many of which are listed in the Bibliography at the conclusion of this volume, is issuing from the press. The present proposal, therefore, calls not for anything new or strange, but for an extension and co-ordination of procedures now quite familiar.

It is evident that the tendency of recent years has been toward the centralization of governmental authority all along the line. Functions have been passed along to successively larger units —from the smaller local units to the county and from both to the states, from the states to regions and from both to the Federal Government. We do not know what the optimal units are for specific governmental purposes, nor do we have any clearly formulated principles to enable us to determine what they are. These, such an investigation as outlined above might provide. The size of the undertaking may be appalling, but its very size offers a challenge to the American people.

W. Brooke Graves, Ph.D., professor of political science at Temple University, Philadelphia, has done extensive writing and research in the field of state government and state administration. He edited "Readings in Public Opinion" (1928), and is the author of "Uniform State Action" (1934) and "American State Government" (1936).

A Bibliography of Intergovernmental Relations in the United States

By Dorothy Campbell Culver

Contents

Federal Relations with Other Units
    Federal-state relations
    Federal-municipal relations
    Grants-in-aid
    Taxation
Interstate Relations
    Interstate co-operation
    Interstate compacts
    Trade barriers
    Tax competition
    Uniform legislation
Regionalism
Interrelations of local units
    Fiscal relations
    Special districts, authorities, etc.
    School districts
    Metropolitan areas
    Rural municipalities
    City-county consolidation

Federal Relations with Other Units

Anderson, William. *The Units of Government in the United States.* Pp. 37. (Publication No. 42.) Chicago: Public Administration Service, 1934.

Ball, Carleton R. *Federal, State and Local Administrative Relationships in Agriculture.* 2 vols. Berkeley: University of California Press, 1938.

Chatters, Carl H. "Cities Look at Their Federal-State Relationships," *Minnesota Municipalities,* 22: 363–67, Nov. 1937.

Gulick, Luther. "Interjurisdictional Co-operation among Public Personnel Agencies." Civil Service Assembly of the United States and Canada, *Proceedings,* 30: 32–33, Oct. 1938.

Leland, Simeon E. "Co-ordination of Federal, State and Local Fiscal Systems," *Municipal Finance,* 6: 35–46, Aug. 1933.

Federal-state relations

American Legislators' Association. *State Legislation to Aid National Recovery: A Survey of Types of State Statutes which Might be Enacted to Supplement Recent Federal Acts.* (Mim.). Chicago: The Association, July 8, 1933.

Barnett, James D. "Co-operation between the Federal and State Governments," *National Municipal Review,* 17: 283–91, May 1928.

Burdine, J. Alton. *National-State Co-operation, with Special Reference to Texas.* Pp. 25. Dallas: Arnold Foundation, 1935.

Clark, Jane P. *The Rise of a New Federalism: Federal-State Co-operation in the United States.* Pp. 347. New York: Columbia University Press, 1938.
    Bibliography, pp. 321–40.
    Discusses informational co-operation: discussion and conference, exchange of service, loan of personnel; agreements and contracts; co-operative use of government personnel; interdependent law and administration; grants-in-aid.

Cohen, Julius H. *Increasing Federal Encroachments upon the Powers and Properties of the States.* Pp. 15. New York: Chamber of Commerce of the State of New York, 1938.

Corwin, Edward S. "National-State Co-operation—Its Present Possibilities," *Yale Law Journal,* 46: 599–623, Feb. 1937.

Gaumnitz, E. W. "Co-ordination of Federal and State Regulation of Milk." Middle States Conference on Milk Control, *Proceedings,* 1935: 103–8.

Graves, W. Brooke. "State Constitutional Provision for Federal-State Co-operation," *The Annals of the American Academy of Political and Social Science,* 181: 142–48, Sept. 1935.

———. "Federal Leadership in State Legislation," *Temple Law Quarterly,* 10: 385–405, July 1936.

———. "The Future of the American States," *American Political Science Review,* 30: 24–50, Feb. 1936.

HOWARD, L. V. "Recent Developments in the Field of Federal-State Co-operation in Agriculture," *Journal of Politics*, 1: 206–12, May 1939.

JOHNSTON, OLIN D. "Should States Surrender Authority to Federal Government in Conduct of Schools?" Governors Conference, *Proceedings*, 29: 58–69, 1937.

KOENIG, LOUIS W. "Federal and State Co-operation under the Constitution," *Michigan Law Review*, 36: 752–85, March 1938.

> Discusses grants-in-aid, supplementary legislation, interstate compacts, reciprocal legislation, interstate regional planning, conference methods, utilization of state administrative agencies by Federal Government.

LEE, F. P. *New Federal-State Relationships.* Pp. 10 (mim.). Charlottesville, Va.: University of Virginia, Institute of Public Affairs, 1938.

PATE, JAMES E. "Federal-State Relations in Planning," *Social Forces*, 15: 187–95, Dec. 1936.

A SYMPOSIUM ON CO-OPERATIVE FEDERALISM. *Iowa Law Review*, 23: 455–616, May 1938.

> "Co-operative Federalism," by Frank R. Strong; "Influence of Congressional Legislation on Legislation in the States," by W. Brooke Graves; "Interdependent Federal and State Laws as a Form of Federal-State Co-operation," by Jane P. Clark; "The Drainage Basin Studies, Co-operative Federalism in Practice," by William E. Warne; "Modern Machinery for Interstate Co-operation," by Henry W. Toll; "Co-operation in Reverse: A Natural State Tendency," by John B. Cheadle.

TEPLE, EDWIN R. "Federal Power over Things which Affect Interstate Commerce," *Ohio State Law Journal*, 4: 56–91, Dec. 1937.

UNITED STATES. FEDERAL COMMITTEE ON APPRENTICE TRAINING. *What the Federal-State Apprentice Training Program Means to Employers.* Pp. 10. (Bulletin No. 1.) Washington, D. C., April 1935.

Federal-municipal relations

BETTERS, PAUL V. "The Federal Government and the Cities: A Problem in Adjustment," *The Annals of the American Academy of Political and Social Science*, 199: 190–98, Sept. 1938.

———. *Federal Services to Municipal Government.* Pp. 100. (Publication No. 24.) New York: Municipal Administration Service, 1931.

———. *Recent Federal-City Relations.* Pp. 145. Chicago: United Conference of Mayors, 1936.

BUTTENHEIM, HAROLD S. "Uncle Sam or Boss Sam," *National Municipal Review*, 23: 654–59, Dec. 1934.

KILPATRICK, WYLIE, and others. "Federal Relations to Urban Governments," in United States, National Resources Committee, *Urban Government*, 55–160. Washington, D. C., 1939.

KILPATRICK, WYLIE. "Federal Regulation of Local Debt," *National Municipal Review*, 26: 283–90, June 1937.

LUDWIG, C. C. "Cities and the National Government under the New Deal," *American Political Science Review*, 29: 640–48, Aug. 1935.

MALLERY, EARL D. "Federal-City Relations in 1938," *Municipal Year Book*, 1939: 147–65.

MERRIAM, CHARLES E. "The Federal Government Recognizes the Cities," *National Municipal Review*, 23: 107–9, 116, Feb. 1934.

OGDEN, GLADYS. "Municipalities and the Federal Works Program," *National Municipal Review*, 26: 62–70, Feb. 1937.

REINHOLD, FRANCES L. "Federal-Municipal Relations: The Road Thus Far," *National Municipal Review*, 25: 452, 458–64, Aug. 1936.

RIDLEY, CLARENCE E., and ORREN NOLTING (Eds.). *What the Depression Has Done to Cities.* Pp. 55. Chicago: International City Managers' Association, 1935.

WALLERSTEIN, MORTON L. "Federal-Municipal Relations—Whither Bound?" *National Municipal Review*, 25: 453–57, Aug. 1936.

Grants-in-aid

BITTERMANN, HENRY J. *State and Federal Grants-in-Aid.* Pp. 550. Chicago: Mentzer, Bush & Co., 1938.
> Relief and social security; highways; agricultural colleges; experiment stations and extension work; vocational education; forest fire protection and forestry extension.

JOHNSEN, JULIA E. (Comp.). *Federal Aid to Education.* Pp. 213. (Reference shelf, Vol. 9, No. 3.) New York: H. W. Wilson, 1933.

KEY, V. O., JR. *The Administration of Federal Grants to States.* Pp. 388. (Studies in administration, Vol. 1.) Chicago: Social Science Research Council, Committee on Public Administration, 1937.

ROSEN, DOROTHY E. *Federal Grants-in-Aid: Selected Bibliography.* Pp. 11 (mim.). (Bibliography No. 7.) Los Angeles: University of Southern California, School of Government, Institute of Government, Committee on Bibliographies, 1938.

ZUBER, LEO J. *Federal Aid in Tennessee.* Pp. 63 (mim.). (Bulletin No. 16.) Nashville: Tennessee State Planning Commission, Feb. 1939.

Taxation

ARMSTRONG, C. E. "Federal Taxation of Other Governments," *Texas Municipalities,* 25: 311–17, Dec. 1938.

DICKINSON, JOHN. "Federal-State Tax Relations: Immunity or Reciprocity; A Critical Review of the Legal Background of the Problem," *State Government,* 12: 66–67, April 1939.

HATTON, ROBERT E. "Reciprocal Immunity of Federal and State Instrumentalities," National Tax Association, *Bulletin,* 24: 146–53, Feb. 1939.

HEER, CLARENCE. "Relations between Federal, State and Local Finances," *American Economic Review,* 26: sup. 174–81, March 1936.

HILLHOUSE, A. M. "Intergovernmental Tax Exemptions," *Municipal Year Book,* 1939: 345–81.

HOLMES, J. HENDREN. "Termination of Reciprocal Tax Exemption," *Taxes—the Tax Magazine,* 17: 281–83, May 1939.

LEPAWSKY, ALBERT. "Co-ordination of National, State and Local Taxation," *Minnesota Municipalities,* 24: 153–55, May 1939.

MAGILL, ROSWELL. "Problem of Intergovernmental Tax Exemption," *Tax Magazine,* 15: 699–703, Dec. 1937.

NEWCOMER, MABEL. "Co-ordination of Federal, State and Local Tax Systems," *The Annals of the American Academy of Political and Social Science,* 183: 39–47, Jan. 1936.

PHILIPSBORN, MARTIN, JR., and HERBERT CANTRILL. "Immunity from Taxation of Governmental Instrumentalities," *Georgetown Law Journal,* 26: 543–73, March 1938.

RIBBLE, F. D. G. "Conflicts between Federal Regulation through Taxes and the States," *Cornell Law Quarterly,* 23: 131–41, Dec. 1937.

SETLOCK, EDWARD J. "Intergovernmental Immunities from Taxation," *Marquette Law Review,* 23: 32–35, Dec. 1938.

SOMERS, PAUL, JR. "Tax Duplications between the Federal and State Governments," National Tax Association, *Bulletin,* 24: 54–63, 74–87, Nov., Dec. 1938.

STOCKWELL, MARVEL. "The Co-ordination of Federal, State and Local Taxation," *Tax Magazine,* 16: 198–200, 232–34, April 1938.

TAX POLICY LEAGUE. *Tax Relations among Governmental Units,* by Roy Blough and others. Pp. 226. New York: The League, 1938.
> Bibliography, pp. 219–26.

WATKINS, WILLIAM R. "The Power of the State and Federal Governments to Tax One Another," *Virginia Law Review,* 24: 475–506, March 1938.

INTERSTATE RELATIONS

The Book of the States, Vol. 3, 1939–40. Pp. 454. Chicago: Council of State Governments, 1939.
> Regional commissions of the Council of State Governments; Federal grants-in-aid to states; interstate trade barriers; state laws which tend to obstruct

interstate commerce; developments in interstate compacts; selected list of uniform state laws.

GRAVES, W. BROOKE. *American State Government.* Pp. 829. New York: Heath, c1936.

>Intergovernmental relations; interstate relations; local units of the states; state centralization.

HARTSHORNE, RICHARD. "Intergovernmental Co-operation—the Way Out," *New Jersey Law Review*, 2: 5–26, Jan. 1936.

TOLL, HENRY W. "Can Interstate Plans Be Effective?" National Planning Conference, *Proceedings*, 1937: 163–73.

Interstate co-operation

CALROW, CHARLES J. "Interstate Co-operation," *National Municipal Review*, 25: 445–51, Aug. 1936.

INDIANA. COMMISSION ON INTERSTATE CO-OPERATION. *Report ... to the Governor and to the General Assembly.* Pp. 34. Indianapolis, 1939.

MASSACHUSETTS. COMMISSION ON INTERSTATE CO-OPERATION. *Report*, 1, Feb. 1938; 2, Feb. 1939. (House Nos. 1802, 2072.) Boston, 1938–39.

NEW JERSEY. COMMISSION ON INTERSTATE CO-OPERATION. *Report*, 1, Jan. 1936–3, Jan. 1938. Trenton, 1936–38.

NEW YORK (STATE). JOINT LEGISLATIVE COMMITTEE ON INTERSTATE CO-OPERATION. *Report*, 1936–38. (Legislative Documents (1936) No. 111, (1937) No. 101, (1938) No. 90.) Albany, 1936–38.

PENNSYLVANIA. JOINT LEGISLATIVE COMMISSION ON INTERSTATE CO-OPERATION. *Report.* Pp. 65. Harrisburg [1937].

Interstate compacts

CARNEGIE ENDOWMENT FOR INTERNATIONAL PEACE. LIBRARY. *Interstate Compacts.* Pp. 4 (mim.). (Brief Reference List No. 2.) Washington, D. C., revised Sept. 20, 1935.

CHAMBER OF COMMERCE OF THE UNITED STATES. Special Committee on State Compacts. *State Compacts, Preliminary Report.* Pp. 15. Washington, D. C., Nov. 1936. *State Compacts, Report.* Pp. 21. Washington, D. C., March 1937.

CLARK, JANE P. "Interstate Compacts and Social Legislation," *Political Science Quarterly*, 50: 502–24, Dec. 1935; 51: 36–60, March 1936.

COUNCIL OF STATE GOVERNMENTS. *Congressional Consent to Interstate Compacts, 1789–1936; State and Federal Statutes Authorizing Compacts.* Pp. 18 (mim.). Chicago, May 29, 1936.

DODD, ALICE M. "Interstate Compacts," *United States Law Review*, 70: 557–78, Oct. 1936; 73: 75–88, Feb. 1939.

DUERBECK, EDWIN M. "Economic Control by Interstate Compact," *Social Forces*, 15: 104–11, Oct. 1936.

>Discusses water problems, labor, oil and gas, Port of New York Authority.

FRANKFURTER, FELIX, and JAMES M. LANDIS. "The Compact Clause of the Constitution—A Study in Interstate Adjustments," *Yale Law Journal*, 34: 685–750, May 1925.

GALLAGHER, HUBERT R. "The Development of Interstate Government," *National Municipal Review*, 26: 345–51, July 1937.

HOWARD, J. T. *Review of References on Interstate Compacts.* Pp. 15 (mim.). (Publication No. 34.) Boston: New England Regional Planning Commission, May 20, 1936.

PRITCHETT, C. HERMAN. "Regional Authorities through Interstate Compacts," *Social Forces*, 14: 200–10, Dec. 1935.

SPENGLER, JOSEPH J. "The Economic Limitations to Certain Uses of Interstate Compacts," *American Political Science Review*, 31: 41–51, Feb. 1937.

TEMPLE UNIVERSITY. DEPARTMENT OF POLITICAL SCIENCE. *Reference List on Interstate Compacts and Interstate Co-operation.* Pp. 11 (mim.). Philadelphia, Feb. 1938.

Trade barriers

ALLRED, JAMES V. "Interstate Tariffs Dam National Prosperity; Laws Restricting Trade among the States Promote Economic Provincialism," *State Government*, 11: 223–24, 234–35, Dec. 1938.

BERCAW, LOUISE O. *State Trade Barriers: Selected References.* Pp. 16 (mim.). (Economic Library List No. 1.) Washington, D. C.: U. S. Bureau of Agricultural Economics, March 1939.

BUELL, RAYMOND L. *Death by Tariff; Protectionism in State and Federal Legislation.* Pp. 40. (Public Policy Pamphlet No. 27.) Chicago: University of Chicago Press, Jan. 1939.

CONFERENCE ON STATE DEFENSE. *The States—at the Cross-roads;* address by Henry Epstein, July 25, 1938. Pp. 19. New York, 1938.

GREEN, THOMAS S., JR. "State Trade Barriers—Portents to National Prosperity," *National Municipal Review,* 28: 411–15, June 1939.

"Interstate Tariffs," *Tax Policy* (Tax Policy League), 6 (7): 1–13, May 1939. References, p. 10 (12 items). Legislative notes, pp. 11–13.

LINDER, ROBERT L. "New Mexico Legal Barriers to Interstate Trade," *New Mexico Business Review,* 8: 119–25, July 1939.

MELDER, FREDERICK E. *State and Local Barriers to Interstate Commerce in the United States: a Study in Economic Sectionalism.* Pp. 181. (University of Maine Studies Ser. 2, No. 43, Nov. 1937.) Orono, 1937.

NATIONAL ASSOCIATION OF MARKETING OFFICIALS. *Trade Barriers, City Markets and Advertising Farm Products:* Proceedings of the 19th Annual Meeting, December 1937. Pp. 60. Trenton, [1938].

NATIONAL CONFERENCE ON INTERSTATE TRADE BARRIERS. *Trade Barriers among the States: Proceedings,* 1939. Pp. 127. Chicago: Council of State Governments, 1939. Bibliography, pp. 121–27.

NATIONAL HIGHWAY USERS CONFERENCE. *State Barriers to Highway Transportation: A Discussion of Ports of Entry, Border Inspection Stations and Restrictive Regulations—a Plea for Reciprocity.* Pp. 24. Washington, D. C., Jan. 1937.

NOYES, CHARLES E. "Barriers against Interstate Commerce," *Editorial Research Reports,* 1 (11): 1–19, March 17, 1939.

SORRELL, VERNON G. "Ports of Entry and Interstate Commerce with Special Reference to the New Mexico Law; with discussion," *New Mexico Business Review,* 8: 93–108, April 1939.

SPENCER, LELAND. "Practice and Theory of Market Exclusion within the United States," *Journal of Farm Economics,* 15: 141–58, Jan. 1933.

"State Trade Barriers in the Making," *State Government,* 12: 49–53, 58–59, March 1939.

TAYLOR, GEORGE R., and others. *Barriers to Internal Trade in Farm Products.* Pp. 104. Washington, D. C.: U. S. Bureau of Agricultural Economics, March 1939.

Tax competition

BROWN, ROBERT C. "Multiple Taxation by the States—What Is Left of It?" *Harvard Law Review,* 48: 407–32, Jan. 1935.

COUNCIL OF STATE GOVERNMENTS. Regional Committee on Conflicting Taxation. *Proceedings of meeting, October 14, 1938.* Pp. 26 (mim.). Chicago 1938.

HAGLUND, CHARLES G. "Double Taxation," *Southern California Law Review,* 8: 79–113, Jan. 1935.

INTERSTATE COMMISSION ON CONFLICTING TAXATION. *Conflicting Taxation: the 1935 Progress Report.* Pp. 202. Chicago: Council of State Governments, 1935.

JOHNSON, GEORGE M. "Multi-state Taxation of Interstate Sales," *California Law Review,* 27: 549–70, July 1939.

MARTIN, JAMES W. "Conflicting Taxation at the Second Interstate Assembly," *American Bar Association Journal,* 21: 207–10, April 1935.

———. "State and Local Policy toward Restriction of Reciprocal Tax Immunity," *Minnesota Municipalities,* 13: 416–19, Dec. 1938.

NASH, FRANCIS C. "And Again Multiple Taxation?" *Georgetown Law Journal,* 26: 288–342, Jan. 1938.

Uniform legislation

GRANT, J. A. C. "The Search for Uniformity of Law," *American Political Science Review,* 32: 1082–98, Dec. 1938.

GRAVES, W. BROOKE. *Uniform State Action: A Possible Substitute for Centralization.* Pp. 368. Chapel Hill: University of North Carolina Press, 1934.

HARGEST, WILLIAM M. "Keeping the Uniform State Laws Uniform," *University of Pennsylvania Law Review*, 76: 178–84, Dec. 1927.

STEVENS, ROBERT S. "Uniform Corporation Laws through Interstate Compacts and Federal Legislation," *Michigan Law Review*, 34: 1063–92, June 1936.

REGIONALISM

DAVIDSON, DONALD. *The Attack on Leviathan: Regionalism and Nationalism in the United States.* Pp. 368. Chapel Hill: University of North Carolina Press, 1938.

———. "Regionalism as Social Science," *Southern Review*, 3: 209–24, Autumn 1937.

———. "Where Regionalism and Sectionalism Meet," *Social Forces*, 13: 23–31, Oct. 1934.

FESLER, JAMES W. "Federal Administrative Regions," *American Political Science Review*, 30: 257–68, April 1936.

———. "Standardization of Federal Administrative Regions," *Social Forces*, 15: 12–21, Oct. 1936.

HERTZLER, J. O. "Some Sociological Aspects of American Regionalism," *Social Forces*, 18: 17–29, Oct. 1939.

KOLLMORGEN, WALTER. "Political Regionalism in the United States—Fact or Myth," *Social Forces*, 15: 111–22, Oct. 1936.

MOORE, HARRY E. "Social Scientists Explore the Region," *Social Forces*, 16: 463–74, Oct. 1937–May 1938.

MUMFORD, LEWIS. "The Theory and Practice of Regionalism," *Sociological Review*, 20: 18–33, Jan. 1928.

MUNRO, WILLIAM B. "Regional Governments for Regional Problems," *The Annals of the American Academy of Political and Social Science*, 185: 123–32, May 1936.

ODUM, HOWARD W. "The Case for Regional-National Social Planning," *Social Forces*, 13: 6–23, Oct. 1934.

———. "Regionalism vs. Sectionalism in the South's Place in the National Economy," *Social Forces*, 12: 338–54, March 1934.

———, and HARRY E. MOORE. *American Regionalism: A Cultural-Historical Approach to National Integration.* Pp. 693. New York: Holt, c1938.
Bibliography, pp. 643–75.

OGBURN, WILLIAM F. "Regions," *Social Forces*, 15: 6–11, Oct. 1936.

RUSSELL, JOHN C. "State Regionalism in New Mexico," *Social Forces*, 16: 268–71, Dec. 1937.

TYLOR, W. RUSSELL. "The Process of Change from Neighborhood to Regional Organization and Its Effect on Rural Life," *Social Forces*, 16: 530–42, Oct. 1937–May 1938.

———. "Regionalism in Practice," *American Journal of Sociology*, 44: 379–90, Nov. 1938.

UNITED STATES. NATIONAL RESOURCES COMMITTEE. *Regional Factors in National Planning and Development.* Pp. 223. Washington, D. C., Dec. 1935.

UNITED STATES. NATIONAL RESOURCES COMMITTEE. URBANISM COMMITTEE. *Urban Government:* Vol. 1 of *Supplementary Report of the Urbanism Committee.* Pp. 303. Washington, D. C., 1939.

VANCE, RUPERT B. *Human Geography of the South: A Study in Regional Resources and Human Adequacy.* Pp. 596. Chapel Hill: University of North Carolina Press, 1932.

INTERRELATIONS OF LOCAL UNITS

ALDERFER, H. F. "Centralization in Pennsylvania," *National Municipal Review*, 27: 189–96, April 1938.
State government absorbing functions of local government.

CHUTE, CHARLTON E. "Co-operative Purchasing in the United States and Canada," *National Municipal Review*, 27: 499–504, Oct. 1938.

GILL, NORMAN N. "Intergovernmental Arrangements," *Municipal Year Book*, 1936: 140–47.

HOFFMAN, SAMUEL D. "A State Department of Local Government: New Jersey . . . Control of Its Local Subdivisions," *National Municipal Review*, 28: 348–54, May 1939.

LANCASTER, LANE W. "State Supervision and Local Administrative Standards," *Southwestern Social Science Quarterly*, 13: 321–32, March 1933.

McCOMBS, CARL E. "Local Self-government and the State," *National Municipal Review*, 26: 168–74, April 1937.

MACCORKLE, STUART A. "State Control over Counties in Texas," *Southwestern Social Science Quarterly*, 17: 161–77, Sept. 1936.

———. "The Theory of State-Municipal Purchasing Arrangements," *Southwestern Social Science Quarterly*, 19: 233–47, Dec. 1938.

MARX, FRITZ M. "Whither Local Self-government? Obsolete Boundaries Must be Abandoned if Local Government Is to Hold Its Own in the Reapportionment of Functions." *Public Management*, 16: 131–35, May 1934.

NEW YORK STATE CONSTITUTIONAL CONVENTION COMMITTEE. *Problems Relating to Home Rule and Local Government*. Pp. 300. (Report No. 11.) Albany, 1938.

———. *State and Local Government in New York*. Pp. 879. (Report No. 4.) Albany, 1938.

PENNSYLVANIA. UNIVERSITY. INSTITUTE OF LOCAL AND STATE GOVERNMENT. *City-State Relations*, prepared for the Philadelphia Charter Commission. Pp. 65 (mim.). (Factual Material Memorandum No. 2.) Philadelphia, Oct. 1937.

PINCHBECK, RAYMOND B. "The State Commission of Local Government," *National Municipal Review*, 28: 80–88, Feb. 1939.

SHENEFIELD, HALE T. "City-County Financial Relations (the No-Man's Land of Public Finance)," *Municipal Finance*, 8: 8–10, May 1936.

WAGER, PAUL W., and others. *Redistributing Functions of State and Local Government*. Pp. 12. (Government Series Lecture No. 12.) New York: National Advisory Council on Radio in Education, Nov. 29, 1932.

Fiscal relations

ALDERFER, H. F. "State Control of County Finance Increases," *National Municipal Review*, 28: 105–10, Feb. 1939.

AMERICAN MUNICIPAL ASSOCIATION. *Financial Relationships between State Governments and Municipalities*. Pp. 10. (Report No. 24.) Chicago, 1933. Reprinted under same title: *Minnesota Municipalities*, 18: 62–67, Feb. 1933.

CARR, ROBERT K. *State Control of Local Finance in Oklahoma*. Pp. 281. Norman: University of Oklahoma Press, 1937.

Bibliography, pp. 270–75.

CROUCH, WINSTON W. *State Aid to Local Government in California*. (University of California at Los Angeles, Publications in Social Sciences 6 (3): 223–422.) Berkeley: University of California Press, 1939.

Bibliography, pp. 413–18.

HAYGOOD, T. F. "State Control of Local Expenditures through Centralization of Financial Statistics," *Tax Magazine*, 301–7, 318–19, 346–47, 353–54, Aug., Sept. 1933.

JONES, HOWARD P. "Effect of the Depression on State-Local Relations," *National Municipal Review*, 25: 465–70, Aug. 1936.

KILPATRICK, WYLIE. "State Administrative Supervision of Local Financial Processes," *Municipal Year Book*, 1936: 340–66.

LANCASTER, LANE W. "State Limitations on Local Indebtedness," *Municipal Year Book*, 1936: 313–27.

LELAND, SIMEON E. "The Need for a Changed Attitude between States and Municipalities," *Municipal Problems* (American Municipal Association), 1932: 47–66.

LUTZ, H. L. "State Supervision of Local Finance," *Journal of Political Economy*, 43: 289–305, June 1935.

MARTIN, RICHARD. *The Financial Relationship of the State and the Towns*. Pp. 31. Manchester: Connecticut League of Municipalities, 1938.

NEW YORK (STATE) COMMISSION ON STATE AID TO MUNICIPAL SUB-DIVISIONS. *Report*, February 1, 1936. Pp. 357. (Legislative Document (1936) No. 58.) Albany, 1936.

NEW YORK (STATE) TAX COMMISSION. *The Fiscal Aspects of State and Local*

Relationships in New York, by Paul E. Malone. Pp. 433. (Special Report No. 13.) Albany, 1937.
    Bibliography, pp. 404–12.
———. *State Grants-in-Aid,* by Russell John Hinckley. Pp. 221. (Special Report No. 9.) Albany, 1935.
    Bibliography, pp. 203–15.
NEWCOMER, MABEL. "Locally Shared State Revenues," *National Municipal Review,* 24: 678–81, Dec. 1935.
STUDENSKI, PAUL. "Constitutional Limitation on Local Indebtedness in New York State," *National Municipal Review,* 27: 299–303, June 1938.
UHL, RAYMOND, and ANTHONY V. SHEA, JR. "State-Administered Locally-Shared Taxes," *Municipal Year Book,* 1936: 367–89.

Special districts, authorities, etc.
BAUM, ROBERT D. "Power District Legislation," *National Municipal Review,* 26: 28–30, Jan. 1937.
BLACH, FRIEDRICH. "Semi-independent Authorities," *Survey Graphic,* 27: 450–55, Sept. 1938.
DAVIS, HORACE A. "Borrowing Machines: The New 'Authority'—Is It Blessing or Menace?" *National Municipal Review,* 24: 328–34, June 1935.
HUTCHINS, WELLS A. *Irrigation Districts; Their Organization, Operation and Financing.* Pp. 93. (Technical Bulletin No. 254.) Washington, D. C.: U. S. Department of Agriculture, June 1931.
ILLINOIS. STATE PLANNING COMMISSION. *Non-taxing Improvement Authorities: An Analysis of Recent Developments.* Pp. 5. Springfield, July 1937.
NATIONAL ASSOCIATION OF REAL ESTATE BOARDS. *Neighborhood Protective and Improvement Districts: A Suggested State Statute.* Pp. 11. Chicago, Sept. 30, 1935.
NEHEMKIS, PETER R., JR. "The Public Authority: Some Legal and Practical Aspects," *Yale Law Journal,* 47: 14–33, Nov. 1937.
NEW YORK STATE CONSTITUTIONAL CONVENTION COMMITTEE. *New York City Government; Functions and Problems.* Pp. 246. (Report No. 5.) Albany, 1938.
    Authorities, pp. 96–107.

"103 Kinds of Special Districts," *Tax Digest,* 13: 162–68, May 1935.
PORTER, KIRK H. "A Plague of Special Districts: Their Services Are Necessary, but Not Their Waste," *National Municipal Review,* 22: 544–47, Nov. 1933.
RICE, JOHN L., and MARGARET W. BARNARD. "Four Years of District Health Administration in New York City," *Milbank Memorial Fund Quarterly,* 253–66, July 1938.
UNITED STATES. HOUSING AUTHORITY. PROJECT PLANNING DIVISION. *Local Housing Authorities.* Pp. 12 (mim.). Washington, D. C., 1938.
UNITED STATES. NATIONAL RESOURCES COMMITTEE. *Drainage Basin Problems and Programs.* Pp. 540. Washington, D. C., Dec. 1936.
UNITED STATES. SOIL CONSERVATION SERVICE. *A Standard State Soil Conservation Districts Law;* prepared at the suggestion of representatives of a number of states. Pp. 64. Washington, D. C., 1936.

School districts
ALVES, HENRY F. "The Study of Local School Units in Ten States," *National Municipal Review,* 27: 86–91, Feb. 1938.
AXTELL, P. H. "The Power to Create and Alter School Districts: Its Source and Limitations," *American School Board Journal,* 23–24, Nov. 1937.
BACON, H. B. "School District Consolidation," *Minnesota Municipalities,* 19: 446–49, Dec. 1934.
GRACE, ALONZO G. "Development of Satisfactory Units of School Administration," *National Municipal Review,* 26: 164–67, April 1937.
HENRY, NELSON B., and JEROME G. KERWIN. *Schools and City Government: A Study of School and Municipal Relationships in Cities of 50,000 or More Population.* Pp. 104. Chicago: University of Chicago, 1938.

Metropolitan areas
DICKINSON, R. E. "The Metropolitan Regions of the United States," *Geographical Review,* 24: 278–91, April 1934.

LEONARD, J. M., and LENT D. UPSON. *The Government of the Detroit Metropolitan Area.* Pp. 121. Lansing: Michigan Commission of Inquiry into County, Township and School District Government, May 1, 1934.

LEPAWSKY, ALBERT. "Redefining the Metropolitan Area," *National Municipal Review,* 25: 417–22, July 1936.

LOS ANGELES. PUBLIC LIBRARY. MUNICIPAL REFERENCE LIBRARY. *Government of Metropolitan Areas: A List of References to Publications Issued since 1928, with Special Reference to Cities of 500,000 Population and Over and to the Adjacent Territory.* Pp. 11 (mim.). Revised Aug. 1, 1935.

LYNAGH, PAULA. *Metropolitan Milwaukee, One Trade Area Burdened with 93 Local Governments: A Study of Economic Unity and Political Decentralization.* Pp. 97. Milwaukee: Milwaukee County Joint Committee on Consolidation, 1936.

MCKENZIE, R. D. *The Metropolitan Community.* Pp. 352. New York: McGraw-Hill, 1933.

MARTIN, ROSCOE C. *Urban Local Government in Texas.* Pp. 357. (Study No. 20.) Austin: University of Texas, Bureau of Research in the Social Sciences, Oct. 1, 1936.

MERRIAM, CHARLES E., and others. *The Government of the Metropolitan Region of Chicago.* Pp. 193. (Social Science Studies No. 26.) Chicago: University of Chicago, 1933.

STUDENSKI, PAUL. *The Government of Metropolitan Areas in the United States.* Pp. 403. New York: National Municipal League, 1930.

Rural municipalities

LANCASTER, LANE W. *Government in Rural America.* Pp. 416. New York: Van Nostrand, 1937.

MANNY, THEODORE B. "Rural Areas for Rural Government," *National Municipal Review,* 21: 481–83, Aug. 1932.

———. *Rural Municipalities: A Sociological Study of Local Government in the United States.* Pp. 343. New York: Century, 1930.
Bibliography, pp. 323–33.

City-county consolidation

AMERICAN BAR ASSOCIATION. SECTION OF MUNICIPAL LAW. *Report of the Committee on Consolidation and Reorganization of City and County Government.* Pp. 10 (mim.). Chicago, 1939.

BOUNDS, ROGER J. *Bibliography on the Reorganization and Consolidation of Local Government.* Pp. 15 (mim.). Washington, D. C.: Chamber of Commerce of the United States, Construction and Civic Development Department, April 1934.

CHUBB, L. R. "The Financial Aspects of City-County Consolidation," *National Municipal Review,* 28: 101–4, Feb. 1939.

PUTNEY, BRYANT. "Consolidation of Local Governments," *Editorial Research Reports,* 2 (8): 149–64, Sept. 1, 1936.

REED, THOMAS H. "City-County Consolidation," *National Municipal Review,* 23: 523–25, Oct. 1934.

WHITNALL, GORDON. "Consolidation by Contract: A Device by Which Local Units May Purchase Services from a Central Government," *State Government,* 8: 41–43, Feb. 1935.

Dorothy Campbell Culver is research assistant and bibliographer of the Bureau of Public Administration, University of California, Berkeley. She has compiled the following publications: "Bibliography of Crime and Criminal Justice, 1927–31" (1934); "Bibliography of Crime and Criminal Justice, 1932–37" (1939); "Methodology of Social Science Research: A Bibliography" (1936); "Land Utilization: A Bibliography" (1935); "Land Utilization: A Bibliography, supplement, 1937" (1937); "An Analysis of State Milk Control Laws" (1937).

AMERICAN FEDERALISM
The Urban Dimension

An Arno Press Collection

Atkinson, Raymond C. **The Federal Role in Unemployment Compensation Administration.** 1941

Benson, George C. S. **The New Centralization.** 1941

Betters, Paul V. **Cities and the 1936 Congress** *and* **Recent Federal-City Relations** with J. Kerwin Williams and Sherwood L. Reeder. 1936

Betters, Paul V. **Federal Services to Municipal Governments.** 1931

Civil Aeronautics Authority. **Airport Survey.** 1939

Colean, Miles L. **Housing for Defense.** 1940

Connery, Robert H. and Richard H. Leach. **The Federal Government and Metropolitan Areas.** 1960

The Council of State Governments. **Federal Grants-In-Aid.** 1949

The Council of State Governments. **Federal-State Relations.** 1949

Dearing, Charles L. **American Highway Policy.** 1941

Federal Aid to the Cities. 1977

Federal-City Relations in the 1930s. 1977

Friedman, Lawrence M. **Government and Slum Housing.** 1968

Graves, W. Brooke, editor. **Intergovernmental Relations in the United States.** 1940

Heer, Clarence. **Federal Aid and the Tax Problem.** 1939

Keith, John A. H. and William C. Bagley. **The Nation and the Schools.** 1920

Lutz, Edward A. **Some Problems and Alternatives in Developing Federal Block Grants to States for Public Welfare Purposes.** 1954

MacDonald, Austin F. **Federal Aid:** A Study of the American Subsidy System. 1928

Martin, Roscoe C. **The Cities and the Federal System.** 1965

Millett, John D. **The Works Progress Administration in New York City.** 1938

Reynolds, Harry. W., Jr., editor. **Intergovernmental Relations in the United States.** 1965

Tax Policy League. **Tax Relations Among Governmental Units.** 1938

Thompson, Walter. **Federal Centralization.** 1923

Tobey, James A. **The National Government and Public Health.** 1926

U.S. Advisory Commission on Intergovernmental Relations. **Metropolitan America.** 1966

U.S. Advisory Commission on Intergovernmental Relations. **The Role of Equalization in Federal Grants.** 1964

U.S. Commission on Intergovernmental Relations. **A Report to the President for Transmittal to the Congress.** 1955

U.S. House Committee on Banking and Currency. **Demonstration Cities, Housing and Urban Development, and Urban Mass Transit.** 1966. Two Vols. in One.

U.S. House Committee on Banking, Currency and Housing. **The New York City Fiscal Crisis:** Selections from *Debt Financing Problems of State and Local Government.* 1975

U.S. House Committee on Government Operations. **Federal-State-Local Relations: Federal Grants-In-Aid** *and* **Federal-State-Local Relations: State and Local Officials.** 1958/1959. Two Vols. in One.

U.S. National Resources Committee, Research Committee on Urbanism. **Interim Report to the National Resources Committee.** 1936

U.S. National Resources Committee. **Urban Government.** 1939

U.S. Senate Committee on Government Operations. **Creative Federalism.** 1967. Three Vols. in One

U.S. Senate Committee on Government Operations. **The Effect of Inflation and Recession on State and Local Governments.** 1975

U.S. Senate Select Committee on Reconstruction and Production. **The Federal Government and the Housing Problem:** Selections from *Reconstruction and Production.* 1921. Two Vols.

U.S. Treasury Department, The Committee on Intergovernmental Fiscal Relations. **Federal, State, and Local Government Fiscal Relations.** 1943

Warren, Charles. **Congress as Santa Claus.** 1932

JK325 .A64 1978A
AMERICAN ACADEMY OF
INTERGOVERNMENTAL
RELATIONS IN THE UNI